THE FRUIT
OF THE
SPIRIT

Books by Sarah Hornsby

At the Name of Jesus
Who I Am in Jesus
Nicaraguense: Poems, Prayers,
  Portraits of a Love Affair

THE FRUIT OF THE SPIRIT

SARAH HORNSBY

Published by
chosen books

FLEMING H. REVELL COMPANY
OLD TAPPAN, NEW JERSEY

Scripture quotations are from:

The Amplified New Testament, © The Lockman Foundation 1954–1958, and used by permission.

The King James Version of the Bible.

The Living Bible, © 1971 by Tyndale House Publishers, Wheaton, Ill. Used by permission.

The New American Standard Bible, © The Lockman Foundation 1960, 1962, 1963, 1968, 1971, 1972, 1973, 1975, 1977. Used by permission.

The New English Bible, © The Delegates of the Oxford University Press, 1961, 1970. Reprinted by permission.

The New King James Version, © 1979, 1980, 1982, Thomas Nelson, Inc., Publishers.

The Holy Bible: New International Version, © 1973, 1978 by the International Bible Society. Used by permission of Zondervan Bible Publishers.

The New Testament in Modern English, Revised Edition—J. B. Phillips, translator, © J. B. Phillips, 1958, 1960, 1972. Used by permission of Macmillan Publishing Co., Inc.

The Revised Standard Version of the Bible, © 1946, 1952, 1971 by the Division of Christian Education of the National Council of the Churches of Christ in the United States of America, and used by permission. All rights reserved.

Library of Congress Cataloging-in-Publication Data

Hornsby, Sarah.
  Fruit of the spirit.

  1. Devotional calendars.   I. Title.
BV4811.H645   1988   242'.2   88-20273
ISBN 0-8007-9138-X

A Chosen Book
Copyright 1988 by Sarah Hornsby

Chosen Books are published by
Fleming H. Revell Company
Old Tappan, New Jersey
Printed in the United States of America

To my sister,
Ebba Anderson Kelbaugh,
and her family,
John, Russ, and Kathie

I would like to thank

Ginie Hazelwood, who carefully proofread these pages with a spirit of gentleness.

Ebba Kelbaugh and Tish Anderson, my mother, for loving wisdom.

Jane Campbell and Ann McMath, my editors, who had faith that now is the time for this book, and encouraged me during its two-and-a-half years in the making.

Susan Bell and Jack Lewis for encouraging me in drawing, when I had always felt my art was not "good enough," and to Dan Hagan for printing advice.

Margie Thornton, Kathie Doyle, Dave MacFarland, and Randy Vanderwilt for patiently teaching me to use a word processor.

Faye Inlow, friend and prayer partner, for patiently enduring.

Matthew, James, Andy, and Jim, who have shaped me; as family we have been planted, weeded, harvested, and pruned in a wonderful cycle of life. Black brothers and sisters and Jesus People in the inner-city streets of Jacksonville, Florida, shared fourteen years of our journey. Brown brothers and sisters, too, of Nicaragua's dusty roads have been a part of the joy that forgiveness releases, and of the peace that grows hand-in-hand with justice.

Half of these pages were written under our palm-thatched roof in Nicaragua our second year there, as I struggled with the poverty around me and felt intensely the injustices toward the poor in that war-torn country. I had to dig deeper wells of listening in order to hear God's voice in such a place, and am thankful that He is always faithful to speak if we but take time to hear. He spoke through the word studies and through the courage and forgiveness of the Nicaraguan Christians.

A central truth I learned is that the Spirit of Jesus walks hand-in-hand with the poor, so if we are to grow in Him, we must be in touch with those in greater need than ourselves. Love contains charity; within peace's definition is justice; humility includes those who are depressed in mind and circumstances.

I had always wondered how Matthew could quote Jesus as saying, "Blessed are the poor in spirit," while Luke quotes only, "Blessed are the poor." Now I see that as we recognize our own poverty and our closeness to those poorer than us, we will find ourselves blessed by being in touch with what God's Kingdom is all about: His will being done on earth as it is in heaven!

Contents

A Word about
Fruit of the Spirit

Each page is designed as a daily meditation on a single scriptural fruit of the Spirit using the theme of the month. Each word in the Scripture passage was studied, using mainly *Strong's Exhaustive Concordance* based on the King James Version of the Bible.

First I paraphrased the Scripture from the word studies. Then I spent time listening for what the Lord seemed to be saying about the Scripture, writing those thoughts as the second half of each devotional. Finally, I drew borders, using a variety of ideas from art sources found in the Lake Blackshear Public Library. Some particularly helpful ones were the illuminated manuscripts and collections of Armenian art treasures in Jerusalem, samples of early Christian art, and art works from a variety of cultures. I also reworked some of my favorite borders from *At the Name of Jesus* and *Who I Am in Jesus*.

Sarah Hornsby

"But the fruit of the Spirit is love, joy, peace, patience, kindness, goodness, faithfulness, gentleness, self-control."

Galatians 5:22–23 (RSV)

THE FRUIT
OF THE
SPIRIT

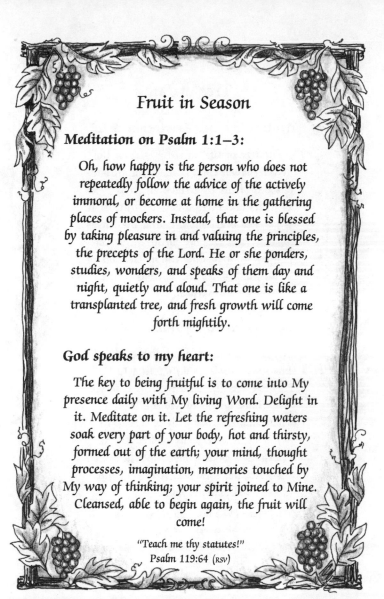

Fruit in Season

Meditation on Psalm 1:1–3:

Oh, how happy is the person who does not repeatedly follow the advice of the actively immoral, or become at home in the gathering places of mockers. Instead, that one is blessed by taking pleasure in and valuing the principles, the precepts of the Lord. He or she ponders, studies, wonders, and speaks of them day and night, quietly and aloud. That one is like a transplanted tree, and fresh growth will come forth mightily.

God speaks to my heart:

The key to being fruitful is to come into My presence daily with My living Word. Delight in it. Meditate on it. Let the refreshing waters soak every part of your body, hot and thirsty, formed out of the earth; your mind, thought processes, imagination, memories touched by My way of thinking; your spirit joined to Mine. Cleansed, able to begin again, the fruit will come!

"Teach me thy statutes!"
Psalm 119:64 (RSV)

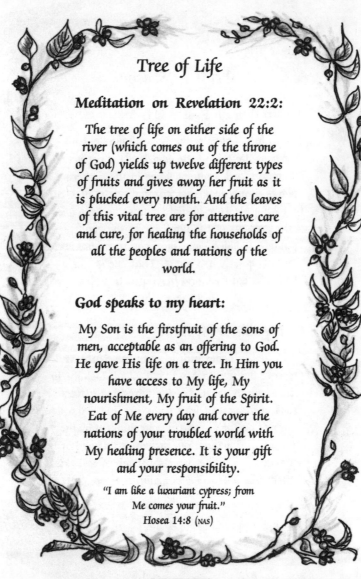

Tree of Life

Meditation on Revelation 22:2:

The tree of life on either side of the river (which comes out of the throne of God) yields up twelve different types of fruits and gives away her fruit as it is plucked every month. And the leaves of this vital tree are for attentive care and cure, for healing the households of all the peoples and nations of the world.

God speaks to my heart:

My Son is the firstfruit of the sons of men, acceptable as an offering to God. He gave His life on a tree. In Him you have access to My life, My nourishment, My fruit of the Spirit. Eat of Me every day and cover the nations of your troubled world with My healing presence. It is your gift and your responsibility.

"I am like a luxuriant cypress; from Me comes your fruit."
Hosea 14:8 (NAS)

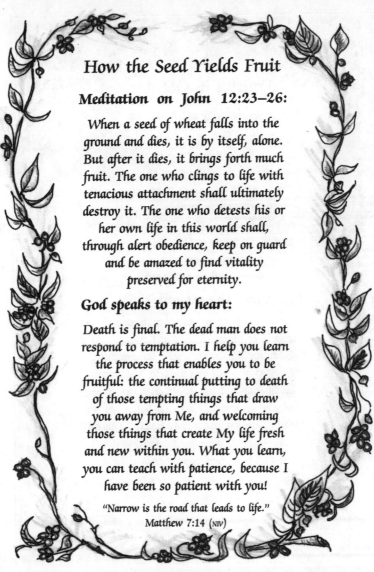

How the Seed Yields Fruit

Meditation on John 12:23–26:

When a seed of wheat falls into the ground and dies, it is by itself, alone. But after it dies, it brings forth much fruit. The one who clings to life with tenacious attachment shall ultimately destroy it. The one who detests his or her own life in this world shall, through alert obedience, keep on guard and be amazed to find vitality preserved for eternity.

God speaks to my heart:

Death is final. The dead man does not respond to temptation. I help you learn the process that enables you to be fruitful: the continual putting to death of those tempting things that draw you away from Me, and welcoming those things that create My life fresh and new within you. What you learn, you can teach with patience, because I have been so patient with you!

"Narrow is the road that leads to life."
Matthew 7:14 (NIV)

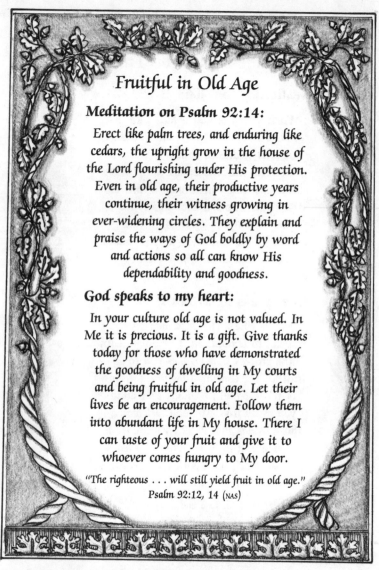

Fruitful in Old Age

Meditation on Psalm 92:14:

Erect like palm trees, and enduring like
cedars, the upright grow in the house of
the Lord flourishing under His protection.
Even in old age, their productive years
continue, their witness growing in
ever-widening circles. They explain and
praise the ways of God boldly by word
and actions so all can know His
dependability and goodness.

God speaks to my heart:

In your culture old age is not valued. In
Me it is precious. It is a gift. Give thanks
today for those who have demonstrated
the goodness of dwelling in My courts
and being fruitful in old age. Let their
lives be an encouragement. Follow them
into abundant life in My house. There I
can taste of your fruit and give it to
whoever comes hungry to My door.

"The righteous . . . will still yield fruit in old age."
Psalm 92:12, 14 (NAS)

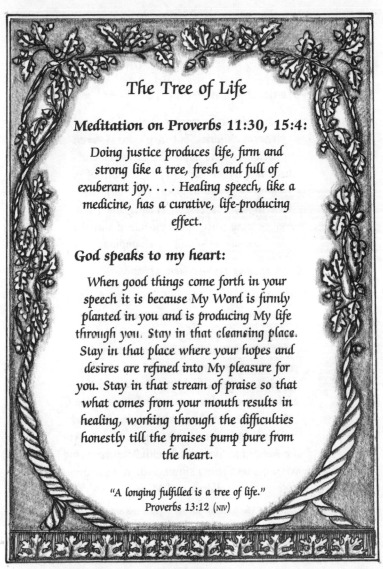

The Tree of Life

Meditation on Proverbs 11:30, 15:4:

Doing justice produces life, firm and strong like a tree, fresh and full of exuberant joy. . . . Healing speech, like a medicine, has a curative, life-producing effect.

God speaks to my heart:

When good things come forth in your speech it is because My Word is firmly planted in you and is producing My life through you. Stay in that cleansing place. Stay in that place where your hopes and desires are refined into My pleasure for you. Stay in that stream of praise so that what comes from your mouth results in healing, working through the difficulties honestly till the praises pump pure from the heart.

"A longing fulfilled is a tree of life."
Proverbs 13:12 (NIV)

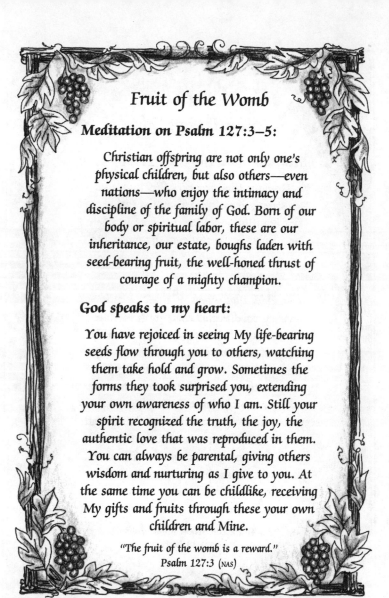

Fruit of the Womb

Meditation on Psalm 127:3–5:

Christian offspring are not only one's
physical children, but also others—even
nations—who enjoy the intimacy and
discipline of the family of God. Born of our
body or spiritual labor, these are our
inheritance, our estate, boughs laden with
seed-bearing fruit, the well-honed thrust of
courage of a mighty champion.

God speaks to my heart:

You have rejoiced in seeing My life-bearing
seeds flow through you to others, watching
them take hold and grow. Sometimes the
forms they took surprised you, extending
your own awareness of who I am. Still your
spirit recognized the truth, the joy, the
authentic love that was reproduced in them.
You can always be parental, giving others
wisdom and nurturing as I give to you. At
the same time you can be childlike, receiving
My gifts and fruits through these your own
children and Mine.

"The fruit of the womb is a reward."
Psalm 127:3 (NAS)

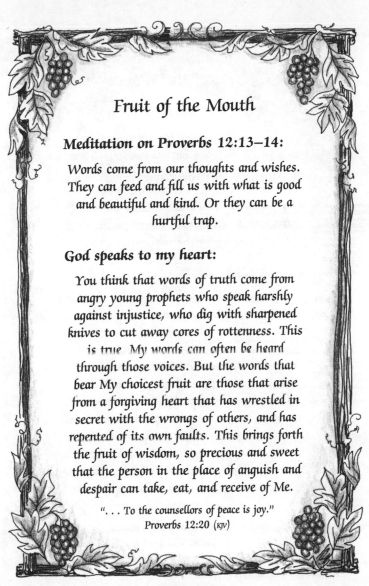

Fruit of the Mouth

Meditation on Proverbs 12:13–14:

Words come from our thoughts and wishes.
They can feed and fill us with what is good
and beautiful and kind. Or they can be a
hurtful trap.

God speaks to my heart:

You think that words of truth come from
angry young prophets who speak harshly
against injustice, who dig with sharpened
knives to cut away cores of rottenness. This
is true. My words can often be heard
through those voices. But the words that
bear My choicest fruit are those that arise
from a forgiving heart that has wrestled in
secret with the wrongs of others, and has
repented of its own faults. This brings forth
the fruit of wisdom, so precious and sweet
that the person in the place of anguish and
despair can take, eat, and receive of Me.

"... To the counsellors of peace is joy."
Proverbs 12:20 (KJV)

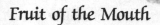

Fruit of the Mouth

Meditation on Proverbs 13:2:

*A person who speaks what is good, cheerful, kind,
and loving, is nourished by those "good" words
and thoughts.*

God speaks to my heart:

*You sometimes like to think you can be good
without Me. This is because you'd rather do what
is right in your own eyes. The result is
disastrous—a treacherous end on the wrong road.
Yet, even after being led through the valley of the
shadow of death, the psalmist could affirm that
goodness accompanied him through it all.
Hang onto Me. I'll help you clean up your
language, imaginations, ambitions.
With Me you don't have to pretend you are
something you are not. I* know *what you are; you
can start from there your praises!*

"A righteous man hates falsehood."
Proverbs 13:5 (RSV)

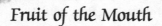

Fruit of the Mouth

Meditation on Proverbs 18:20–21:

Death or life? What I love, what I consistently give my affection to with all my energies, determines whether I am nourished by words that result in death or life.

God speaks to my heart:

You have felt wounds made by words that murder in their anger. You have seen fragile spirits shake before venom-spewing "friends" who later act as if they have done nothing. The poison causes festering and must be cleansed. Death walks in that pain.

You have authority in My name to bind this evil coming from the poisonous words, and to bind up the wounded. Don't give up. Love and forgive until the oil of My Spirit releases those roots of past grievances. I will not rest until every one of My children has come to maturity in the use of the tongue.

"He delivered me. . . ."
Psalm 18:17 (KJV)

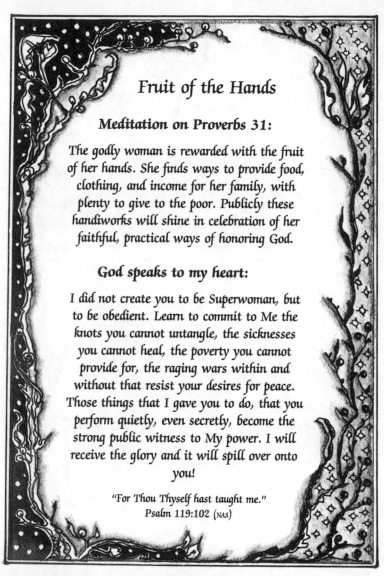

Fruit of the Hands

Meditation on Proverbs 31:

The godly woman is rewarded with the fruit of her hands. She finds ways to provide food, clothing, and income for her family, with plenty to give to the poor. Publicly these handiworks will shine in celebration of her faithful, practical ways of honoring God.

God speaks to my heart:

I did not create you to be Superwoman, but to be obedient. Learn to commit to Me the knots you cannot untangle, the sicknesses you cannot heal, the poverty you cannot provide for, the raging wars within and without that resist your desires for peace. Those things that I gave you to do, that you perform quietly, even secretly, become the strong public witness to My power. I will receive the glory and it will spill over onto you!

"For Thou Thyself hast taught me."
Psalm 119:102 (NAS)

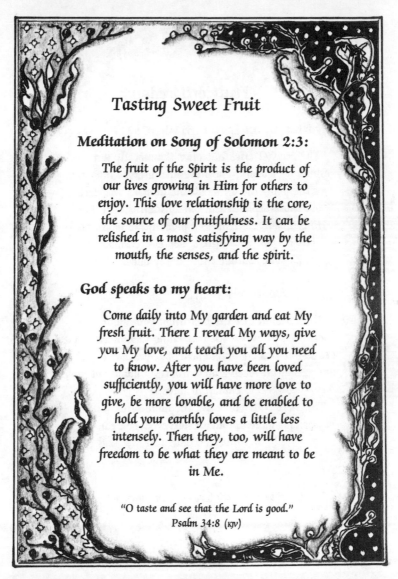

Tasting Sweet Fruit

Meditation on Song of Solomon 2:3:

The fruit of the Spirit is the product of our lives growing in Him for others to enjoy. This love relationship is the core, the source of our fruitfulness. It can be relished in a most satisfying way by the mouth, the senses, and the spirit.

God speaks to my heart:

Come daily into My garden and eat My fresh fruit. There I reveal My ways, give you My love, and teach you all you need to know. After you have been loved sufficiently, you will have more love to give, be more lovable, and be enabled to hold your earthly loves a little less intensely. Then they, too, will have freedom to be what they are meant to be in Me.

"O taste and see that the Lord is good."
Psalm 34:8 (KJV)

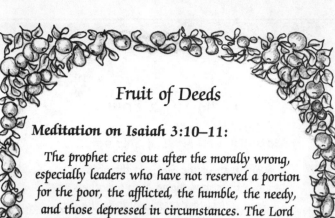

Fruit of Deeds

Meditation on Isaiah 3:10–11:

The prophet cries out after the morally wrong, especially leaders who have not reserved a portion for the poor, the afflicted, the humble, the needy, and those depressed in circumstances. The Lord Himself will contend and judge those who crush His people, who bruise, oppress, crumble, or discourage those lowly ones.

God speaks to my heart:

Do not shut out the poor from your sight. Let their need be ever with you, to do them good—not because it is a commandment, but because it is My desire that all receive good from My hand and have enough to give.

The more fruit you give, the more seeds will be planted for more abundant harvests. You can never give too much!

"[The] poor man cried, and the Lord heard him."
Psalm 34:6 (kjv)

Fruit of Prayer

Meditation on Isaiah 57:17–18:

God has been provoked to an outburst of rage by
the dishonest, unjust gain of His people. Those
who have seen this and wept for His people will
receive the fruit of their prayers when God, who
perceives everything exactly as it is, heals His
people. He will mend by stitching as a physician,
repair, make whole, and enable them to be
confronted with a true and complete repentance
that makes full restitution.

God speaks to my heart:

If you have My heart, you will cry, weep, yearn
for My people to return to Me. Though you have
joy with Me and your family in Me, you also feel
an unplumbed depth of sadness, a yearning for
those to return, to be restored, to be made whole,
to see Me in the poor. Ask for them to return, for
you ask with My Shepherd's heart.

"The Lord has heard my cry for mercy."
Psalm 6:9 (NIV)

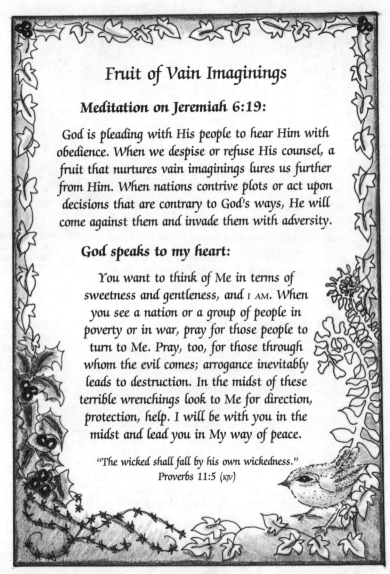

Fruit of Vain Imaginings

Meditation on Jeremiah 6:19:

God is pleading with His people to hear Him with obedience. When we despise or refuse His counsel, a fruit that nurtures vain imaginings lures us further from Him. When nations contrive plots or act upon decisions that are contrary to God's ways, He will come against them and invade them with adversity.

God speaks to my heart:

You want to think of Me in terms of sweetness and gentleness, and I AM. When you see a nation or a group of people in poverty or in war, pray for those people to turn to Me. Pray, too, for those through whom the evil comes; arrogance inevitably leads to destruction. In the midst of these terrible wrenchings look to Me for direction, protection, help. I will be with you in the midst and lead you in My way of peace.

"The wicked shall fall by his own wickedness."
Proverbs 11:5 (kjv)

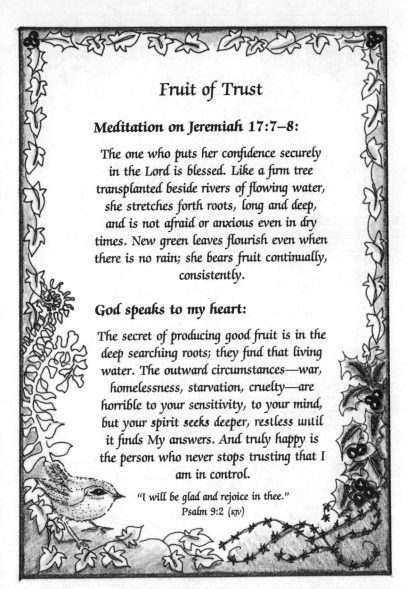

Fruit of Trust

Meditation on Jeremiah 17:7–8:

The one who puts her confidence securely
in the Lord is blessed. Like a firm tree
transplanted beside rivers of flowing water,
she stretches forth roots, long and deep,
and is not afraid or anxious even in dry
times. New green leaves flourish even when
there is no rain; she bears fruit continually,
consistently.

God speaks to my heart:

The secret of producing good fruit is in the
deep searching roots; they find that living
water. The outward circumstances—war,
homelessness, starvation, cruelty—are
horrible to your sensitivity, to your mind,
but your spirit seeks deeper, restless until
it finds My answers. And truly happy is
the person who never stops trusting that I
am in control.

"I will be glad and rejoice in thee."
Psalm 9:2 (KJV)

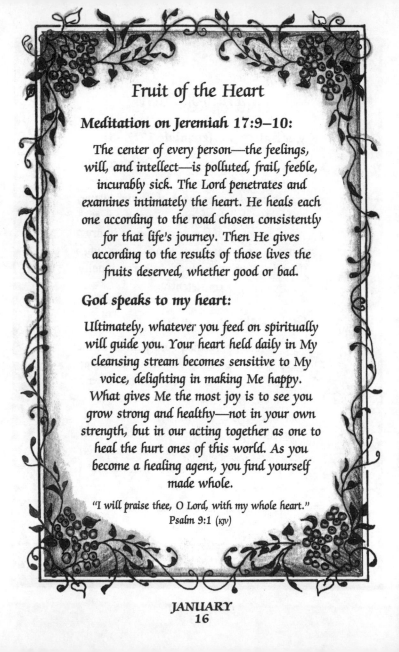

Fruit of the Heart

Meditation on Jeremiah 17:9–10:

The center of every person—the feelings,
will, and intellect—is polluted, frail, feeble,
incurably sick. The Lord penetrates and
examines intimately the heart. He heals each
one according to the road chosen consistently
for that life's journey. Then He gives
according to the results of those lives the
fruits deserved, whether good or bad.

God speaks to my heart:

Ultimately, whatever you feed on spiritually
will guide you. Your heart held daily in My
cleansing stream becomes sensitive to My
voice, delighting in making Me happy.
What gives Me the most joy is to see you
grow strong and healthy—not in your own
strength, but in our acting together as one to
heal the hurt ones of this world. As you
become a healing agent, you find yourself
made whole.

"I will praise thee, O Lord, with my whole heart."
Psalm 9:1 (KJV)

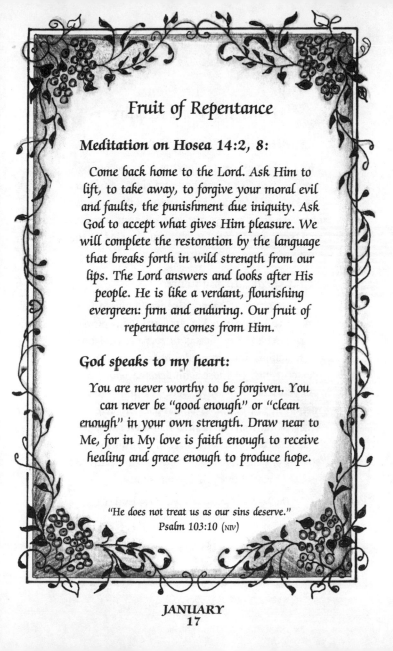

Fruit of Repentance

Meditation on Hosea 14:2, 8:

Come back home to the Lord. Ask Him to
lift, to take away, to forgive your moral evil
and faults, the punishment due iniquity. Ask
God to accept what gives Him pleasure. We
will complete the restoration by the language
that breaks forth in wild strength from our
lips. The Lord answers and looks after His
people. He is like a verdant, flourishing
evergreen: firm and enduring. Our fruit of
repentance comes from Him.

God speaks to my heart:

You are never worthy to be forgiven. You
can never be "good enough" or "clean
enough" in your own strength. Draw near to
Me, for in My love is faith enough to receive
healing and grace enough to produce hope.

"He does not treat us as our sins deserve."
Psalm 103:10 (NIV)

Fruit the Lord Requires

Meditation on Micah 6:8:

The Lord seeks companionship with people who walk in ways that are just and right. As lovers are kind and compassionate, especially to those subject to their power, we also without arrogance or assertiveness may accompany the God of the universe!

God speaks to my heart:

The most precious commodity in the world is the ability to walk with Me, to learn what pleases Me, to know My responses to every circumstance: to temptation, to needs, to injustices, to persecutions, to those who demand your time. As you learn My ways, you will find yourself delighting in impulses of compassion, like the Good Samaritan, or desires for restitution, like Zacchaeus. You will crave the intimacy of "stream of consciousness" conversation with Me, your Lover God, continually.

"The Lord is gracious and full of compassion."
Psalm 111:4 (KJV)

Receiving the Seed

Meditation on Mark 4:20:

Those most fruitful are like good soil:
beautiful, valuable, useful. When the good
seed of God's Word is extended, they listen
with understanding; they receive, accept,
admit, and delight in it.

God speaks to my heart:

When the ground is new, hard with rocks,
weeds, and roots, it takes time, persistence,
and constant guarding to make a garden.
I am a good gardener and know the precise
formula for your maximum productions. I
know the plants you need beside you, the
time to plant, the time to rest. I desire to
harvest the most that is possible from the
seeds I plant, to feed the hungry.

"The trees of the Lord are well watered."
Psalm 104:16 (NIV)

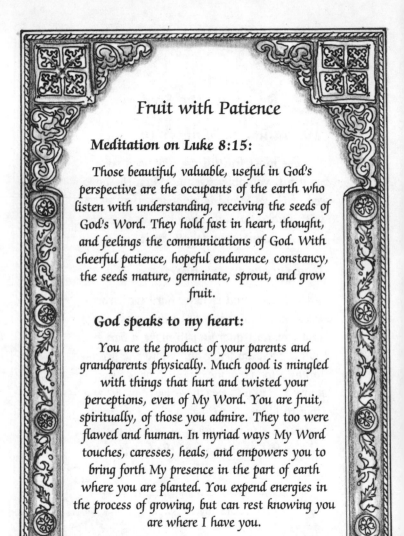

Fruit with Patience

Meditation on Luke 8:15:

Those beautiful, valuable, useful in God's perspective are the occupants of the earth who listen with understanding, receiving the seeds of God's Word. They hold fast in heart, thought, and feelings the communications of God. With cheerful patience, hopeful endurance, constancy, the seeds mature, germinate, sprout, and grow fruit.

God speaks to my heart:

You are the product of your parents and grandparents physically. Much good is mingled with things that hurt and twisted your perceptions, even of My Word. You are fruit, spiritually, of those you admire. They too were flawed and human. In myriad ways My Word touches, caresses, heals, and empowers you to bring forth My presence in the part of earth where you are planted. You expend energies in the process of growing, but can rest knowing you are where I have you.

"[He] satisfies you with good as long as you live."
Psalm 103:5 (RSV)

Pruned to Be More Fruitful

Meditation on John 15:2:

The branch that does not bear fruit or endure,
the Lord will remove. And He will purge,
cleanse, and prune so that there will be more
excellent fruit—greatly excelling in number,
quantity, or quality. Gladly now you are made
clean, pure by God's Word; good thoughts,
reasoning, and motives are put into action.

God speaks to my heart:

To cut from your life what appears to flourish
may seem cruel. Trust the Master Gardener. I
will prune only that which can be effectively
removed in order to allow that which remains
opportunity for a surging of vitality. Ultimately
you will burst forth with more select fruit. If you
allow Me to cut away parts of yourself that you
have loved, you will find Me faithful to give
them back to you richer and fuller than before.

"By this my Father is glorified, that you bear much fruit."
John 15:8 (RSV)

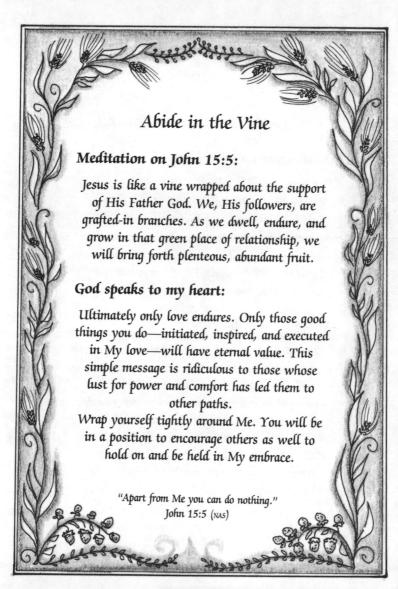

Abide in the Vine

Meditation on John 15:5:

Jesus is like a vine wrapped about the support of His Father God. We, His followers, are grafted-in branches. As we dwell, endure, and grow in that green place of relationship, we will bring forth plenteous, abundant fruit.

God speaks to my heart:

Ultimately only love endures. Only those good things you do—initiated, inspired, and executed in My love—will have eternal value. This simple message is ridiculous to those whose lust for power and comfort has led them to other paths.

Wrap yourself tightly around Me. You will be in a position to encourage others as well to hold on and be held in My embrace.

"Apart from Me you can do nothing."
John 15:5 (NAS)

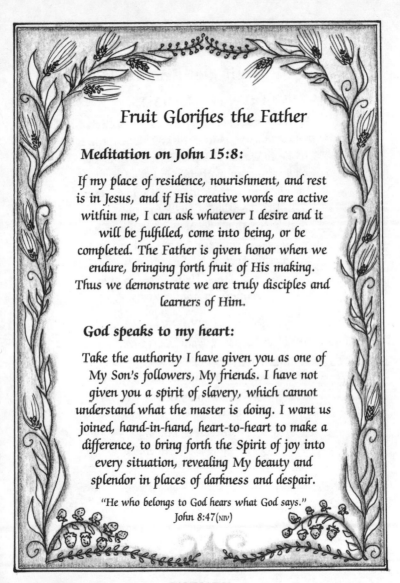

Fruit Glorifies the Father

Meditation on John 15:8:

If my place of residence, nourishment, and rest is in Jesus, and if His creative words are active within me, I can ask whatever I desire and it will be fulfilled, come into being, or be completed. The Father is given honor when we endure, bringing forth fruit of His making. Thus we demonstrate we are truly disciples and learners of Him.

God speaks to my heart:

Take the authority I have given you as one of My Son's followers, My friends. I have not given you a spirit of slavery, which cannot understand what the master is doing. I want us joined, hand-in-hand, heart-to-heart to make a difference, to bring forth the Spirit of joy into every situation, revealing My beauty and splendor in places of darkness and despair.

"He who belongs to God hears what God says."
John 8:47(NIV)

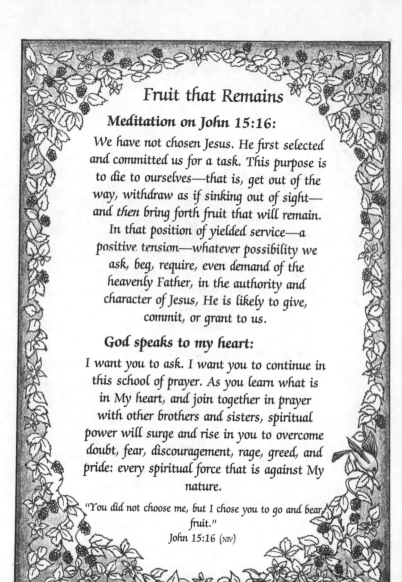

Fruit that Remains

Meditation on John 15:16:

We have not chosen Jesus. He first selected and committed us for a task. This purpose is to die to ourselves—that is, get out of the way, withdraw as if sinking out of sight— and *then* bring forth fruit that will remain.

In that position of yielded service—a positive tension—whatever possibility we ask, beg, require, even demand of the heavenly Father, in the authority and character of Jesus, He is likely to give, commit, or grant to us.

God speaks to my heart:

I want you to ask. I want you to continue in this school of prayer. As you learn what is in My heart, and join together in prayer with other brothers and sisters, spiritual power will surge and rise in you to overcome doubt, fear, discouragement, rage, greed, and pride: every spiritual force that is against My nature.

"You did not choose me, but I chose you to go and bear fruit."
John 15:16 (NIV)

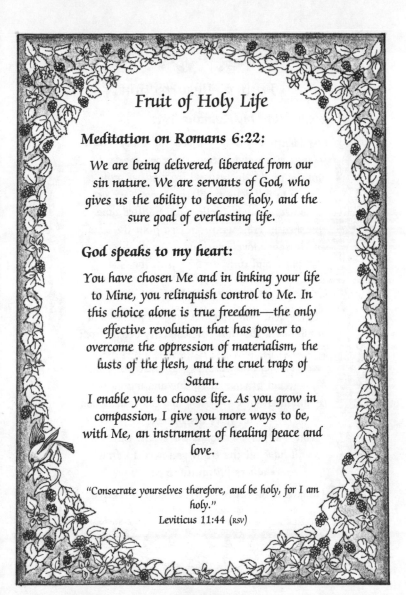

Fruit of Holy Life

Meditation on Romans 6:22:

We are being delivered, liberated from our sin nature. We are servants of God, who gives us the ability to become holy, and the sure goal of everlasting life.

God speaks to my heart:

You have chosen Me and in linking your life to Mine, you relinquish control to Me. In this choice alone is true freedom—the only effective revolution that has power to overcome the oppression of materialism, the lusts of the flesh, and the cruel traps of Satan.

I enable you to choose life. As you grow in compassion, I give you more ways to be, with Me, an instrument of healing peace and love.

"Consecrate yourselves therefore, and be holy, for I am holy."
Leviticus 11:44 (RSV)

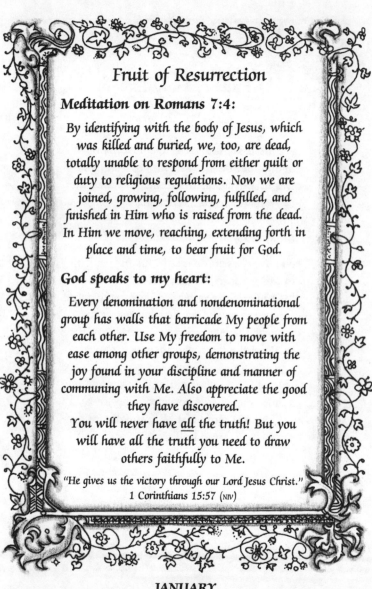

Fruit of Resurrection

Meditation on Romans 7:4:

By identifying with the body of Jesus, which was killed and buried, we, too, are dead, totally unable to respond from either guilt or duty to religious regulations. Now we are joined, growing, following, fulfilled, and finished in Him who is raised from the dead. In Him we move, reaching, extending forth in place and time, to bear fruit for God.

God speaks to my heart:

Every denomination and nondenominational group has walls that barricade My people from each other. Use My freedom to move with ease among other groups, demonstrating the joy found in your discipline and manner of communing with Me. Also appreciate the good they have discovered.

You will never have <u>all</u> the truth! But you will have all the truth you need to draw others faithfully to Me.

"He gives us the victory through our Lord Jesus Christ."
1 Corinthians 15:57 (NIV)

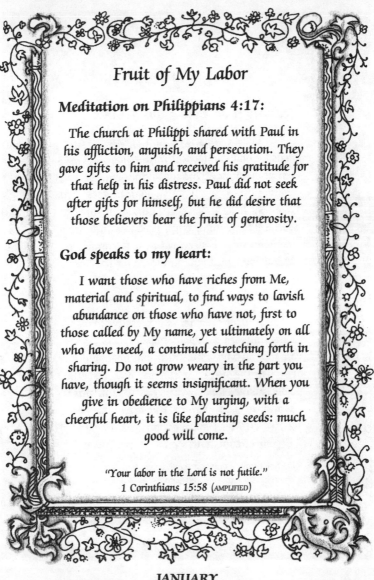

Fruit of My Labor

Meditation on Philippians 4:17:

The church at Philippi shared with Paul in his affliction, anguish, and persecution. They gave gifts to him and received his gratitude for that help in his distress. Paul did not seek after gifts for himself, but he did desire that those believers bear the fruit of generosity.

God speaks to my heart:

I want those who have riches from Me, material and spiritual, to find ways to lavish abundance on those who have not, first to those called by My name, yet ultimately on all who have need, a continual stretching forth in sharing. Do not grow weary in the part you have, though it seems insignificant. When you give in obedience to My urging, with a cheerful heart, it is like planting seeds: much good will come.

"Your labor in the Lord is not futile."
1 Corinthians 15:58 (AMPLIFIED)

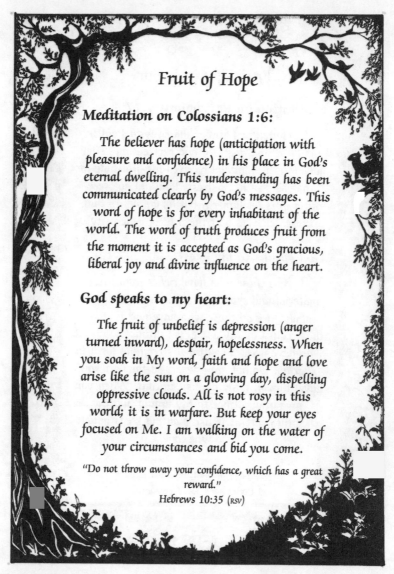

Fruit of Hope

Meditation on Colossians 1:6:

The believer has hope (anticipation with pleasure and confidence) in his place in God's eternal dwelling. This understanding has been communicated clearly by God's messages. This word of hope is for every inhabitant of the world. The word of truth produces fruit from the moment it is accepted as God's gracious, liberal joy and divine influence on the heart.

God speaks to my heart:

The fruit of unbelief is depression (anger turned inward), despair, hopelessness. When you soak in My word, faith and hope and love arise like the sun on a glowing day, dispelling oppressive clouds. All is not rosy in this world; it is in warfare. But keep your eyes focused on Me. I am walking on the water of your circumstances and bid you come.

"Do not throw away your confidence, which has a great reward."
Hebrews 10:35 (RSV)

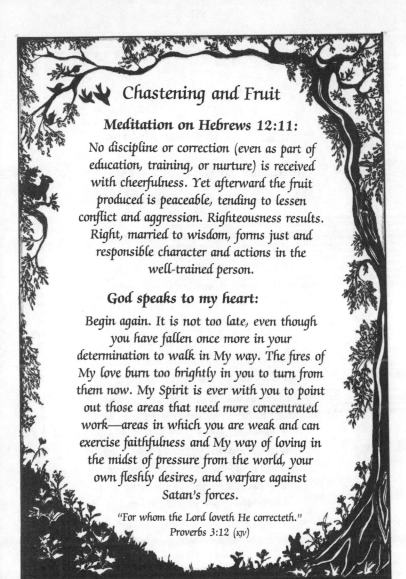

Chastening and Fruit

Meditation on Hebrews 12:11:

No discipline or correction (even as part of
education, training, or nurture) is received
with cheerfulness. Yet afterward the fruit
produced is peaceable, tending to lessen
conflict and aggression. Righteousness results.
Right, married to wisdom, forms just and
responsible character and actions in the
well-trained person.

God speaks to my heart:

Begin again. It is not too late, even though
you have fallen once more in your
determination to walk in My way. The fires of
My love burn too brightly in you to turn from
them now. My Spirit is ever with you to point
out those areas that need more concentrated
work—areas in which you are weak and can
exercise faithfulness and My way of loving in
the midst of pressure from the world, your
own fleshly desires, and warfare against
Satan's forces.

"For whom the Lord loveth He correcteth."
Proverbs 3:12 (kjv)

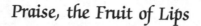

Praise, the Fruit of Lips

Meditation on Hebrews 13:15:

Let us with increasing intensity bring to
God the sacrifice of praise, telling the
story of what He has done, continually,
in every way possible, through the whole
of our lives. Our lips as the pouring
place, we offer thanks, disclose our faults
for cleansing, and promise Him devotion,
as in a betrothal covenant.

God speaks to my heart:

I am with you. I am in you to draw you
further in and higher and deeper and
wider in Me. You are limited only by
your own willingness. This is My love
relationship with you. My love is by
definition all-inclusive, reaching out,
joining heart to heart in the truth and
power and glory of My presence.

"Bless the Lord, O my soul, and forget none of His
benefits."
Psalm 103:2 (NAS)

Wisdom Bears Good Fruit

Meditation on James 3:17:

God's wisdom includes feelings that inspire
sympathy and reasoning that results in
understanding. It is pure, clean, innocent,
modest, chaste, blameless, consecrated. Wisdom
is peaceable: seeking to lessen conflict and
aggression, working toward unity. It is gentle:
quiet, restful, appropriate, mild, patient, yielding.
It is agreeable: trusting, friendly, rich in
compassion and tender actions. Wisdom does not
play favorites. Wisdom is sincere, speaking and
acting honestly. How fruitful, rewarding, and
good is wisdom!

God speaks to my heart:

If you have wisdom, you love. If you love, you
are wise. If you have true wisdom, you will bless
and be blessed. Wisdom is a gift, but it will
grow in you as you experience My love. Ask Me
for it. I have already wrapped it up and put your
name on it!

"[Wisdom] yields better returns than gold."
Proverbs 3:14 (NIV)

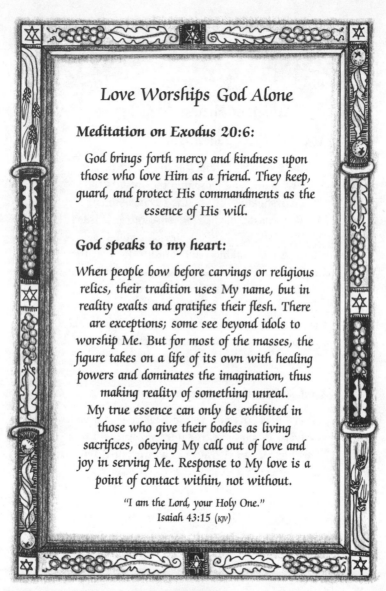

Love Worships God Alone

Meditation on Exodus 20:6:

God brings forth mercy and kindness upon those who love Him as a friend. They keep, guard, and protect His commandments as the essence of His will.

God speaks to my heart:

When people bow before carvings or religious relics, their tradition uses My name, but in reality exalts and gratifies their flesh. There are exceptions; some see beyond idols to worship Me. But for most of the masses, the figure takes on a life of its own with healing powers and dominates the imagination, thus making reality of something unreal.

My true essence can only be exhibited in those who give their bodies as living sacrifices, obeying My call out of love and joy in serving Me. Response to My love is a point of contact within, not without.

"I am the Lord, your Holy One."
Isaiah 43:15 (KJV)

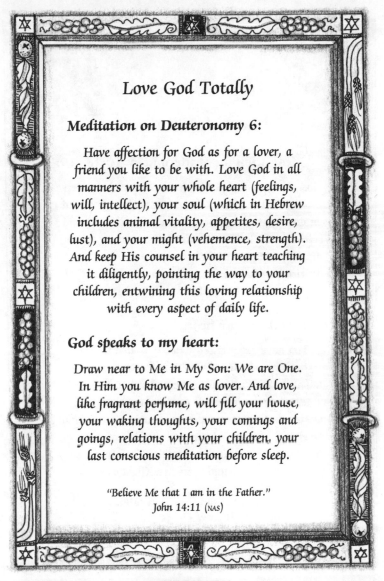

Love God Totally

Meditation on Deuteronomy 6:

Have affection for God as for a lover, a friend you like to be with. Love God in all manners with your whole heart (feelings, will, intellect), your soul (which in Hebrew includes animal vitality, appetites, desire, lust), and your might (vehemence, strength). And keep His counsel in your heart teaching it diligently, pointing the way to your children, entwining this loving relationship with every aspect of daily life.

God speaks to my heart:

Draw near to Me in My Son: We are One. In Him you know Me as lover. And love, like fragrant perfume, will fill your house, your waking thoughts, your comings and goings, relations with your children, your last conscious meditation before sleep.

"Believe Me that I am in the Father."
John 14:11 (NAS)

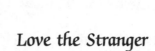

Love the Stranger

Meditation on Deuteronomy 10:18–19:

God accomplishes justice from the pleas of lonely orphans and widows, those bereaved or discarded in divorce, the desolate. He has affection for and befriends the foreigner, alien, and stranger, giving healing and food and clothing. So we, too, must befriend, welcome, love the stranger just as God does.

God speaks to my heart:

You have experienced what it is like to be a stranger—the loneliness, the frustration with language and cultural barriers. Yet you have also tasted of the joy made possible by hands and hearts reaching across the gulf, patiently teaching, receiving, sharing. When you find Me at work in the other, what unity is possible! True spirituality gleams, bringing in My Kingdom.

"Do not neglect to show hospitality to strangers."
Hebrews 13:2 (RSV)

Loving God's Name

Meditation on Psalm 5:11:

All who trust in the Lord—confide in Him, hope in Him, flee to Him for protection—will rejoice because God defends them. Acclamations of joy, as in triumph of battle, will rise. All who commit their physical desires into His care will jump for joy!

God speaks to my heart:

You are in a battle that rages on many fronts at once. Sometimes you feel about to be overcome physically, emotionally, spiritually. My rhythm for you includes opportunities for resting as well as for fighting in the front lines. Sometimes I call you to do what you feel is beyond your endurance, but what I ask of you I enable you to complete in joy.

"After [Abraham] had patiently endured. . . ."
Hebrews 6:15 (KJV)

Secure in God's Love

Meditation on Psalm 18:1–3:

My will, my desire, is to love God with passion.
He is my strength; like a cliff He is a refuge, a
strong, precipitous fortress. I will call out to
Him expressing my need, for He is my husband.
He is good, mighty, worthy of all my boasting. I
will celebrate Him even if my praise seems
foolish to others. I want my gratitude to shine,
for in Him I am safe from my enemies who hate
me.

God speaks to my heart:

David's words are even more meaningful now
because Jesus' blood has secured a lock on those
promises that no man and no power of hell can
break. But you must not give in to bitterness,
anger, or unforgiveness, for that is the same as
opening a doorway for the enemy.

"For thy Maker is thine husband."
Isaiah 54:5 (KJV)

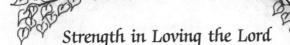

Strength in Loving the Lord

Meditation on Psalm 31:23–24:

Have affection for Him with all your energy, you who
are kind. The Lord protects those who are steady in
their trust. He completes those whose pride is in
what God has done through them. Be cheerful in your
strength, bountiful in help, kindly in conquering. He
will strengthen you physically and mentally when you
trust patiently and confidently in Him.

God speaks to my heart:

Your own self-righteousness is worse than nothing,
enmity to all that God is. In your failure and
weakness, in the midst of ridicule, find and declare
My strength. Receive My holiness as a gift, seeing
yourself as I made you to be. Rejoice as you are
cleansed, set free to begin again, building on the
foundations of those who have believed and not given
up.

"They shall obtain gladness and joy."
Isaiah 51:11 (KJV)

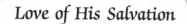

Love of His Salvation

Meditation on Psalm 40:16–17:

You who are committed to searching out the Lord's presence in worship, rejoice and be merry-hearted. You have given Him your energies of love, your desires for deep, intimate friendship. He is the perfect lover who understands totally, who is attentive, passionate. He drew you to His heart, rescuing you from fleshly lusts and Satanic bondages. In Him you found deliverance, help, safety, victory. So let what your mind dwells on, what comes out of your mouth, and the reports you publish, speak one theme: honor the Lord more and more, twisting away from glorifying anything not of or like Him.

God speaks to my heart:

Sometimes you realize how destitute, how desperately needy you are. Let My thoughts permeate your being with My value system, My estimation of your worth.

"The Lord is my light and my salvation."
Psalm 27:1 (KJV)

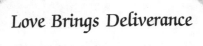

Love Brings Deliverance

Meditation on Psalm 91:14–16:

You join yourself to Him as you delight in and
desire His love. He then places you on an
inaccessible height, a stronghold from your
enemies, a safe place. Because you have known
Him (with senses, mental capacities, intuitive
and imaginative abilities, spiritual discernment)
as a familiar friend or kinsman, you perceive
His presence with you, His true identity and
character. He will pay attention to you,
answering you. He will be with you in tight
places when the adversary presses close or in
times of anguish. He will strip you of every
unnecessary thing, strengthen and equip you so
that you are ready, armed, prepared.

God speaks to my heart:

My respect for you will honor you. Your days
will stretch out in fullness, and you will see
My salvation, victory, prosperity, saving health.

"Wait on the Lord: be of good courage."
Psalm 27:14 (kjv)

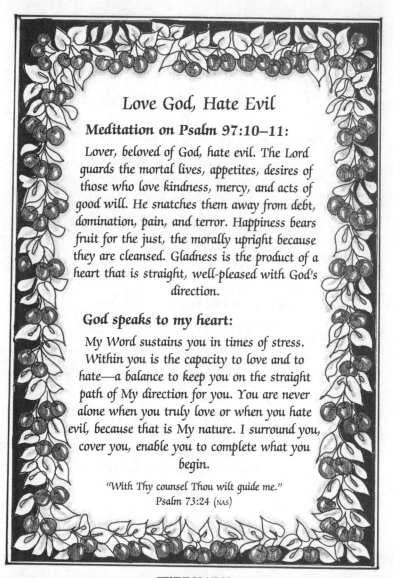

Love God, Hate Evil

Meditation on Psalm 97:10–11:

Lover, beloved of God, hate evil. The Lord guards the mortal lives, appetites, desires of those who love kindness, mercy, and acts of good will. He snatches them away from debt, domination, pain, and terror. Happiness bears fruit for the just, the morally upright because they are cleansed. Gladness is the product of a heart that is straight, well-pleased with God's direction.

God speaks to my heart:

My Word sustains you in times of stress. Within you is the capacity to love and to hate—a balance to keep you on the straight path of My direction for you. You are never alone when you truly love or when you hate evil, because that is My nature. I surround you, cover you, enable you to complete what you begin.

"With Thy counsel Thou wilt guide me."
Psalm 73:24 (NAS)

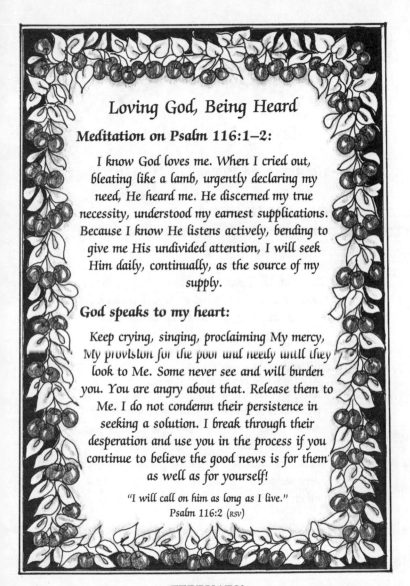

Loving God, Being Heard

Meditation on Psalm 116:1–2:

I know God loves me. When I cried out,
bleating like a lamb, urgently declaring my
need, He heard me. He discerned my true
necessity, understood my earnest supplications.
Because I know He listens actively, bending to
give me His undivided attention, I will seek
Him daily, continually, as the source of my
supply.

God speaks to my heart:

Keep crying, singing, proclaiming My mercy,
My provision for the poor and needy until they
look to Me. Some never see and will burden
you. You are angry about that. Release them to
Me. I do not condemn their persistence in
seeking a solution. I break through their
desperation and use you in the process if you
continue to believe the good news is for them
as well as for yourself!

"I will call on him as long as I live."
Psalm 116:2 (RSV)

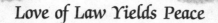

Love of Law Yields Peace

Meditation on Psalm 119:165–167:

Abundant peace, prosperity, safety, rest, and happiness belong to those who love God's Law. This is the lifestyle that results from following biblical precepts. Nothing exists that is able to cause these people to stumble.

Every obstacle can be overcome. The psalmist prays, "I love Your Word and ways wholly. All my course of life, mode of action, and conversation are fully exposed in Your sight."

God speaks to my heart:

I want you to rest in My righteousness and not feel you need to prove your loyalty to Me by doing more. Certainly from time to time you will evaluate your direction and accomplishments. But let My peace flood over every wounded and weary place. The gratitude others see in you will draw them more than many great works.

"Give heed to his commandments."
Exodus 15:26 (RSV)

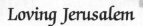

Loving Jerusalem

Meditation on Psalm 122:6:

All who love Jerusalem will be tranquil, secure,
seeking its good, desiring God's presence there
as in Solomon's time when Shekinah glory filled
the Temple. . . . Jerusalem: where Jesus was
dedicated as a baby and the curtain to the Holy
of Holies was torn at His death; where the
Spirit of God was poured out onto ordinary
people, not just in the Temple but in the
streets; where beggars were made whole,
walked, leaped, and praised God!

What does it mean to love Jerusalem, to love
Israel? There is loyalty, but there is also a deep,
passionate concern that God's ways of peace
and faith and love spring forth, uninhibited by
legalism and militarism.

God speaks to my heart:

That tension requires intercession and the
commitment not to give up despite all the
violence. Through those prayers I work glorious
things in you and bring forth the Israel of God.

"Peace shall be upon Israel."
Psalm 125:5 (KJV)

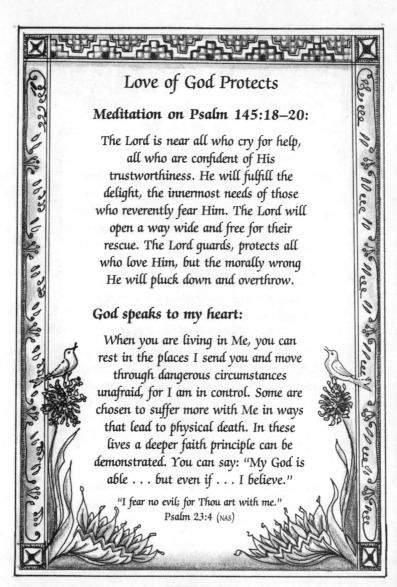

Love of God Protects

Meditation on Psalm 145:18–20:

The Lord is near all who cry for help,
all who are confident of His
trustworthiness. He will fulfill the
delight, the innermost needs of those
who reverently fear Him. The Lord will
open a way wide and free for their
rescue. The Lord guards, protects all
who love Him, but the morally wrong
He will pluck down and overthrow.

God speaks to my heart:

When you are living in Me, you can
rest in the places I send you and move
through dangerous circumstances
unafraid, for I am in control. Some are
chosen to suffer more with Me in ways
that lead to physical death. In these
lives a deeper faith principle can be
demonstrated. You can say: "My God is
able . . . but even if . . . I believe."

"I fear no evil; for Thou art with me."
Psalm 23:4 (NAS)

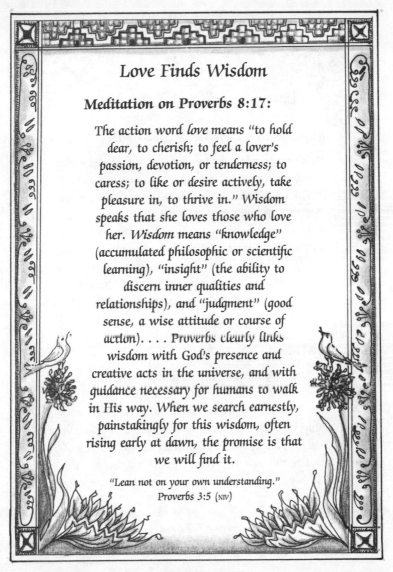

Love Finds Wisdom

Meditation on Proverbs 8:17:

The action word *love* means "to hold dear, to cherish; to feel a lover's passion, devotion, or tenderness; to caress; to like or desire actively, take pleasure in, to thrive in." Wisdom speaks that she loves those who love her. *Wisdom* means "knowledge" (accumulated philosophic or scientific learning), "insight" (the ability to discern inner qualities and relationships), and "judgment" (good sense, a wise attitude or course of action). . . . Proverbs clearly links wisdom with God's presence and creative acts in the universe, and with guidance necessary for humans to walk in His way. When we search earnestly, painstakingly for this wisdom, often rising early at dawn, the promise is that we will find it.

"Lean not on your own understanding."
Proverbs 3:5 (NIV)

Love the Wife of Your Youth

Meditation on Proverbs 5:18–19:

"Let thy fountain be blessed. . . ." A fountain can be a source of water, tears, woman's blood, offspring, wisdom, or happiness. Husband, thank God for "the wife of thy youth." Praise her. Cause to make merry the woman you first chose as bride. Be healed in this relationship and consider your wife affectionately as partner. Let her breasts slake your thirst, abundantly satisfy your fleshly appetites. Constantly, regularly be intoxicated, enraptured with her love!

God speaks to my heart:

Many marriages grow stale and unbearable in patterns of rejection, anger, and retribution, thus making a new "affair" with someone else seem alluring. Seek new ways to find heights of pleasure and depths of joy in each other as you grow and change through the years. This is a demonstration of My love relationship with you, forgiveness in action.

"Let marriage be held in honor."
Hebrews 13:4 (RSV)

Love Covers All Sins

Meditation on Proverbs 10:12:

Hatred, which is intense hostility usually borne of fear or anger or a sense of injury, stirs itself up into discord, quarrels, and contentions. But love (true affection and friendship) fills up the hollows, conceals, hides, covers. This love does not ignore, punish, or gossip about sins, but in secret intercession repeatedly touches the object of prayer with the acceptance and encouragement needed to set the person or nation free from rebellion and transgression.

God speaks to my heart:

You have felt My hand restrain and discipline you when you deliberately or accidentally walked in the wrong direction. Love rests in a covering of forgiveness, patience, and eternal hope.

"Love one another, as I have loved you."
John 15:12 (KJV)

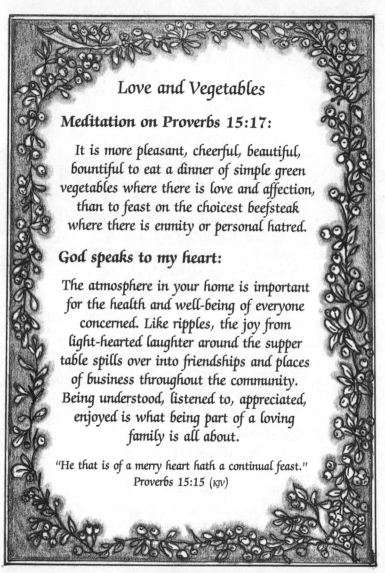

Love and Vegetables

Meditation on Proverbs 15:17:

It is more pleasant, cheerful, beautiful,
bountiful to eat a dinner of simple green
vegetables where there is love and affection,
than to feast on the choicest beefsteak
where there is enmity or personal hatred.

God speaks to my heart:

The atmosphere in your home is important
for the health and well-being of everyone
concerned. Like ripples, the joy from
light-hearted laughter around the supper
table spills over into friendships and places
of business throughout the community.
Being understood, listened to, appreciated,
enjoyed is what being part of a loving
family is all about.

"He that is of a merry heart hath a continual feast."
Proverbs 15:15 (KJV)

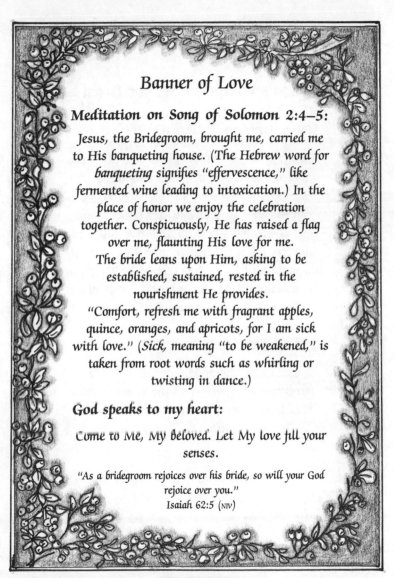

Banner of Love

Meditation on Song of Solomon 2:4–5:

Jesus, the Bridegroom, brought me, carried me
to His banqueting house. (The Hebrew word for
banqueting signifies "effervescence," like
fermented wine leading to intoxication.) In the
place of honor we enjoy the celebration
together. Conspicuously, He has raised a flag
over me, flaunting His love for me.
The bride leans upon Him, asking to be
established, sustained, rested in the
nourishment He provides.
"Comfort, refresh me with fragrant apples,
quince, oranges, and apricots, for I am sick
with love." (*Sick*, meaning "to be weakened," is
taken from root words such as whirling or
twisting in dance.)

God speaks to my heart:

Come to Me, My beloved. Let My love fill your
senses.

"As a bridegroom rejoices over his bride, so will your God
rejoice over you."
Isaiah 62:5 (NIV)

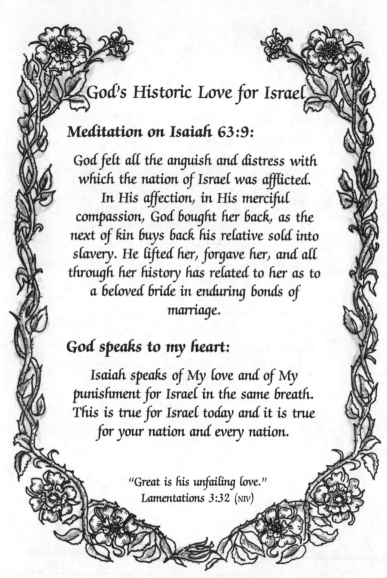

God's Historic Love for Israel

Meditation on Isaiah 63:9:

God felt all the anguish and distress with
which the nation of Israel was afflicted.
In His affection, in His merciful
compassion, God bought her back, as the
next of kin buys back his relative sold into
slavery. He lifted her, forgave her, and all
through her history has related to her as to
a beloved bride in enduring bonds of
marriage.

God speaks to my heart:

Isaiah speaks of My love and of My
punishment for Israel in the same breath.
This is true for Israel today and it is true
for your nation and every nation.

"Great is his unfailing love."
Lamentations 3:32 (NIV)

Prepared for Love

Meditation on Song of Solomon 4:10:

Jesus sees us, His bride, through eyes of love as perfect. To Him our love is more merry, more precious than bubbling wine. The gift of our rich, perfumed anointing oil is better than all other spices and sweet odors.

God speaks to my heart:

When you have prepared yourself to be with Me, when you have received My Holy Spirit's breath and bathed in His sweet, softening lotion, what a joy it is to be together! It is important that you take time to love yourself enough to receive My love. From this fullness a refreshing stream flows to others and witnesses to the fact that I am love, for they will see that you are loved.

"I was glad when they said unto me, Let us go into the house of the Lord."
Psalm 122:1 (kjv)

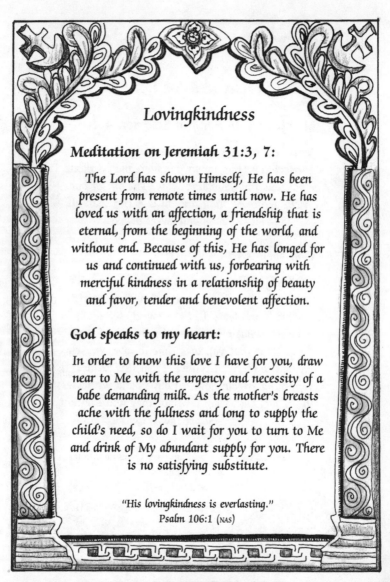

Lovingkindness

Meditation on Jeremiah 31:3, 7:

The Lord has shown Himself, He has been present from remote times until now. He has loved us with an affection, a friendship that is eternal, from the beginning of the world, and without end. Because of this, He has longed for us and continued with us, forbearing with merciful kindness in a relationship of beauty and favor, tender and benevolent affection.

God speaks to my heart:

In order to know this love I have for you, draw near to Me with the urgency and necessity of a babe demanding milk. As the mother's breasts ache with the fullness and long to supply the child's need, so do I wait for you to turn to Me and drink of My abundant supply for you. There is no satisfying substitute.

"His lovingkindness is everlasting."
Psalm 106:1 (NAS)

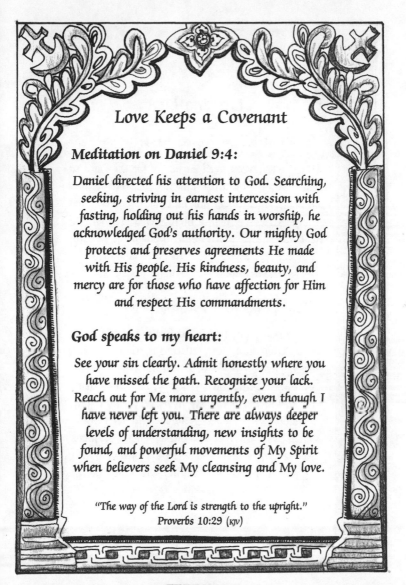

Love Keeps a Covenant

Meditation on Daniel 9:4:

Daniel directed his attention to God. Searching, seeking, striving in earnest intercession with fasting, holding out his hands in worship, he acknowledged God's authority. Our mighty God protects and preserves agreements He made with His people. His kindness, beauty, and mercy are for those who have affection for Him and respect His commandments.

God speaks to my heart:

See your sin clearly. Admit honestly where you have missed the path. Recognize your lack. Reach out for Me more urgently, even though I have never left you. There are always deeper levels of understanding, new insights to be found, and powerful movements of My Spirit when believers seek My cleansing and My love.

"The way of the Lord is strength to the upright."
Proverbs 10:29 (KJV)

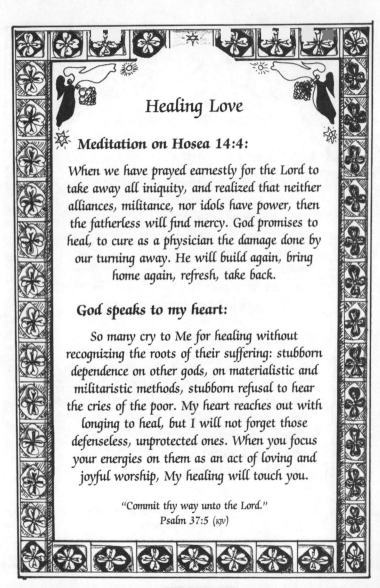

Healing Love

Meditation on Hosea 14:4:

When we have prayed earnestly for the Lord to take away all iniquity, and realized that neither alliances, militance, nor idols have power, then the fatherless will find mercy. God promises to heal, to cure as a physician the damage done by our turning away. He will build again, bring home again, refresh, take back.

God speaks to my heart:

So many cry to Me for healing without recognizing the roots of their suffering: stubborn dependence on other gods, on materialistic and militaristic methods, stubborn refusal to hear the cries of the poor. My heart reaches out with longing to heal, but I will not forget those defenseless, unprotected ones. When you focus your energies on them as an act of loving and joyful worship, My healing will touch you.

"Commit thy way unto the Lord."
Psalm 37:5 (kjv)

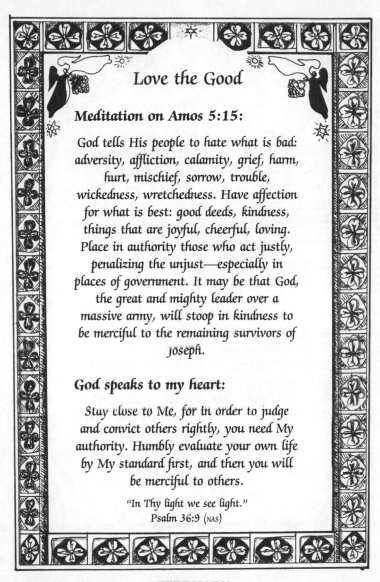

Love the Good

Meditation on Amos 5:15:

God tells His people to hate what is bad: adversity, affliction, calamity, grief, harm, hurt, mischief, sorrow, trouble, wickedness, wretchedness. Have affection for what is best: good deeds, kindness, things that are joyful, cheerful, loving. Place in authority those who act justly, penalizing the unjust—especially in places of government. It may be that God, the great and mighty leader over a massive army, will stoop in kindness to be merciful to the remaining survivors of Joseph.

God speaks to my heart:

Stay close to Me, for in order to judge and convict others rightly, you need My authority. Humbly evaluate your own life by My standard first, and then you will be merciful to others.

"In Thy light we see light."
Psalm 36:9 (NAS)

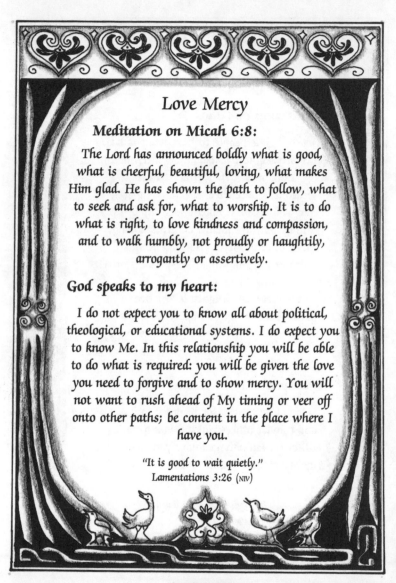

Love Mercy

Meditation on Micah 6:8:

The Lord has announced boldly what is good,
what is cheerful, beautiful, loving, what makes
Him glad. He has shown the path to follow, what
to seek and ask for, what to worship. It is to do
what is right, to love kindness and compassion,
and to walk humbly, not proudly or haughtily,
arrogantly or assertively.

God speaks to my heart:

I do not expect you to know all about political,
theological, or educational systems. I do expect you
to know Me. In this relationship you will be able
to do what is required: you will be given the love
you need to forgive and to show mercy. You will
not want to rush ahead of My timing or veer off
onto other paths; be content in the place where I
have you.

"It is good to wait quietly."
Lamentations 3:26 (NIV)

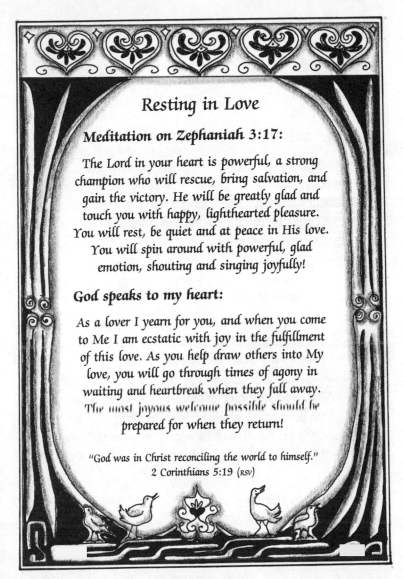

Resting in Love

Meditation on Zephaniah 3:17:

The Lord in your heart is powerful, a strong
champion who will rescue, bring salvation, and
gain the victory. He will be greatly glad and
touch you with happy, lighthearted pleasure.
You will rest, be quiet and at peace in His love.
You will spin around with powerful, glad
emotion, shouting and singing joyfully!

God speaks to my heart:

As a lover I yearn for you, and when you come
to Me I am ecstatic with joy in the fulfillment
of this love. As you help draw others into My
love, you will go through times of agony in
waiting and heartbreak when they fall away.
The most joyous welcome possible should be
prepared for when they return!

"God was in Christ reconciling the world to himself."
2 Corinthians 5:19 (RSV)

Love Corrects

Meditation on Proverbs 3:12:

The one God loves, He corrects (convicts, rebukes, reproves, convinces of just action) as a loving father his son. Do not reject or refuse the Lord's warning, instruction, restraint, or discipline. Do not be anxious. Do not sever yourself from His correction.

God speaks to my heart:

You can never cast the first stone at others because when you search your mind and heart, you see the greater measure of My mercy, compassion, and forgiveness toward you. Let Me do the correcting and judging in every case, for I alone do it rightly, without self-interest. Bring back the prodigals and include your own failures in this cleansing love as a witness to My power to make all things new.

"Whoever loves discipline loves knowledge."
Proverbs 12:1 (NIV)

A Friend Loves

Meditation on Proverbs 17:17:

A true friend, one attached to another by affection or esteem, loves totally, at all times, continually. That friend who stays close in times of adversity, tightness, trouble, anguish, affliction, distress, or rivalry, becomes dearer than a brother or sister.

God speaks to my heart:

Love is always costly. It is painful to go through childbirth, but how much richer your life is for having children. Every person you love will cause you pain at times. My nature in you always urges you to keep pushing, keep stretching toward more and deeper love relationships that forgive your own failings as well as those of others. When My love is reproduced in the earth, My Kingdom is come!

"Filled with compassion, Jesus reached out his hand."
Mark 1:41 (NIV)

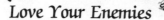

Love Your Enemies

Meditation on Matthew 5:44:

Love (as a decision) your enemies, those who
are hateful, actively hostile. Bless, speak
well of those who curse and detest you. Do
good, be honest and fair to them. Pray,
holding your mind toward those who
threaten, insult, slander, and falsely accuse
you, who follow after you to harass,
persecute, or injure you.

God speaks to my heart:

The love I call you to is a lifetime decision
to see others through My eyes of
compassion, even when they are wounding
you terribly. Every human stands before Me
in need of forgiveness. When your enemies in
the midst of their hate and evil are
confronted by love, the shock can be just the
thing to cause them to desire My presence,
painful though the cleansing be.

"Jesus said, 'Father, forgive them, for they do not know
what they are doing.' "
Luke 23:34 (NIV)

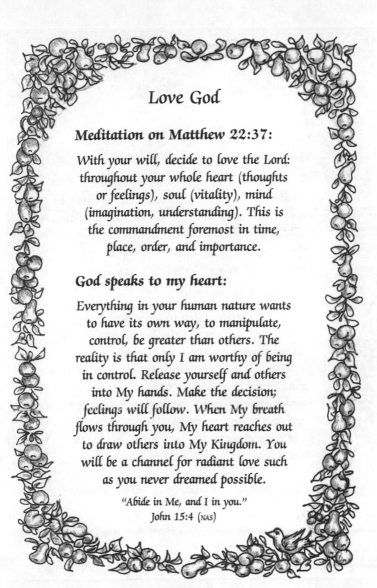

Love God

Meditation on Matthew 22:37:

With your will, decide to love the Lord:
throughout your whole heart (thoughts
or feelings), soul (vitality), mind
(imagination, understanding). This is
the commandment foremost in time,
place, order, and importance.

God speaks to my heart:

Everything in your human nature wants
to have its own way, to manipulate,
control, be greater than others. The
reality is that only I am worthy of being
in control. Release yourself and others
into My hands. Make the decision;
feelings will follow. When My breath
flows through you, My heart reaches out
to draw others into My Kingdom. You
will be a channel for radiant love such
as you never dreamed possible.

"Abide in Me, and I in you."
John 15:4 (NAS)

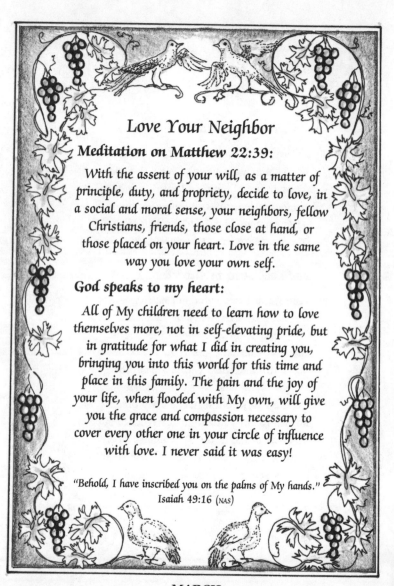

Love Your Neighbor

Meditation on Matthew 22:39:

With the assent of your will, as a matter of principle, duty, and propriety, decide to love, in a social and moral sense, your neighbors, fellow Christians, friends, those close at hand, or those placed on your heart. Love in the same way you love your own self.

God speaks to my heart:

All of My children need to learn how to love themselves more, not in self-elevating pride, but in gratitude for what I did in creating you, bringing you into this world for this time and place in this family. The pain and the joy of your life, when flooded with My own, will give you the grace and compassion necessary to cover every other one in your circle of influence with love. I never said it was easy!

"Behold, I have inscribed you on the palms of My hands."
Isaiah 49:16 (NAS)

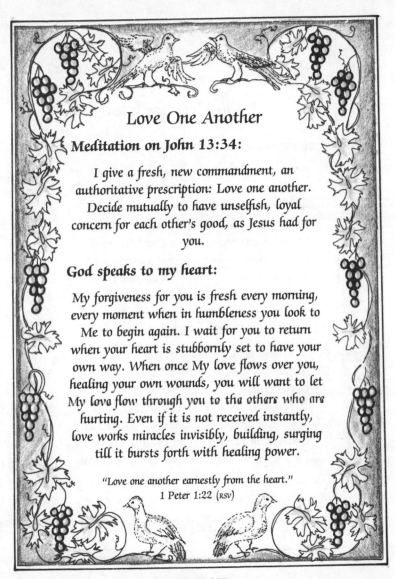

Love One Another

Meditation on John 13:34:

I give a fresh, new commandment, an authoritative prescription: Love one another. Decide mutually to have unselfish, loyal concern for each other's good, as Jesus had for you.

God speaks to my heart:

My forgiveness for you is fresh every morning, every moment when in humbleness you look to Me to begin again. I wait for you to return when your heart is stubbornly set to have your own way. When once My love flows over you, healing your own wounds, you will want to let My love flow through you to the others who are hurting. Even if it is not received instantly, love works miracles invisibly, building, surging till it bursts forth with healing power.

"Love one another earnestly from the heart."
1 Peter 1:22 (RSV)

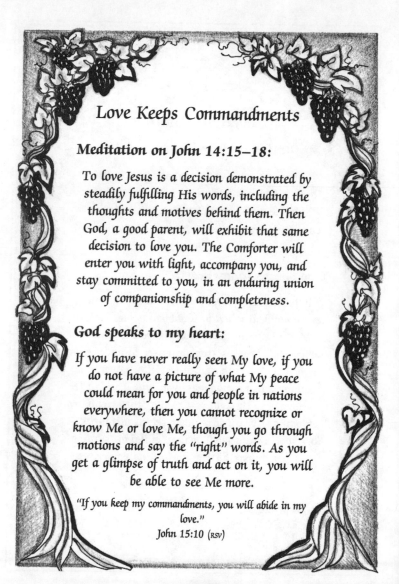

Love Keeps Commandments

Meditation on John 14:15–18:

To love Jesus is a decision demonstrated by steadily fulfilling His words, including the thoughts and motives behind them. Then God, a good parent, will exhibit that same decision to love you. The Comforter will enter you with light, accompany you, and stay committed to you, in an enduring union of companionship and completeness.

God speaks to my heart:

If you have never really seen My love, if you do not have a picture of what My peace could mean for you and people in nations everywhere, then you cannot recognize or know Me or love Me, though you go through motions and say the "right" words. As you get a glimpse of truth and act on it, you will be able to see Me more.

"If you keep my commandments, you will abide in my love."
John 15:10 (RSV)

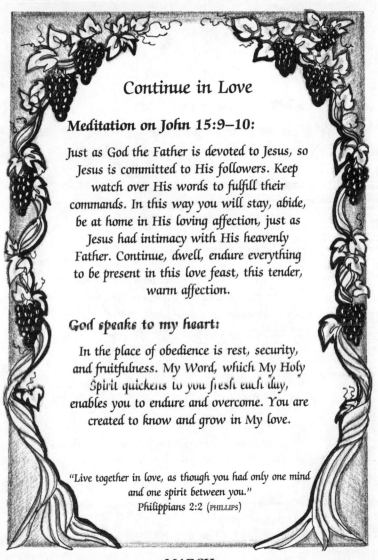

Continue in Love

Meditation on John 15:9–10:

Just as God the Father is devoted to Jesus, so
Jesus is committed to His followers. Keep
watch over His words to fulfill their
commands. In this way you will stay, abide,
be at home in His loving affection, just as
Jesus had intimacy with His heavenly
Father. Continue, dwell, endure everything
to be present in this love feast, this tender,
warm affection.

God speaks to my heart:

In the place of obedience is rest, security,
and fruitfulness. My Word, which My Holy
Spirit quickens to you fresh each day,
enables you to endure and overcome. You are
created to know and grow in My love.

"Live together in love, as though you had only one mind
and one spirit between you."
Philippians 2:2 (PHILLIPS)

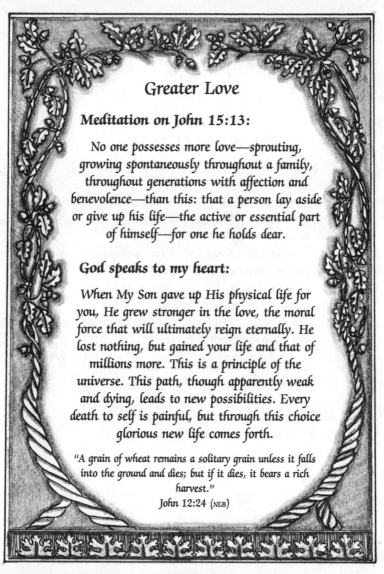

Greater Love

Meditation on John 15:13:

No one possesses more love—sprouting, growing spontaneously throughout a family, throughout generations with affection and benevolence—than this: that a person lay aside or give up his life—the active or essential part of himself—for one he holds dear.

God speaks to my heart:

When My Son gave up His physical life for you, He grew stronger in the love, the moral force that will ultimately reign eternally. He lost nothing, but gained your life and that of millions more. This is a principle of the universe. This path, though apparently weak and dying, leads to new possibilities. Every death to self is painful, but through this choice glorious new life comes forth.

"A grain of wheat remains a solitary grain unless it falls into the ground and dies; but if it dies, it bears a rich harvest."
John 12:24 (NEB)

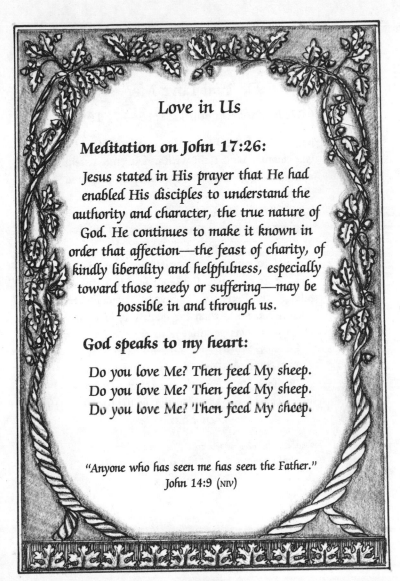

Love in Us

Meditation on John 17:26:

Jesus stated in His prayer that He had enabled His disciples to understand the authority and character, the true nature of God. He continues to make it known in order that affection—the feast of charity, of kindly liberality and helpfulness, especially toward those needy or suffering—may be possible in and through us.

God speaks to my heart:

Do you love Me? Then feed My sheep.
Do you love Me? Then feed My sheep.
Do you love Me? Then feed My sheep.

"Anyone who has seen me has seen the Father."
John 14:9 (NIV)

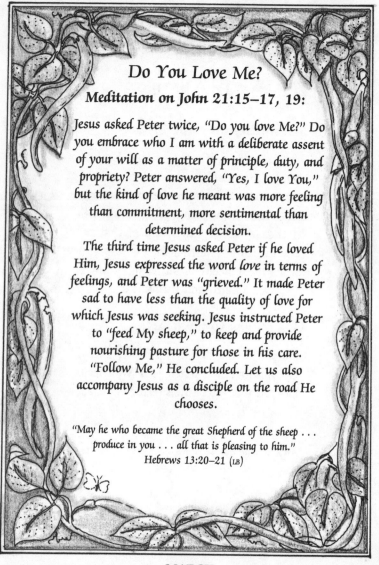

Do You Love Me?

Meditation on John 21:15–17, 19:

Jesus asked Peter twice, "Do you love Me?" Do you embrace who I am with a deliberate assent of your will as a matter of principle, duty, and propriety? Peter answered, "Yes, I love You," but the kind of love he meant was more feeling than commitment, more sentimental than determined decision.

The third time Jesus asked Peter if he loved Him, Jesus expressed the word *love* in terms of feelings, and Peter was "grieved." It made Peter sad to have less than the quality of love for which Jesus was seeking. Jesus instructed Peter to "feed My sheep," to keep and provide nourishing pasture for those in his care. "Follow Me," He concluded. Let us also accompany Jesus as a disciple on the road He chooses.

"May he who became the great Shepherd of the sheep . . . produce in you . . . all that is pleasing to him."
Hebrews 13:20–21 (LB)

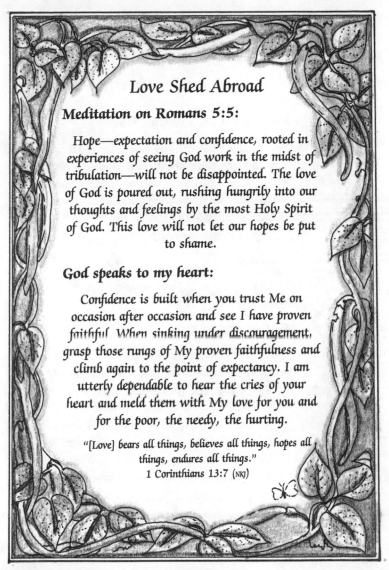

Love Shed Abroad

Meditation on Romans 5:5:

Hope—expectation and confidence, rooted in experiences of seeing God work in the midst of tribulation—will not be disappointed. The love of God is poured out, rushing hungrily into our thoughts and feelings by the most Holy Spirit of God. This love will not let our hopes be put to shame.

God speaks to my heart:

Confidence is built when you trust Me on occasion after occasion and see I have proven faithful. When sinking under discouragement, grasp those rungs of My proven faithfulness and climb again to the point of expectancy. I am utterly dependable to hear the cries of your heart and meld them with My love for you and for the poor, the needy, the hurting.

"[Love] bears all things, believes all things, hopes all things, endures all things."
1 Corinthians 13:7 (NKJ)

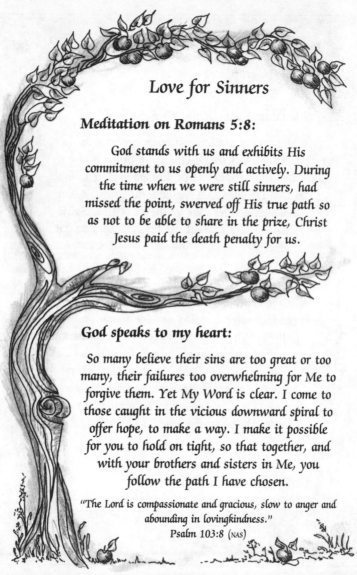

Love for Sinners

Meditation on Romans 5:8:

God stands with us and exhibits His commitment to us openly and actively. During the time when we were still sinners, had missed the point, swerved off His true path so as not to be able to share in the prize, Christ Jesus paid the death penalty for us.

God speaks to my heart:

So many believe their sins are too great or too many, their failures too overwhelming for Me to forgive them. Yet My Word is clear. I come to those caught in the vicious downward spiral to offer hope, to make a way. I make it possible for you to hold on tight, so that together, and with your brothers and sisters in Me, you follow the path I have chosen.

"The Lord is compassionate and gracious, slow to anger and abounding in lovingkindness."
Psalm 103:8 (NAS)

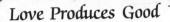

Love Produces Good

Meditation on Romans 8:28:

We, with only a casual understanding, can perceive that the whole of the Logos—the active Word and motives of God—benefits us thoroughly when we are in a love relationship with God marked by doing good to others—those God has chosen us to touch in a specific place and time. His proposed intentions are set forth and exposed like the shewbread in the Temple.

God speaks to my heart:

You have often heard this verse in the context of My working things out for you when you are in troubling circumstances. That is true, but it is only a byproduct of the lifestyle that lays itself down for others, that fulfills My purposes.

"Beloved, let us love one another, for love is of God."
1 John 4:7 (NKJ)

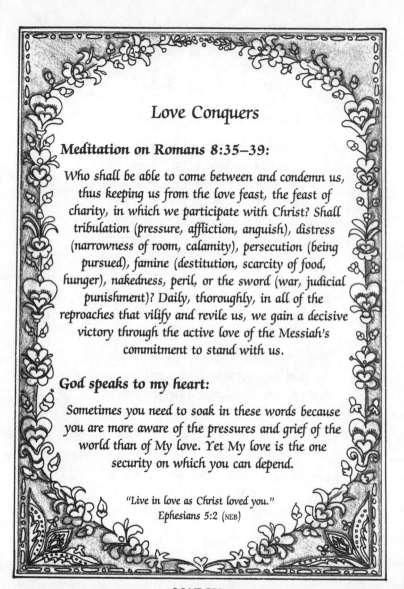

Love Conquers

Meditation on Romans 8:35–39:

Who shall be able to come between and condemn us,
thus keeping us from the love feast, the feast of
charity, in which we participate with Christ? Shall
tribulation (pressure, affliction, anguish), distress
(narrowness of room, calamity), persecution (being
pursued), famine (destitution, scarcity of food,
hunger), nakedness, peril, or the sword (war, judicial
punishment)? Daily, thoroughly, in all of the
reproaches that vilify and revile us, we gain a decisive
victory through the active love of the Messiah's
commitment to stand with us.

God speaks to my heart:

Sometimes you need to soak in these words because
you are more aware of the pressures and grief of the
world than of My love. Yet My love is the one
security on which you can depend.

"Live in love as Christ loved you."
Ephesians 5:2 (NEB)

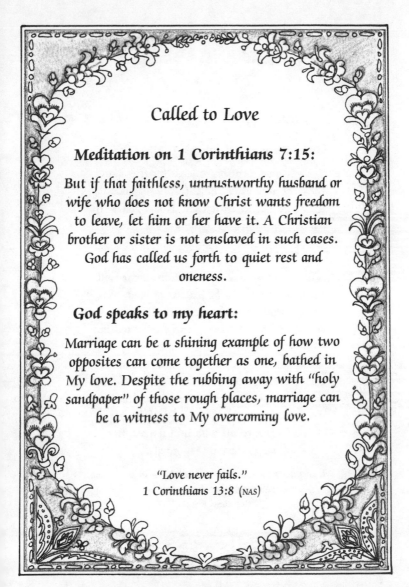

Called to Love

Meditation on 1 Corinthians 7:15:

But if that faithless, untrustworthy husband or wife who does not know Christ wants freedom to leave, let him or her have it. A Christian brother or sister is not enslaved in such cases. God has called us forth to quiet rest and oneness.

God speaks to my heart:

Marriage can be a shining example of how two opposites can come together as one, bathed in My love. Despite the rubbing away with "holy sandpaper" of those rough places, marriage can be a witness to My overcoming love.

"Love never fails."
1 Corinthians 13:8 (NAS)

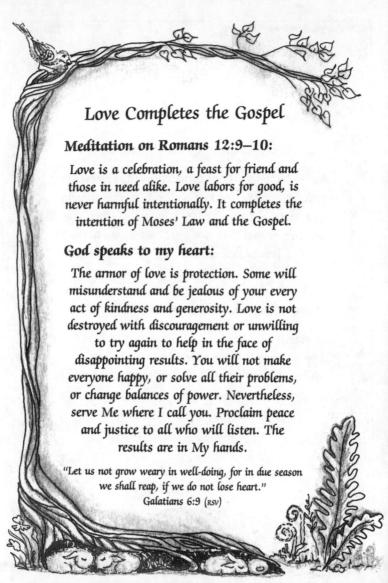

Love Completes the Gospel

Meditation on Romans 12:9–10:

Love is a celebration, a feast for friend and those in need alike. Love labors for good, is never harmful intentionally. It completes the intention of Moses' Law and the Gospel.

God speaks to my heart:

The armor of love is protection. Some will misunderstand and be jealous of your every act of kindness and generosity. Love is not destroyed with discouragement or unwilling to try again to help in the face of disappointing results. You will not make everyone happy, or solve all their problems, or change balances of power. Nevertheless, serve Me where I call you. Proclaim peace and justice to all who will listen. The results are in My hands.

"Let us not grow weary in well-doing, for in due season we shall reap, if we do not lose heart."
Galatians 6:9 (RSV)

Love Constrains

Meditation on 2 Corinthians 5:14:

The love feast, the affectionate generosity of
Jesus, holds us together. If one died for all,
then all were dead; He died for all and was
raised. Now we no longer live for ourselves
but for Him.

God speaks to my heart:

Every day is a gift. How dare you waste
your life frivolously or in drudgery being
enslaved to any cause or person? No! Your
life is Mine, holy! In My yoke alone, pulling
with those I join with you, is satisfaction,
whether or not your plans for each loved one
work out the way you want. Until you make
this choice, you will find yourself chafing at
bitter circumstances. Part of your load is
prayer, plowing deep with My Spirit, so that
their seeds will grow. But no matter what
decision they make, you can choose obedient
joy!

"I have been crucified with Christ."
Galatians 2:20 (NIV)

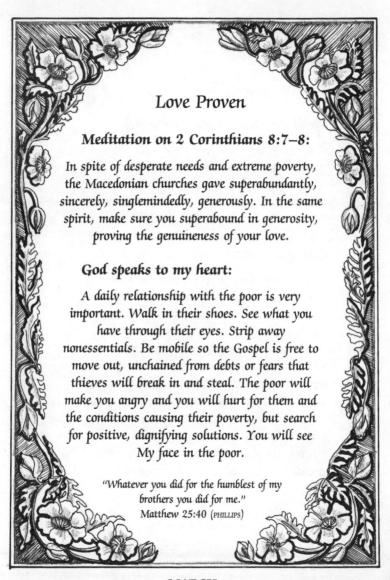

Love Proven

Meditation on 2 Corinthians 8:7–8:

In spite of desperate needs and extreme poverty, the Macedonian churches gave superabundantly, sincerely, singlemindedly, generously. In the same spirit, make sure you superabound in generosity, proving the genuineness of your love.

God speaks to my heart:

A daily relationship with the poor is very important. Walk in their shoes. See what you have through their eyes. Strip away nonessentials. Be mobile so the Gospel is free to move out, unchained from debts or fears that thieves will break in and steal. The poor will make you angry and you will hurt for them and the conditions causing their poverty, but search for positive, dignifying solutions. You will see My face in the poor.

"Whatever you did for the humblest of my brothers you did for me."
Matthew 25:40 (PHILLIPS)

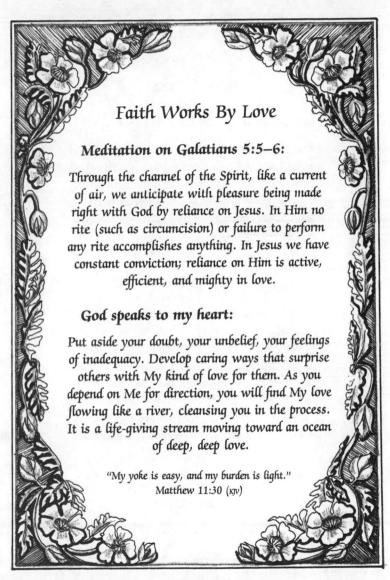

Faith Works By Love

Meditation on Galatians 5:5–6:

Through the channel of the Spirit, like a current of air, we anticipate with pleasure being made right with God by reliance on Jesus. In Him no rite (such as circumcision) or failure to perform any rite accomplishes anything. In Jesus we have constant conviction; reliance on Him is active, efficient, and mighty in love.

God speaks to my heart:

Put aside your doubt, your unbelief, your feelings of inadequacy. Develop caring ways that surprise others with My kind of love for them. As you depend on Me for direction, you will find My love flowing like a river, cleansing you in the process. It is a life-giving stream moving toward an ocean of deep, deep love.

"My yoke is easy, and my burden is light."
Matthew 11:30 (KJV)

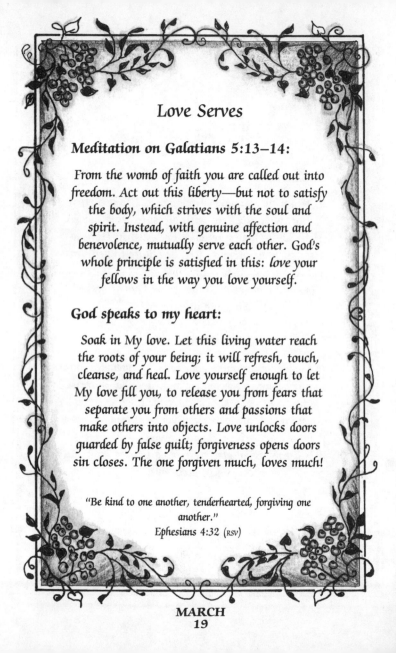

Love Serves

Meditation on Galatians 5:13–14:

From the womb of faith you are called out into freedom. Act out this liberty—but not to satisfy the body, which strives with the soul and spirit. Instead, with genuine affection and benevolence, mutually serve each other. God's whole principle is satisfied in this: love your fellows in the way you love yourself.

God speaks to my heart:

Soak in My love. Let this living water reach the roots of your being; it will refresh, touch, cleanse, and heal. Love yourself enough to let My love fill you, to release you from fears that separate you from others and passions that make others into objects. Love unlocks doors guarded by false guilt; forgiveness opens doors sin closes. The one forgiven much, loves much!

"Be kind to one another, tenderhearted, forgiving one another."
Ephesians 4:32 (RSV)

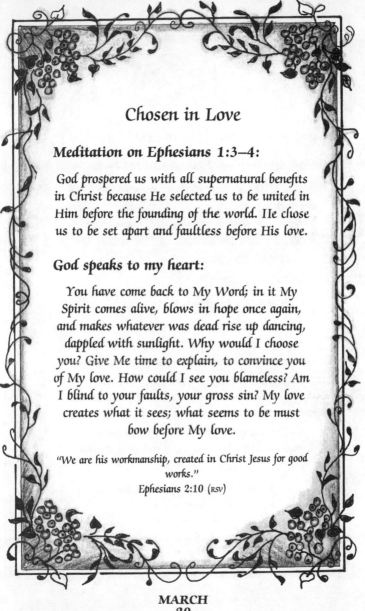

Chosen in Love

Meditation on Ephesians 1:3–4:

God prospered us with all supernatural benefits
in Christ because He selected us to be united in
Him before the founding of the world. He chose
us to be set apart and faultless before His love.

God speaks to my heart:

You have come back to My Word; in it My
Spirit comes alive, blows in hope once again,
and makes whatever was dead rise up dancing,
dappled with sunlight. Why would I choose
you? Give Me time to explain, to convince you
of My love. How could I see you blameless? Am
I blind to your faults, your gross sin? My love
creates what it sees; what seems to be must
bow before My love.

"We are his workmanship, created in Christ Jesus for good
works."
Ephesians 2:10 (RSV)

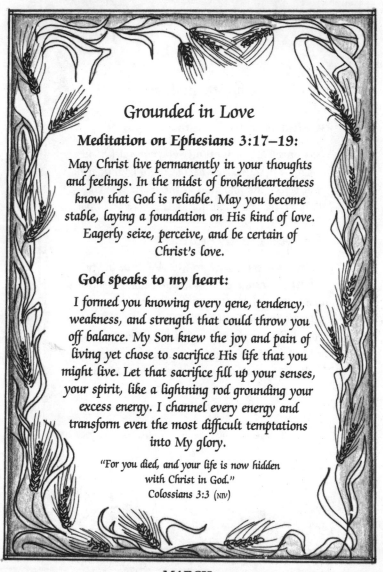

Grounded in Love

Meditation on Ephesians 3:17–19:

May Christ live permanently in your thoughts
and feelings. In the midst of brokenheartedness
know that God is reliable. May you become
stable, laying a foundation on His kind of love.
Eagerly seize, perceive, and be certain of
Christ's love.

God speaks to my heart:

I formed you knowing every gene, tendency,
weakness, and strength that could throw you
off balance. My Son knew the joy and pain of
living yet chose to sacrifice His life that you
might live. Let that sacrifice fill up your senses,
your spirit, like a lightning rod grounding your
excess energy. I channel every energy and
transform even the most difficult temptations
into My glory.

"For you died, and your life is now hidden
with Christ in God."
Colossians 3:3 (NIV)

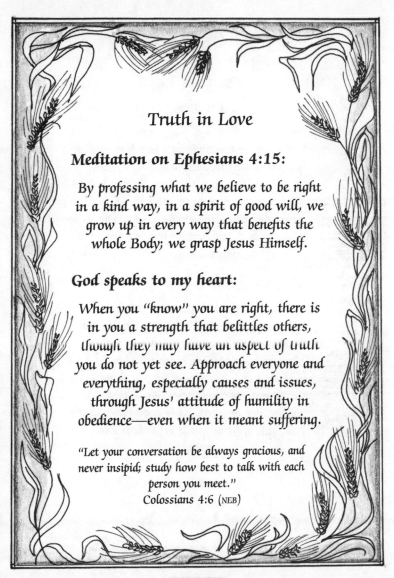

Truth in Love

Meditation on Ephesians 4:15:

By professing what we believe to be right
in a kind way, in a spirit of good will, we
grow up in every way that benefits the
whole Body; we grasp Jesus Himself.

God speaks to my heart:

When you "know" you are right, there is
in you a strength that belittles others,
though they may have an aspect of truth
you do not yet see. Approach everyone and
everything, especially causes and issues,
through Jesus' attitude of humility in
obedience—even when it meant suffering.

"Let your conversation be always gracious, and
never insipid; study how best to talk with each
person you meet."
Colossians 4:6 (NEB)

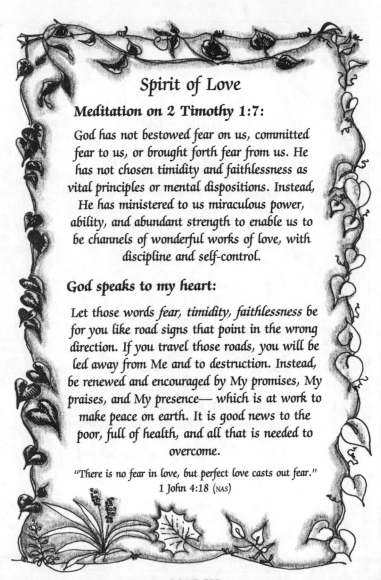

Spirit of Love

Meditation on 2 Timothy 1:7:

God has not bestowed fear on us, committed fear to us, or brought forth fear from us. He has not chosen timidity and faithlessness as vital principles or mental dispositions. Instead, He has ministered to us miraculous power, ability, and abundant strength to enable us to be channels of wonderful works of love, with discipline and self-control.

God speaks to my heart:

Let those words *fear, timidity, faithlessness* be for you like road signs that point in the wrong direction. If you travel those roads, you will be led away from Me and to destruction. Instead, be renewed and encouraged by My promises, My praises, and My presence— which is at work to make peace on earth. It is good news to the poor, full of health, and all that is needed to overcome.

"There is no fear in love, but perfect love casts out fear."
1 John 4:18 (NAS)

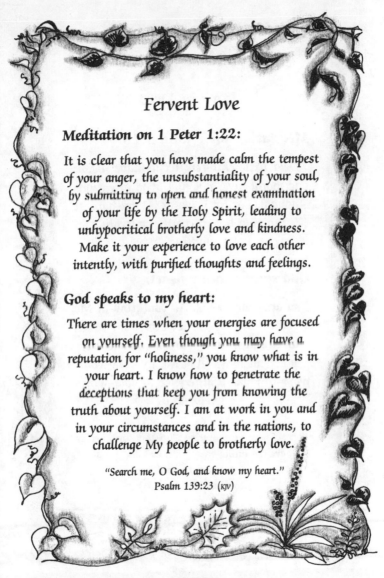

Fervent Love

Meditation on 1 Peter 1:22:

It is clear that you have made calm the tempest
of your anger, the unsubstantiality of your soul,
by submitting to open and honest examination
of your life by the Holy Spirit, leading to
unhypocritical brotherly love and kindness.
Make it your experience to love each other
intently, with purified thoughts and feelings.

God speaks to my heart:

There are times when your energies are focused
on yourself. Even though you may have a
reputation for "holiness," you know what is in
your heart. I know how to penetrate the
deceptions that keep you from knowing the
truth about yourself. I am at work in you and
in your circumstances and in the nations, to
challenge My people to brotherly love.

"Search me, O God, and know my heart."
Psalm 139:23 (KJV)

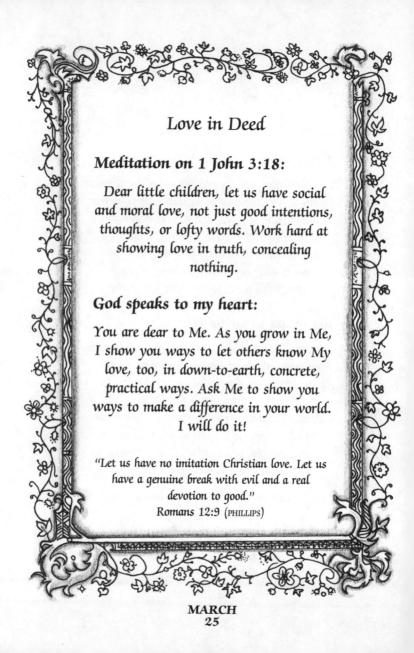

Love in Deed

Meditation on 1 John 3:18:

Dear little children, let us have social and moral love, not just good intentions, thoughts, or lofty words. Work hard at showing love in truth, concealing nothing.

God speaks to my heart:

You are dear to Me. As you grow in Me, I show you ways to let others know My love, too, in down-to-earth, concrete, practical ways. Ask Me to show you ways to make a difference in your world. I will do it!

"Let us have no imitation Christian love. Let us have a genuine break with evil and a real devotion to good."
Romans 12:9 (PHILLIPS)

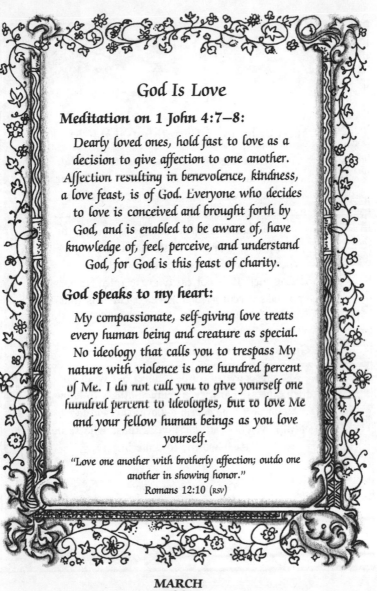

God Is Love

Meditation on 1 John 4:7–8:

Dearly loved ones, hold fast to love as a decision to give affection to one another. Affection resulting in benevolence, kindness, a love feast, is of God. Everyone who decides to love is conceived and brought forth by God, and is enabled to be aware of, have knowledge of, feel, perceive, and understand God, for God is this feast of charity.

God speaks to my heart:

My compassionate, self-giving love treats every human being and creature as special. No ideology that calls you to trespass My nature with violence is one hundred percent of Me. I do not call you to give yourself one hundred percent to ideologies, but to love Me and your fellow human beings as you love yourself.

"Love one another with brotherly affection; outdo one another in showing honor."
Romans 12:10 (RSV)

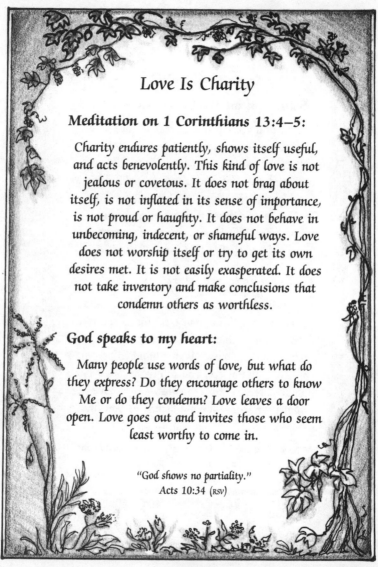

Love Is Charity

Meditation on 1 Corinthians 13:4–5:

Charity endures patiently, shows itself useful,
and acts benevolently. This kind of love is not
jealous or covetous. It does not brag about
itself, is not inflated in its sense of importance,
is not proud or haughty. It does not behave in
unbecoming, indecent, or shameful ways. Love
does not worship itself or try to get its own
desires met. It is not easily exasperated. It does
not take inventory and make conclusions that
condemn others as worthless.

God speaks to my heart:

Many people use words of love, but what do
they express? Do they encourage others to know
Me or do they condemn? Love leaves a door
open. Love goes out and invites those who seem
least worthy to come in.

"God shows no partiality."
Acts 10:34 (RSV)

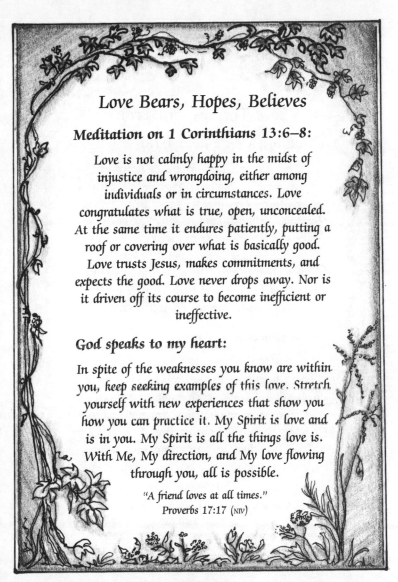

Love Bears, Hopes, Believes

Meditation on 1 Corinthians 13:6–8:

Love is not calmly happy in the midst of
injustice and wrongdoing, either among
individuals or in circumstances. Love
congratulates what is true, open, unconcealed.
At the same time it endures patiently, putting a
roof or covering over what is basically good.
Love trusts Jesus, makes commitments, and
expects the good. Love never drops away. Nor is
it driven off its course to become inefficient or
ineffective.

God speaks to my heart:

In spite of the weaknesses you know are within
you, keep seeking examples of this love. Stretch
yourself with new experiences that show you
how you can practice it. My Spirit is love and
is in you. My Spirit is all the things love is.
With Me, My direction, and My love flowing
through you, all is possible.

"A friend loves at all times."
Proverbs 17:17 (NIV)

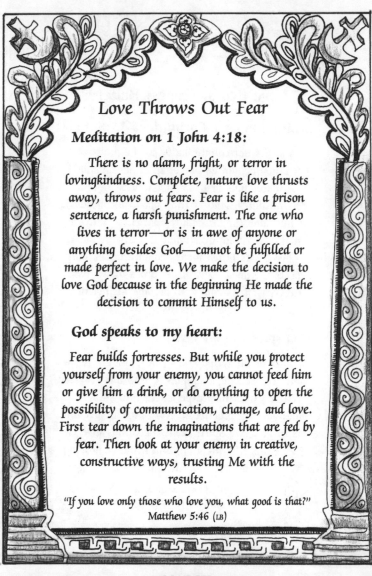

Love Throws Out Fear

Meditation on 1 John 4:18:

There is no alarm, fright, or terror in lovingkindness. Complete, mature love thrusts away, throws out fears. Fear is like a prison sentence, a harsh punishment. The one who lives in terror—or is in awe of anyone or anything besides God—cannot be fulfilled or made perfect in love. We make the decision to love God because in the beginning He made the decision to commit Himself to us.

God speaks to my heart:

Fear builds fortresses. But while you protect yourself from your enemy, you cannot feed him or give him a drink, or do anything to open the possibility of communication, change, and love. First tear down the imaginations that are fed by fear. Then look at your enemy in creative, constructive ways, trusting Me with the results.

"If you love only those who love you, what good is that?"
Matthew 5:46 (LB)

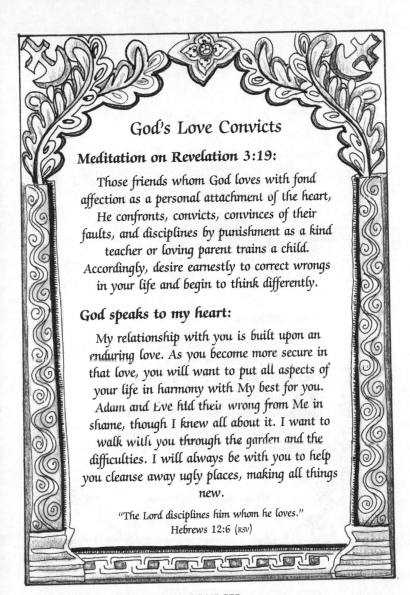

God's Love Convicts

Meditation on Revelation 3:19:

Those friends whom God loves with fond affection as a personal attachment of the heart, He confronts, convicts, convinces of their faults, and disciplines by punishment as a kind teacher or loving parent trains a child. Accordingly, desire earnestly to correct wrongs in your life and begin to think differently.

God speaks to my heart:

My relationship with you is built upon an enduring love. As you become more secure in that love, you will want to put all aspects of your life in harmony with My best for you. Adam and Eve hid their wrong from Me in shame, though I knew all about it. I want to walk with you through the garden and the difficulties. I will always be with you to help you cleanse away ugly places, making all things new.

"The Lord disciplines him whom he loves."
Hebrews 12:6 (RSV)

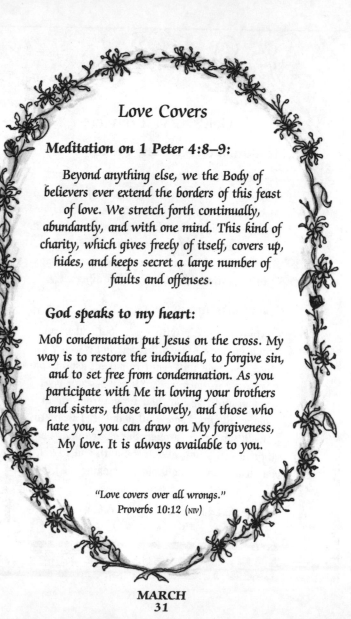

Love Covers

Meditation on 1 Peter 4:8–9:

Beyond anything else, we the Body of
believers ever extend the borders of this feast
of love. We stretch forth continually,
abundantly, and with one mind. This kind of
charity, which gives freely of itself, covers up,
hides, and keeps secret a large number of
faults and offenses.

God speaks to my heart:

Mob condemnation put Jesus on the cross. My
way is to restore the individual, to forgive sin,
and to set free from condemnation. As you
participate with Me in loving your brothers
and sisters, those unlovely, and those who
hate you, you can draw on My forgiveness,
My love. It is always available to you.

"Love covers over all wrongs."
Proverbs 10:12 (NIV)

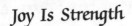

Joy Is Strength

Meditation on Nehemiah 8:8–10:

The elder read in the book of God's Law to
the people as if they were being addressed by
name, as if God were meeting them, stinging,
wounding them. The people understood and
wept sorrowfully. Nehemiah told them that
this day was sacred, set apart for the Lord, so
they were not to grieve, worry, or be angry
with themselves. The gladness and rejoicing of
the Lord was their rock, fortress, defense—
and ours.

God speaks to my heart:

Before fullness of joy comes an utter
recognition of how you fell short. In that
place that is wounded when you wrestle with
Me, I touch you and cause you to walk before
Me humbly, full of thanksgiving. Without
sincere repentance, joy is a hollow and fragile
shell.

"The joy of the Lord is your strength."
Nehemiah 8:10 (kjv)

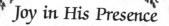

Joy in His Presence

Meditation on Psalm 16:11:

The Lord will instruct me by showing me the
well-trodden road (like one taken by a
caravan) of fresh-springing life. Where His
face and favor are turned toward me is
satisfaction and exceeding gladness,
pleasurable glee. In the strength of His hand
are sweet delights as we travel toward the
goal, confident in His victory.

God speaks to my heart:

Circumstances at times seem to overwhelm
your good intentions and suddenly, like a
storm on the Sea of Galilee, your emotions
rise up, threatening to overturn all the good
that was before. I have called you, I am with
you through it all to bring you into the place
I have prepared. Look for Me in the midst of
your daily path and you will be able to find
the joy in it.

"Thou dost show me the path of life."
Psalm 16:11 (RSV)

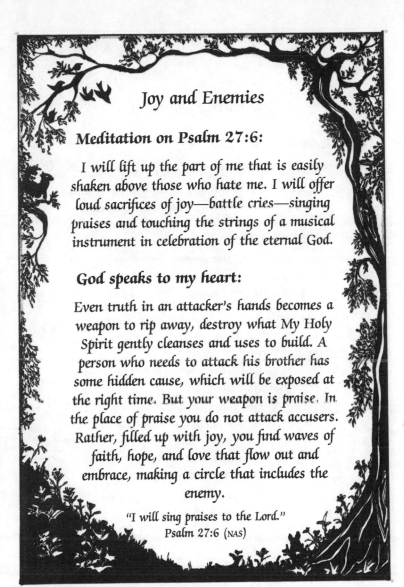

Joy and Enemies

Meditation on Psalm 27:6:

I will lift up the part of me that is easily shaken above those who hate me. I will offer loud sacrifices of joy—battle cries—singing praises and touching the strings of a musical instrument in celebration of the eternal God.

God speaks to my heart:

Even truth in an attacker's hands becomes a weapon to rip away, destroy what My Holy Spirit gently cleanses and uses to build. A person who needs to attack his brother has some hidden cause, which will be exposed at the right time. But your weapon is praise. In the place of praise you do not attack accusers. Rather, filled up with joy, you find waves of faith, hope, and love that flow out and embrace, making a circle that includes the enemy.

"I will sing praises to the Lord."
Psalm 27:6 (NAS)

Joy in the Morning

Meditation on Psalm 30:5:

The passionate wrath of God lasts only a short
time, like a wink of the eye. Delight in His will is
freshness and strength of life. The continual
overflow of tears may last during the darkness, but
the cry of joy and triumph will break forth with
the dawn.

God speaks to my heart:

Evil and suffering have drawn a thick curtain that
obscures reality. My Son broke through the darkest
curtain of torture and death and emerged in the
morning victorious. If you have chosen to be with
suffering brothers and sisters in the midst of their
pain, to cry with them for liberation from their
miseries of poverty and cruelty, know I am there
with you.
Though you share their dark night, you will also
share their joy in the dawning.

"Joy cometh in the morning."
Psalm 30:5 (kjv)

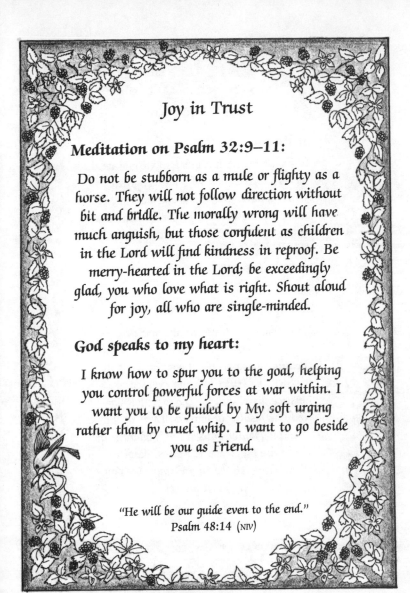

Joy in Trust

Meditation on Psalm 32:9–11:

Do not be stubborn as a mule or flighty as a
horse. They will not follow direction without
bit and bridle. The morally wrong will have
much anguish, but those confident as children
in the Lord will find kindness in reproof. Be
merry-hearted in the Lord; be exceedingly
glad, you who love what is right. Shout aloud
for joy, all who are single-minded.

God speaks to my heart:

I know how to spur you to the goal, helping
you control powerful forces at war within. I
want you to be guided by My soft urging
rather than by cruel whip. I want to go beside
you as Friend.

"He will be our guide even to the end."
Psalm 48:14 (NIV)

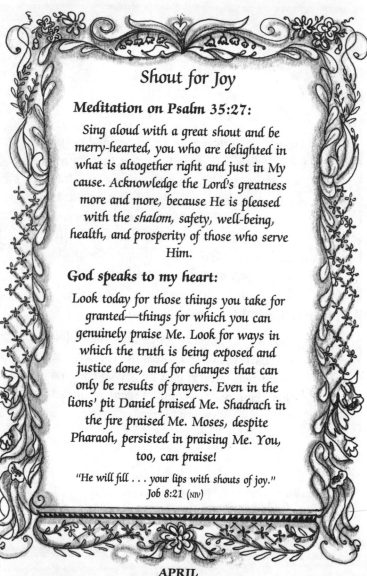

Shout for Joy

Meditation on Psalm 35:27:

Sing aloud with a great shout and be merry-hearted, you who are delighted in what is altogether right and just in My cause. Acknowledge the Lord's greatness more and more, because He is pleased with the *shalom*, safety, well-being, health, and prosperity of those who serve Him.

God speaks to my heart:

Look today for those things you take for granted—things for which you can genuinely praise Me. Look for ways in which the truth is being exposed and justice done, and for changes that can only be results of prayers. Even in the lions' pit Daniel praised Me. Shadrach in the fire praised Me. Moses, despite Pharaoh, persisted in praising Me. You, too, can praise!

"He will fill . . . your lips with shouts of joy."
Job 8:21 (NIV)

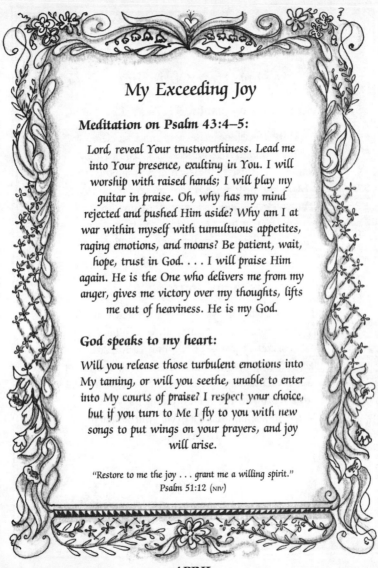

My Exceeding Joy

Meditation on Psalm 43:4–5:

Lord, reveal Your trustworthiness. Lead me
into Your presence, exulting in You. I will
worship with raised hands; I will play my
guitar in praise. Oh, why has my mind
rejected and pushed Him aside? Why am I at
war within myself with tumultuous appetites,
raging emotions, and moans? Be patient, wait,
hope, trust in God. . . . I will praise Him
again. He is the One who delivers me from my
anger, gives me victory over my thoughts, lifts
me out of heaviness. He is my God.

God speaks to my heart:

Will you release those turbulent emotions into
My taming, or will you seethe, unable to enter
into My courts of praise? I respect your choice,
but if you turn to Me I fly to you with new
songs to put wings on your prayers, and joy
will arise.

"Restore to me the joy . . . grant me a willing spirit."
Psalm 51:12 (NIV)

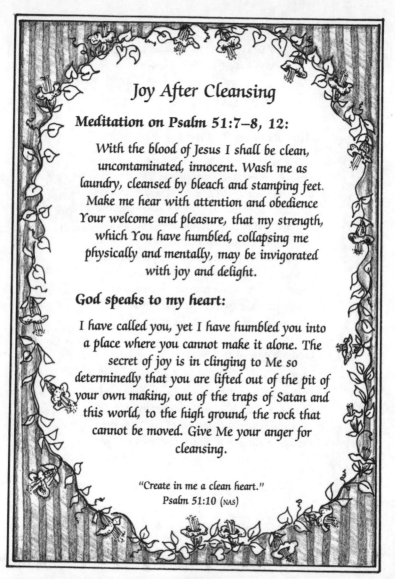

Joy After Cleansing

Meditation on Psalm 51:7–8, 12:

With the blood of Jesus I shall be clean,
uncontaminated, innocent. Wash me as
laundry, cleansed by bleach and stamping feet.
Make me hear with attention and obedience
Your welcome and pleasure, that my strength,
which You have humbled, collapsing me
physically and mentally, may be invigorated
with joy and delight.

God speaks to my heart:

I have called you, yet I have humbled you into
a place where you cannot make it alone. The
secret of joy is in clinging to Me so
determinedly that you are lifted out of the pit of
your own making, out of the traps of Satan and
this world, to the high ground, the rock that
cannot be moved. Give Me your anger for
cleansing.

"Create in me a clean heart."
Psalm 51:10 (NAS)

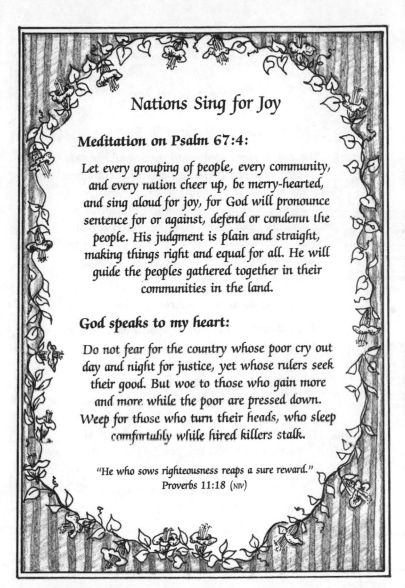

Nations Sing for Joy

Meditation on Psalm 67:4:

Let every grouping of people, every community,
and every nation cheer up, be merry-hearted,
and sing aloud for joy, for God will pronounce
sentence for or against, defend or condemn the
people. His judgment is plain and straight,
making things right and equal for all. He will
guide the peoples gathered together in their
communities in the land.

God speaks to my heart:

Do not fear for the country whose poor cry out
day and night for justice, yet whose rulers seek
their good. But woe to those who gain more
and more while the poor are pressed down.
Weep for those who turn their heads, who sleep
comfortably while hired killers stalk.

"He who sows righteousness reaps a sure reward."
Proverbs 11:18 (NIV)

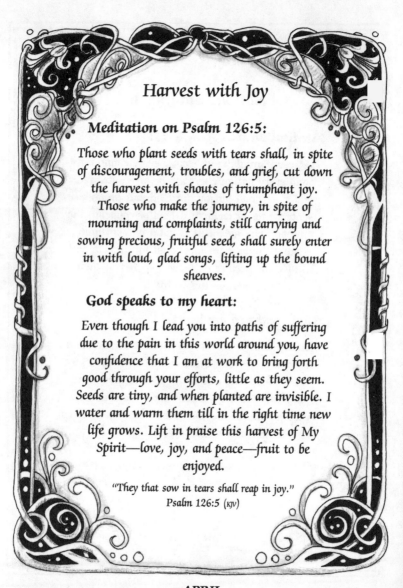

Harvest with Joy

Meditation on Psalm 126:5:

Those who plant seeds with tears shall, in spite of discouragement, troubles, and grief, cut down the harvest with shouts of triumphant joy. Those who make the journey, in spite of mourning and complaints, still carrying and sowing precious, fruitful seed, shall surely enter in with loud, glad songs, lifting up the bound sheaves.

God speaks to my heart:

Even though I lead you into paths of suffering due to the pain in this world around you, have confidence that I am at work to bring forth good through your efforts, little as they seem. Seeds are tiny, and when planted are invisible. I water and warm them till in the right time new life grows. Lift in praise this harvest of My Spirit—love, joy, and peace—fruit to be enjoyed.

"They that sow in tears shall reap in joy."
Psalm 126:5 (KJV)

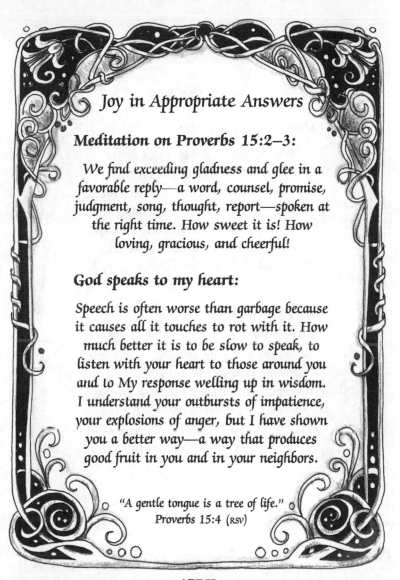

Joy in Appropriate Answers

Meditation on Proverbs 15:2–3:

We find exceeding gladness and glee in a favorable reply—a word, counsel, promise, judgment, song, thought, report—spoken at the right time. How sweet it is! How loving, gracious, and cheerful!

God speaks to my heart:

Speech is often worse than garbage because it causes all it touches to rot with it. How much better it is to be slow to speak, to listen with your heart to those around you and to My response welling up in wisdom. I understand your outbursts of impatience, your explosions of anger, but I have shown you a better way—a way that produces good fruit in you and in your neighbors.

"A gentle tongue is a tree of life."
Proverbs 15:4 (RSV)

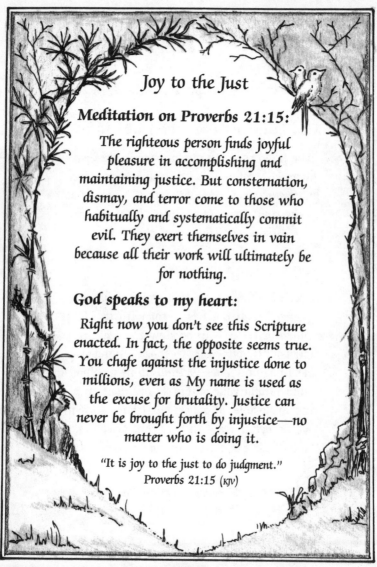

Joy to the Just

Meditation on Proverbs 21:15:

The righteous person finds joyful pleasure in accomplishing and maintaining justice. But consternation, dismay, and terror come to those who habitually and systematically commit evil. They exert themselves in vain because all their work will ultimately be for nothing.

God speaks to my heart:

Right now you don't see this Scripture enacted. In fact, the opposite seems true. You chafe against the injustice done to millions, even as My name is used as the excuse for brutality. Justice can never be brought forth by injustice—no matter who is doing it.

"It is joy to the just to do judgment."
Proverbs 21:15 (KJV)

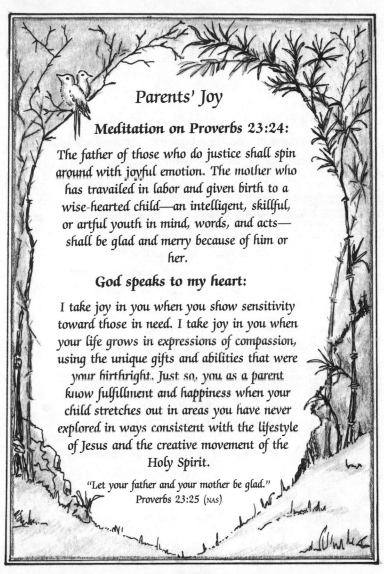

Parents' Joy

Meditation on Proverbs 23:24:

The father of those who do justice shall spin around with joyful emotion. The mother who has travailed in labor and given birth to a wise-hearted child—an intelligent, skillful, or artful youth in mind, words, and acts—shall be glad and merry because of him or her.

God speaks to my heart:

I take joy in you when you show sensitivity toward those in need. I take joy in you when your life grows in expressions of compassion, using the unique gifts and abilities that were your birthright. Just so, you as a parent know fulfillment and happiness when your child stretches out in areas you have never explored in ways consistent with the lifestyle of Jesus and the creative movement of the Holy Spirit.

"Let your father and your mother be glad."
Proverbs 23:25 (NAS)

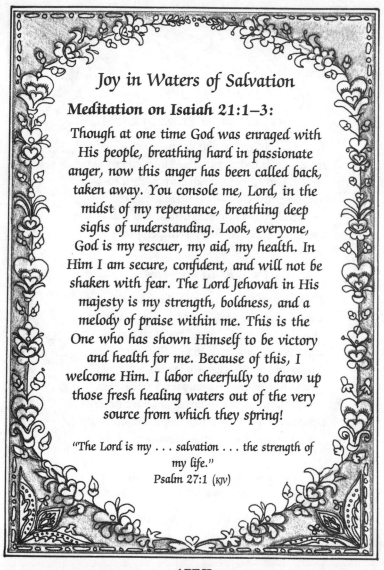

Joy in Waters of Salvation

Meditation on Isaiah 21:1–3:

Though at one time God was enraged with
His people, breathing hard in passionate
anger, now this anger has been called back,
taken away. You console me, Lord, in the
midst of my repentance, breathing deep
sighs of understanding. Look, everyone,
God is my rescuer, my aid, my health. In
Him I am secure, confident, and will not be
shaken with fear. The Lord Jehovah in His
majesty is my strength, boldness, and a
melody of praise within me. This is the
One who has shown Himself to be victory
and health for me. Because of this, I
welcome Him. I labor cheerfully to draw up
those fresh healing waters out of the very
source from which they spring!

"The Lord is my . . . salvation . . . the strength of
my life."
Psalm 27:1 (KJV)

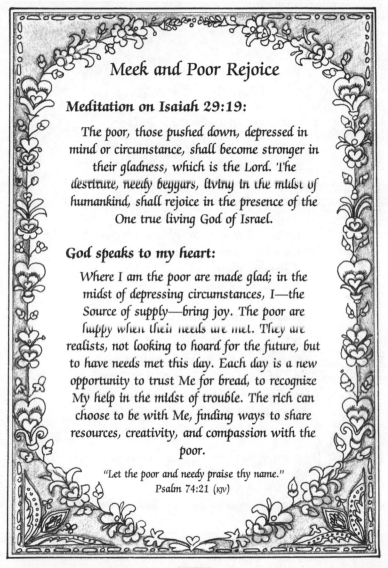

Meek and Poor Rejoice

Meditation on Isaiah 29:19:

The poor, those pushed down, depressed in mind or circumstance, shall become stronger in their gladness, which is the Lord. The destitute, needy beggars, living in the midst of humankind, shall rejoice in the presence of the One true living God of Israel.

God speaks to my heart:

Where I am the poor are made glad; in the midst of depressing circumstances, I—the Source of supply—bring joy. The poor are happy when their needs are met. They are realists, not looking to hoard for the future, but to have needs met this day. Each day is a new opportunity to trust Me for bread, to recognize My help in the midst of trouble. The rich can choose to be with Me, finding ways to share resources, creativity, and compassion with the poor.

"Let the poor and needy praise thy name."
Psalm 74:21 (KJV)

Desert Shall Rejoice

Meditation on Isaiah 35:1–2:

The dry pasture and the parched barren places
shall be cheerful and the sterile plain shall
show gladness by breaking forth with abundant
wild roses. They shall flourish and spin around
happily, singing in the revolution of the
seasons. The splendor of Lebanon shall be
restored to it, the magnificent beauty of Carmel
and Sharon. They shall see the splendor of the
Lord and the magnificent beauty of our God.

God speaks to my heart:

It is in My perfect purposes for worthless,
abandoned land to be productive, to be restored
to useful beauty. The earth is crying out in
agony, yearning for the sons of God to exhibit
My nature in their care of the land, growing
good things for the good of all.

"Water will gush forth . . . and streams in the desert."
Isaiah 35:6 (NIV)

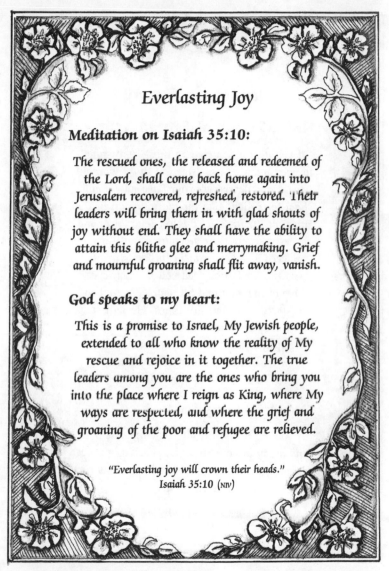

Everlasting Joy

Meditation on Isaiah 35:10:

The rescued ones, the released and redeemed of
the Lord, shall come back home again into
Jerusalem recovered, refreshed, restored. Their
leaders will bring them in with glad shouts of
joy without end. They shall have the ability to
attain this blithe glee and merrymaking. Grief
and mournful groaning shall flit away, vanish.

God speaks to my heart:

This is a promise to Israel, My Jewish people,
extended to all who know the reality of My
rescue and rejoice in it together. The true
leaders among you are the ones who bring you
into the place where I reign as King, where My
ways are respected, and where the grief and
groaning of the poor and refugee are relieved.

"Everlasting joy will crown their heads."
Isaiah 35:10 (NIV)

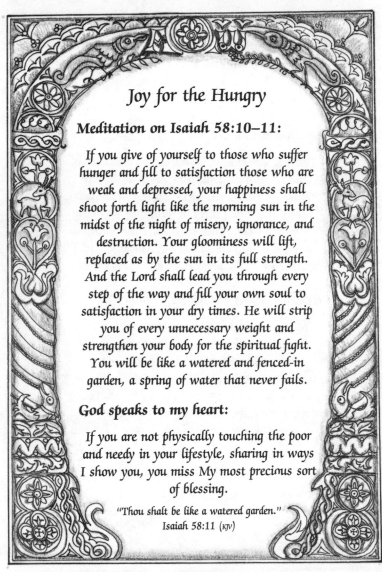

Joy for the Hungry

Meditation on Isaiah 58:10–11:

If you give of yourself to those who suffer hunger and fill to satisfaction those who are weak and depressed, your happiness shall shoot forth light like the morning sun in the midst of the night of misery, ignorance, and destruction. Your gloominess will lift, replaced as by the sun in its full strength. And the Lord shall lead you through every step of the way and fill your own soul to satisfaction in your dry times. He will strip you of every unnecessary weight and strengthen your body for the spiritual fight. You will be like a watered and fenced-in garden, a spring of water that never fails.

God speaks to my heart:

If you are not physically touching the poor and needy in your lifestyle, sharing in ways I show you, you miss My most precious sort of blessing.

"Thou shalt be like a watered garden."
Isaiah 58:11 (KJV)

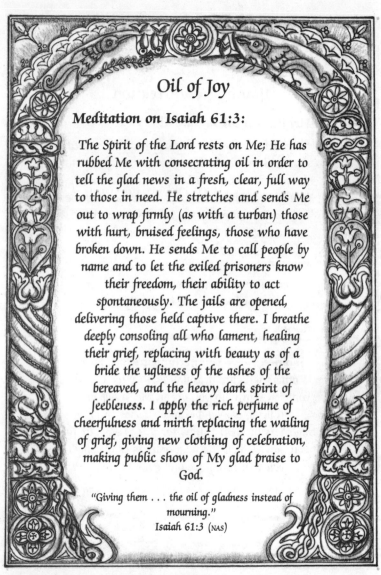

Oil of Joy

Meditation on Isaiah 61:3:

The Spirit of the Lord rests on Me; He has rubbed Me with consecrating oil in order to tell the glad news in a fresh, clear, full way to those in need. He stretches and sends Me out to wrap firmly (as with a turban) those with hurt, bruised feelings, those who have broken down. He sends Me to call people by name and to let the exiled prisoners know their freedom, their ability to act spontaneously. The jails are opened, delivering those held captive there. I breathe deeply consoling all who lament, healing their grief, replacing with beauty as of a bride the ugliness of the ashes of the bereaved, and the heavy dark spirit of feebleness. I apply the rich perfume of cheerfulness and mirth replacing the wailing of grief, giving new clothing of celebration, making public show of My glad praise to God.

"Giving them . . . the oil of gladness instead of mourning."
Isaiah 61:3 (NAS)

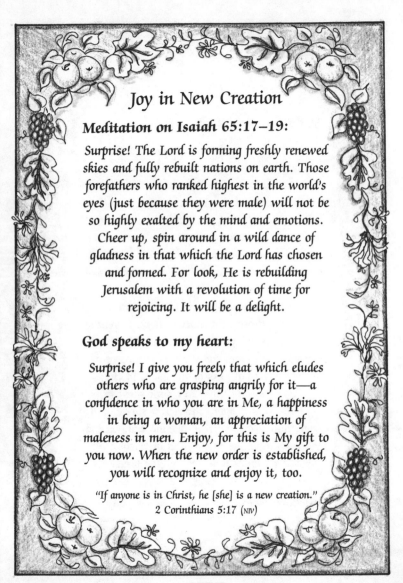

Joy in New Creation

Meditation on Isaiah 65:17–19:

*Surprise! The Lord is forming freshly renewed
skies and fully rebuilt nations on earth. Those
forefathers who ranked highest in the world's
eyes (just because they were male) will not be
so highly exalted by the mind and emotions.
Cheer up, spin around in a wild dance of
gladness in that which the Lord has chosen
and formed. For look, He is rebuilding
Jerusalem with a revolution of time for
rejoicing. It will be a delight.*

God speaks to my heart:

*Surprise! I give you freely that which eludes
others who are grasping angrily for it—a
confidence in who you are in Me, a happiness
in being a woman, an appreciation of
maleness in men. Enjoy, for this is My gift to
you now. When the new order is established,
you will recognize and enjoy it, too.*

"If anyone is in Christ, he [she] is a new creation."
2 Corinthians 5:17 (NIV)

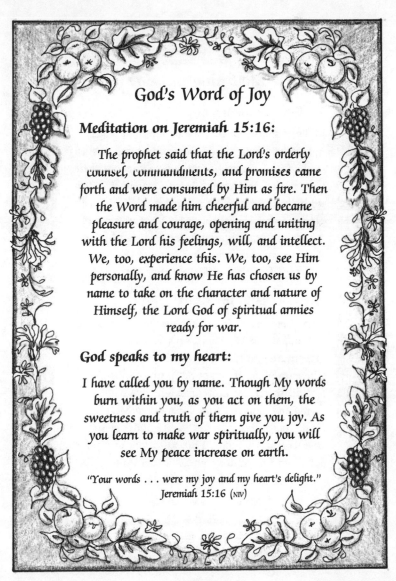

God's Word of Joy

Meditation on Jeremiah 15:16:

The prophet said that the Lord's orderly
counsel, commandments, and promises came
forth and were consumed by Him as fire. Then
the Word made him cheerful and became
pleasure and courage, opening and uniting
with the Lord his feelings, will, and intellect.
We, too, experience this. We, too, see Him
personally, and know He has chosen us by
name to take on the character and nature of
Himself, the Lord God of spiritual armies
ready for war.

God speaks to my heart:

I have called you by name. Though My words
burn within you, as you act on them, the
sweetness and truth of them give you joy. As
you learn to make war spiritually, you will
see My peace increase on earth.

"Your words . . . were my joy and my heart's delight."
Jeremiah 15:16 (NIV)

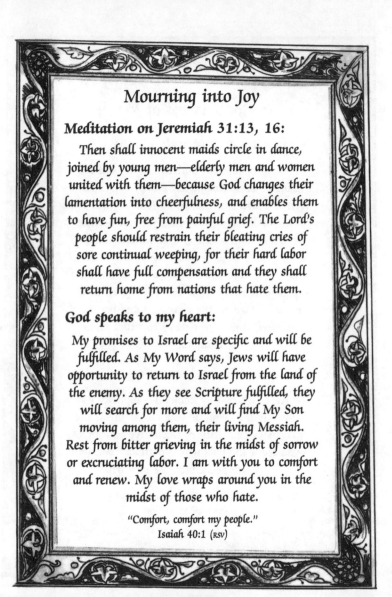

Mourning into Joy

Meditation on Jeremiah 31:13, 16:

Then shall innocent maids circle in dance,
joined by young men—elderly men and women
united with them—because God changes their
lamentation into cheerfulness, and enables them
to have fun, free from painful grief. The Lord's
people should restrain their bleating cries of
sore continual weeping, for their hard labor
shall have full compensation and they shall
return home from nations that hate them.

God speaks to my heart:

My promises to Israel are specific and will be
fulfilled. As My Word says, Jews will have
opportunity to return to Israel from the land of
the enemy. As they see Scripture fulfilled, they
will search for more and will find My Son
moving among them, their living Messiah.
Rest from bitter grieving in the midst of sorrow
or excruciating labor. I am with you to comfort
and renew. My love wraps around you in the
midst of those who hate.

"Comfort, comfort my people."
Isaiah 40:1 (RSV)

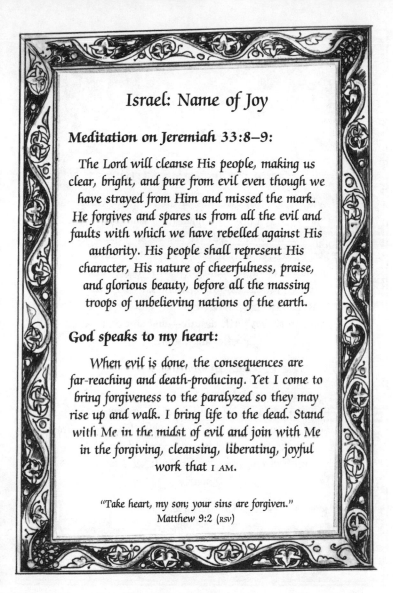

Israel: Name of Joy

Meditation on Jeremiah 33:8–9:

The Lord will cleanse His people, making us
clear, bright, and pure from evil even though we
have strayed from Him and missed the mark.
He forgives and spares us from all the evil and
faults with which we have rebelled against His
authority. His people shall represent His
character, His nature of cheerfulness, praise,
and glorious beauty, before all the massing
troops of unbelieving nations of the earth.

God speaks to my heart:

When evil is done, the consequences are
far-reaching and death-producing. Yet I come to
bring forgiveness to the paralyzed so they may
rise up and walk. I bring life to the dead. Stand
with Me in the midst of evil and join with Me
in the forgiving, cleansing, liberating, joyful
work that I AM.

"Take heart, my son; your sins are forgiven."
Matthew 9:2 (RSV)

Joyful in God

Meditation on Isaiah 61:10:

I will shine with gladness in the Lord. All that is in me—the vitality and appetites—shall spin with joyful emotion in God. He has covered me with robes of deliverance, liberty, prosperity, with outer garments of righteousness, justice to the needy, virtue, kindness, and gentleness. God will ultimately cause what is right, and hymns of praise to spring forth despite—and amazing—the unbelieving nations.

God speaks to my heart:

There is an integral connection between My blessing you and your union and harmony with the poor. As you discover how to apply this wisdom in your life, you will have even greater joy. Others will find joy, too, for they will see I am their source.

"I . . . will clothe you with festal robes."
Zechariah 3:4 (NAS)

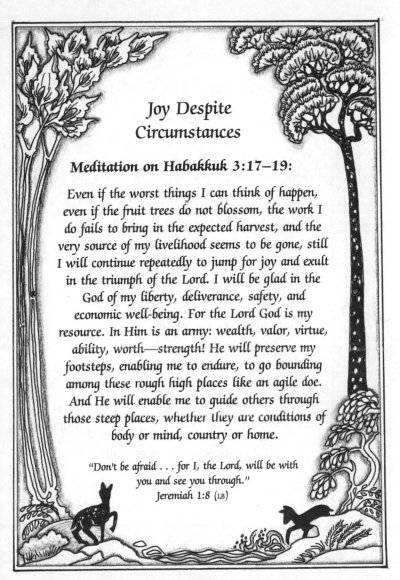

Joy Despite Circumstances

Meditation on Habakkuk 3:17–19:

Even if the worst things I can think of happen,
even if the fruit trees do not blossom, the work I
do fails to bring in the expected harvest, and the
very source of my livelihood seems to be gone, still
I will continue repeatedly to jump for joy and exult
in the triumph of the Lord. I will be glad in the
God of my liberty, deliverance, safety, and
economic well-being. For the Lord God is my
resource. In Him is an army: wealth, valor, virtue,
ability, worth—strength! He will preserve my
footsteps, enabling me to endure, to go bounding
among these rough high places like an agile doe.
And He will enable me to guide others through
those steep places, whether they are conditions of
body or mind, country or home.

"Don't be afraid . . . for I, the Lord, will be with
you and see you through."
Jeremiah 1:8 (LB)

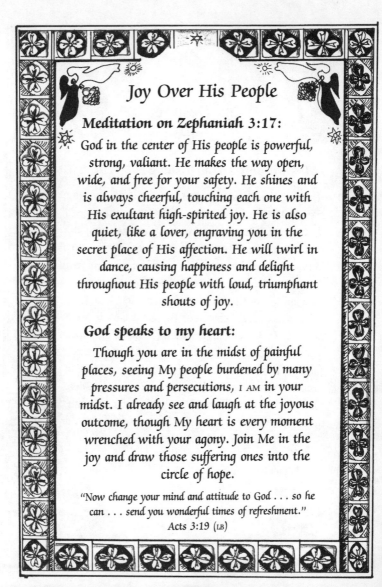

Joy Over His People

Meditation on Zephaniah 3:17:

God in the center of His people is powerful, strong, valiant. He makes the way open, wide, and free for your safety. He shines and is always cheerful, touching each one with His exultant high-spirited joy. He is also quiet, like a lover, engraving you in the secret place of His affection. He will twirl in dance, causing happiness and delight throughout His people with loud, triumphant shouts of joy.

God speaks to my heart:

Though you are in the midst of painful places, seeing My people burdened by many pressures and persecutions, I AM in your midst. I already see and laugh at the joyous outcome, though My heart is every moment wrenched with your agony. Join Me in the joy and draw those suffering ones into the circle of hope.

"Now change your mind and attitude to God . . . so he can . . . send you wonderful times of refreshment."
Acts 3:19 (LB)

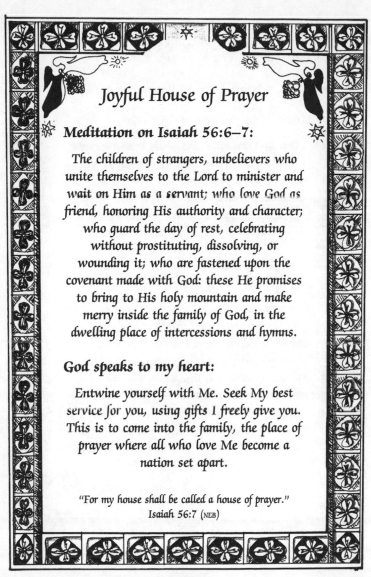

Joyful House of Prayer

Meditation on Isaiah 56:6–7:

The children of strangers, unbelievers who unite themselves to the Lord to minister and wait on Him as a servant; who love God as friend, honoring His authority and character; who guard the day of rest, celebrating without prostituting, dissolving, or wounding it; who are fastened upon the covenant made with God: these He promises to bring to His holy mountain and make merry inside the family of God, in the dwelling place of intercessions and hymns.

God speaks to my heart:

Entwine yourself with Me. Seek My best service for you, using gifts I freely give you. This is to come into the family, the place of prayer where all who love Me become a nation set apart.

"For my house shall be called a house of prayer."
Isaiah 56:7 (NEB)

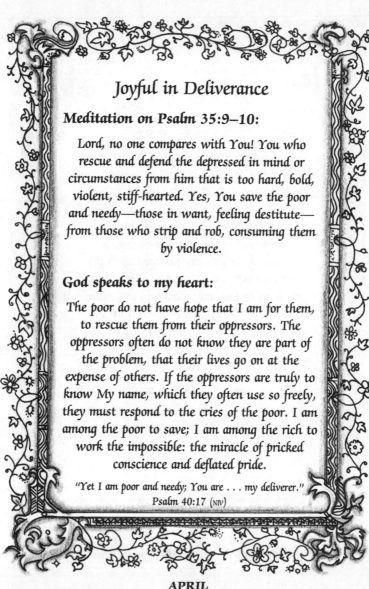

Joyful in Deliverance

Meditation on Psalm 35:9–10:

Lord, no one compares with You! You who
rescue and defend the depressed in mind or
circumstances from him that is too hard, bold,
violent, stiff-hearted. Yes, You save the poor
and needy—those in want, feeling destitute—
from those who strip and rob, consuming them
by violence.

God speaks to my heart:

The poor do not have hope that I am for them,
to rescue them from their oppressors. The
oppressors often do not know they are part of
the problem, that their lives go on at the
expense of others. If the oppressors are truly to
know My name, which they often use so freely,
they must respond to the cries of the poor. I am
among the poor to save; I am among the rich to
work the impossible: the miracle of pricked
conscience and deflated pride.

"Yet I am poor and needy; You are . . . my deliverer."
Psalm 40:17 (NIV)

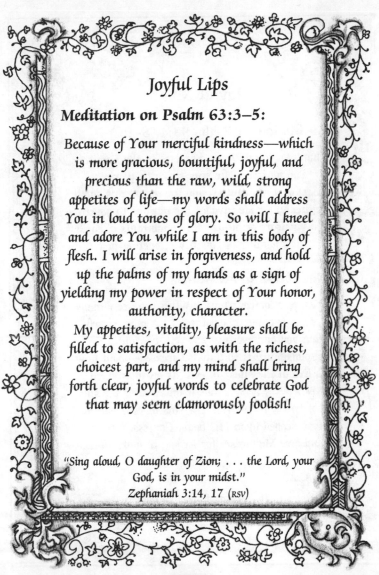

Joyful Lips

Meditation on Psalm 63:3–5:

Because of Your merciful kindness—which is more gracious, bountiful, joyful, and precious than the raw, wild, strong appetites of life—my words shall address You in loud tones of glory. So will I kneel and adore You while I am in this body of flesh. I will arise in forgiveness, and hold up the palms of my hands as a sign of yielding my power in respect of Your honor, authority, character.

My appetites, vitality, pleasure shall be filled to satisfaction, as with the richest, choicest part, and my mind shall bring forth clear, joyful words to celebrate God that may seem clamorously foolish!

"Sing aloud, O daughter of Zion; . . . the Lord, your God, is in your midst."
Zephaniah 3:14, 17 (RSV)

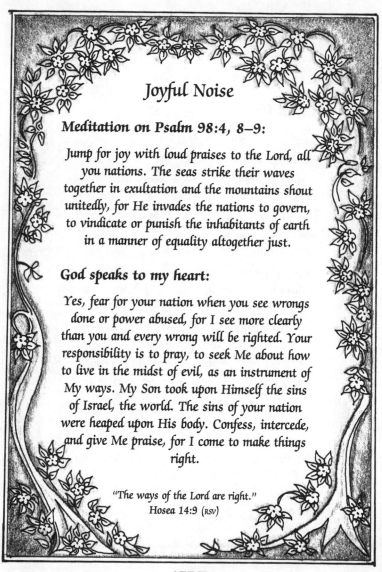

Joyful Noise

Meditation on Psalm 98:4, 8–9:

Jump for joy with loud praises to the Lord, all
you nations. The seas strike their waves
together in exultation and the mountains shout
unitedly, for He invades the nations to govern,
to vindicate or punish the inhabitants of earth
in a manner of equality altogether just.

God speaks to my heart:

Yes, fear for your nation when you see wrongs
done or power abused, for I see more clearly
than you and every wrong will be righted. Your
responsibility is to pray, to seek Me about how
to live in the midst of evil, as an instrument of
My ways. My Son took upon Himself the sins
of Israel, the world. The sins of your nation
were heaped upon His body. Confess, intercede,
and give Me praise, for I come to make things
right.

"The ways of the Lord are right."
Hosea 14:9 (RSV)

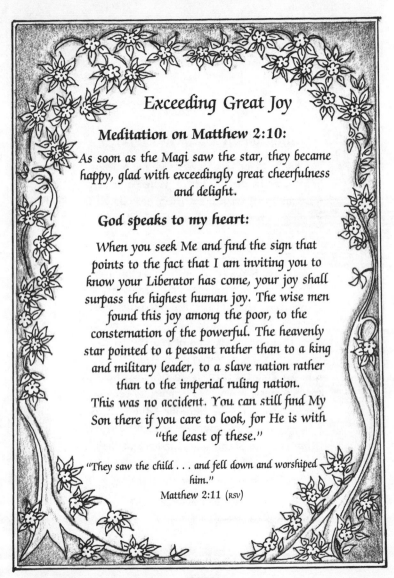

Exceeding Great Joy

Meditation on Matthew 2:10:

As soon as the Magi saw the star, they became happy, glad with exceedingly great cheerfulness and delight.

God speaks to my heart:

When you seek Me and find the sign that points to the fact that I am inviting you to know your Liberator has come, your joy shall surpass the highest human joy. The wise men found this joy among the poor, to the consternation of the powerful. The heavenly star pointed to a peasant rather than to a king and military leader, to a slave nation rather than to the imperial ruling nation.

This was no accident. You can still find My Son there if you care to look, for He is with "the least of these."

"They saw the child . . . and fell down and worshiped him."
Matthew 2:11 (RSV)

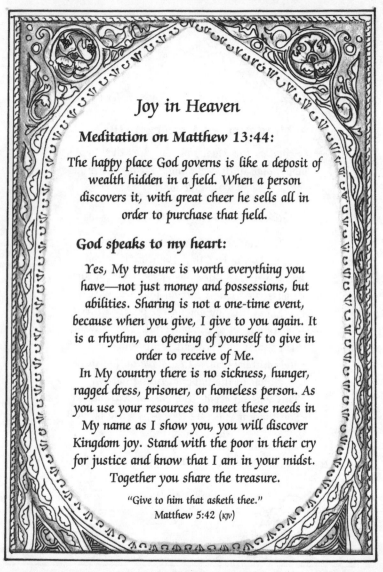

Joy in Heaven

Meditation on Matthew 13:44:

The happy place God governs is like a deposit of
wealth hidden in a field. When a person
discovers it, with great cheer he sells all in
order to purchase that field.

God speaks to my heart:

Yes, My treasure is worth everything you
have—not just money and possessions, but
abilities. Sharing is not a one-time event,
because when you give, I give to you again. It
is a rhythm, an opening of yourself to give in
order to receive of Me.

In My country there is no sickness, hunger,
ragged dress, prisoner, or homeless person. As
you use your resources to meet these needs in
My name as I show you, you will discover
Kingdom joy. Stand with the poor in their cry
for justice and know that I am in your midst.
Together you share the treasure.

"Give to him that asketh thee."
Matthew 5:42 (KJV)

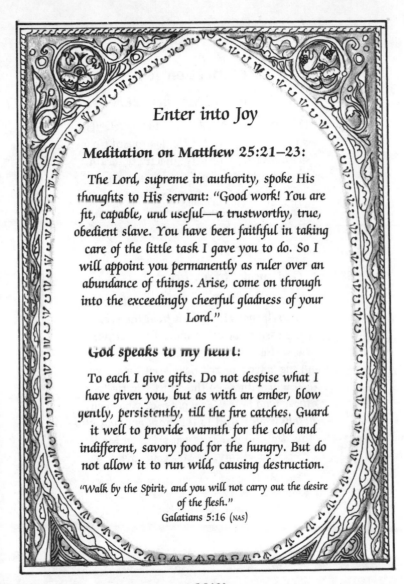

Enter into Joy

Meditation on Matthew 25:21–23:

The Lord, supreme in authority, spoke His thoughts to His servant: "Good work! You are fit, capable, and useful—a trustworthy, true, obedient slave. You have been faithful in taking care of the little task I gave you to do. So I will appoint you permanently as ruler over an abundance of things. Arise, come on through into the exceedingly cheerful gladness of your Lord."

God speaks to my heart:

To each I give gifts. Do not despise what I have given you, but as with an ember, blow gently, persistently, till the fire catches. Guard it well to provide warmth for the cold and indifferent, savory food for the hungry. But do not allow it to run wild, causing destruction.

"Walk by the Spirit, and you will not carry out the desire of the flesh."
Galatians 5:16 (NAS)

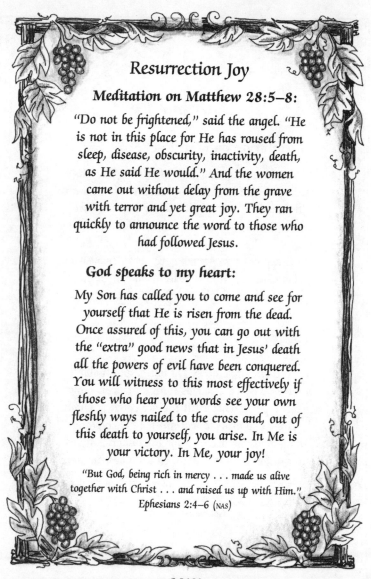

Resurrection Joy

Meditation on Matthew 28:5–8:

"Do not be frightened," said the angel. "He is not in this place for He has roused from sleep, disease, obscurity, inactivity, death, as He said He would." And the women came out without delay from the grave with terror and yet great joy. They ran quickly to announce the word to those who had followed Jesus.

God speaks to my heart:

My Son has called you to come and see for yourself that He is risen from the dead. Once assured of this, you can go out with the "extra" good news that in Jesus' death all the powers of evil have been conquered. You will witness to this most effectively if those who hear your words see your own fleshly ways nailed to the cross and, out of this death to yourself, you arise. In Me is your victory. In Me, your joy!

"But God, being rich in mercy . . . made us alive together with Christ . . . and raised us up with Him."
Ephesians 2:4–6 (NAS)

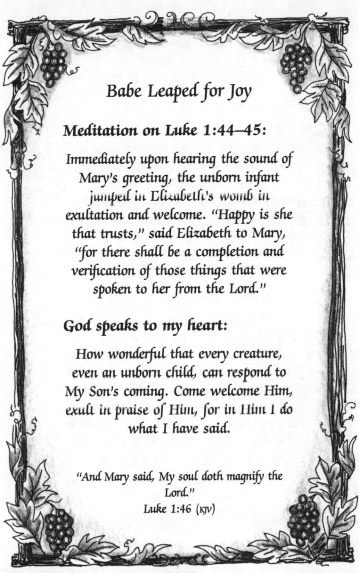

Babe Leaped for Joy

Meditation on Luke 1:44–45:

Immediately upon hearing the sound of
Mary's greeting, the unborn infant
jumped in Elizabeth's womb in
exultation and welcome. "Happy is she
that trusts," said Elizabeth to Mary,
"for there shall be a completion and
verification of those things that were
spoken to her from the Lord."

God speaks to my heart:

How wonderful that every creature,
even an unborn child, can respond to
My Son's coming. Come welcome Him,
exult in praise of Him, for in Him I do
what I have said.

"And Mary said, My soul doth magnify the
Lord."
Luke 1:46 (KJV)

Joy in Persecution

Meditation on Luke 6:22–23:

Be happy whenever humans detest you, severing
you from their groups, taunting you and
reviling your character, calling you morally
derelict, or vicious, or of the devil, driving you
out because of Jesus. In that judgment be
cheerful. Be calmly happy. Jump and skip for
gladness. Your pay for service to Jesus is
plenteous in the happy heavenly household
of God.

God speaks to my heart:

In the "normal" Christian life there will be
people who persecute you because Satan hates
Me; there will also be people who come against
things in you that need correction. You need
wisdom to tell the difference. It is never fun to
experience rejection and abuse of your character,
but if you endure, these lessons will sharpen
your effectiveness. I help you find the door
opening into maturity; it is very low.

"Pray for those who persecute you, to show that you are
the children of your Father."
Matthew 5:44–45 (AMPLIFIED)

Hear the Word with Joy

Meditation on Luke 8:13:

When the seeds of the Word fall on some, they understand and accept with cheerfulness the Living Word, Jesus, offered to them, but they have no stability, no root, as if they were sitting on rock. For a while faith and trust grow, but in the time of testing—examination provoked by experience of evil—they desert, withdraw themselves from that place.

God speaks to my heart:

Time and pressure make rock, but when a rock is submitted to the hammer, it can be made pliable and usable. "Rock" people harden themselves in defense, hoping for protection from the threatening outside, but My way is vulnerability, openness. Rocks cannot be healed from the oppressions that formed them, but people can. My love makes change possible.

". . . Having heard the word, keep it, and bring forth fruit
with patience."
Luke 8:15 (KJV)

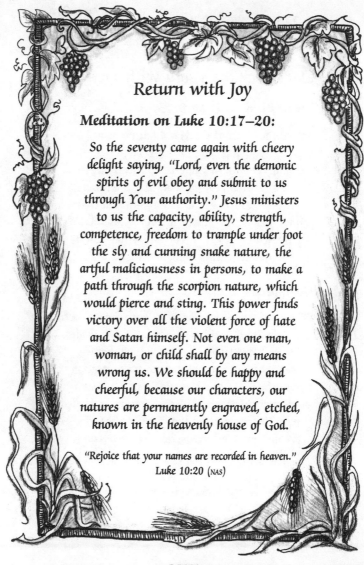

Return with Joy

Meditation on Luke 10:17–20:

So the seventy came again with cheery delight saying, "Lord, even the demonic spirits of evil obey and submit to us through Your authority." Jesus ministers to us the capacity, ability, strength, competence, freedom to trample under foot the sly and cunning snake nature, the artful maliciousness in persons, to make a path through the scorpion nature, which would pierce and sting. This power finds victory over all the violent force of hate and Satan himself. Not even one man, woman, or child shall by any means wrong us. We should be happy and cheerful, because our characters, our natures are permanently engraved, etched, known in the heavenly house of God.

"Rejoice that your names are recorded in heaven."
Luke 10:20 (NAS)

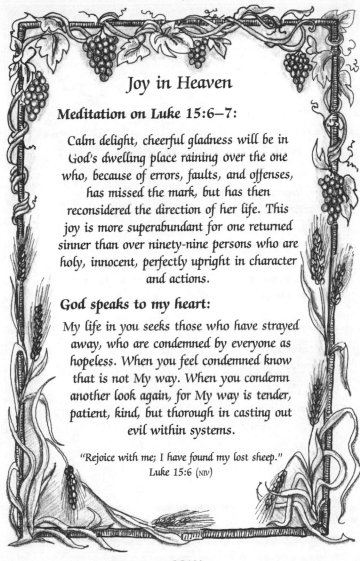

Joy in Heaven

Meditation on Luke 15:6–7:

Calm delight, cheerful gladness will be in
God's dwelling place raining over the one
who, because of errors, faults, and offenses,
has missed the mark, but has then
reconsidered the direction of her life. This
joy is more superabundant for one returned
sinner than over ninety-nine persons who are
holy, innocent, perfectly upright in character
and actions.

God speaks to my heart:

My life in you seeks those who have strayed
away, who are condemned by everyone as
hopeless. When you feel condemned know
that is not My way. When you condemn
another look again, for My way is tender,
patient, kind, but thorough in casting out
evil within systems.

"Rejoice with me; I have found my lost sheep."
Luke 15:6 (NIV)

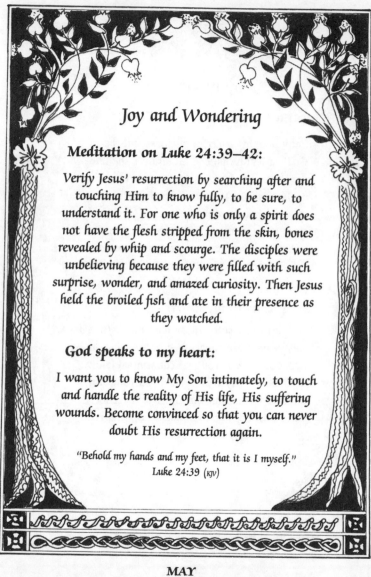

Joy and Wondering

Meditation on Luke 24:39–42:

Verify Jesus' resurrection by searching after and touching Him to know fully, to be sure, to understand it. For one who is only a spirit does not have the flesh stripped from the skin, bones revealed by whip and scourge. The disciples were unbelieving because they were filled with such surprise, wonder, and amazed curiosity. Then Jesus held the broiled fish and ate in their presence as they watched.

God speaks to my heart:

I want you to know My Son intimately, to touch and handle the reality of His life, His suffering wounds. Become convinced so that you can never doubt His resurrection again.

"Behold my hands and my feet, that it is I myself."
Luke 24:39 (kjv)

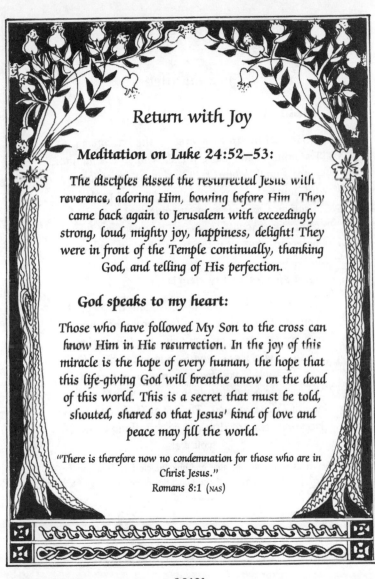

Return with Joy

Meditation on Luke 24:52–53:

The disciples kissed the resurrected Jesus with reverence, adoring Him, bowing before Him They came back again to Jerusalem with exceedingly strong, loud, mighty joy, happiness, delight! They were in front of the Temple continually, thanking God, and telling of His perfection.

God speaks to my heart:

Those who have followed My Son to the cross can know Him in His resurrection. In the joy of this miracle is the hope of every human, the hope that this life-giving God will breathe anew on the dead of this world. This is a secret that must be told, shouted, shared so that Jesus' kind of love and peace may fill the world.

"There is therefore now no condemnation for those who are in Christ Jesus."
Romans 8:1 (NAS)

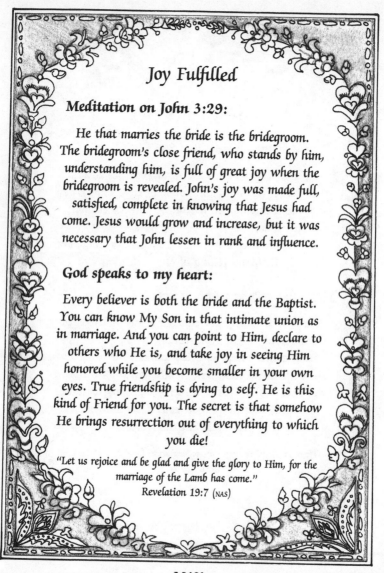

Joy Fulfilled

Meditation on John 3:29:

He that marries the bride is the bridegroom.
The bridegroom's close friend, who stands by him,
understanding him, is full of great joy when the
bridegroom is revealed. John's joy was made full,
satisfied, complete in knowing that Jesus had
come. Jesus would grow and increase, but it was
necessary that John lessen in rank and influence.

God speaks to my heart:

Every believer is both the bride and the Baptist.
You can know My Son in that intimate union as
in marriage. And you can point to Him, declare to
others who He is, and take joy in seeing Him
honored while you become smaller in your own
eyes. True friendship is dying to self. He is this
kind of Friend for you. The secret is that somehow
He brings resurrection out of everything to which
you die!

"Let us rejoice and be glad and give the glory to Him, for the
marriage of the Lamb has come."
Revelation 19:7 (NAS)

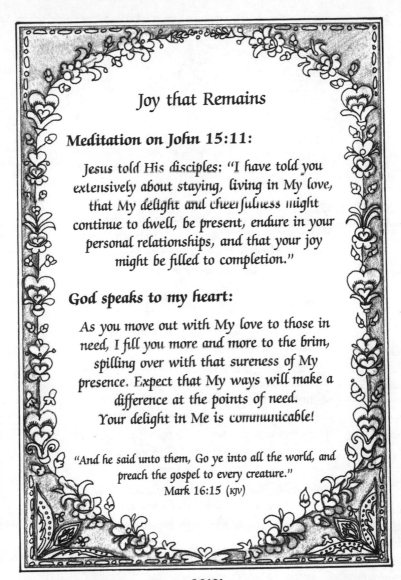

Joy that Remains

Meditation on John 15:11:

Jesus told His disciples: "I have told you extensively about staying, living in My love, that My delight and cheerfulness might continue to dwell, be present, endure in your personal relationships, and that your joy might be filled to completion."

God speaks to my heart:

As you move out with My love to those in need, I fill you more and more to the brim, spilling over with that sureness of My presence. Expect that My ways will make a difference at the points of need. Your delight in Me is communicable!

"And he said unto them, Go ye into all the world, and preach the gospel to every creature."
Mark 16:15 (KJV)

Sorrow into Joy

Meditation on John 16:22–23:

Right now you are dejected with grief, but once
again Jesus will look you in the eyes and you
will be happy. No one can remove that gladness
from you. And then, anything you desire, ask
the Father for in Jesus' name, authority, and
character. He will grant, minister, bring forth
the adventure in you.

God speaks to my heart:

In the midst of depression you cannot sense My
Son's presence. But when you look into His
eyes, you will see hope and reason for joy, for
life. As you learn His nature, you will be able
to know the prayers that are His, which I
delight to give. Our purpose becomes one: to set
free those who are bound, to open blind eyes, to
be provision for the poor, to share the good
news of My love.

"Surely he has borne our griefs and carried our sorrows . . .
and with his stripes we are healed."
Isaiah 53:4–5 (RSV)

Joy None Can Take

Meditation on John 16:22–23:

Now you have heaviness, grief, but once again
Jesus will look at you with wide-open eyes and
your heart will cheer up. Absolutely no one can
take away your delight. Whatever you request
as a favor of the Father in the authority and
character of Jesus, He will grant, deliver,
minister to you.

God speaks to my heart:

When you look only at the darkness—the evil
at work in your nation and in the world, people
profiting from fear—it is easy to despair.
Remember, I have overcome the source, the root
of evil, and you must consistently be a part of
that overcoming. Despair asks Me nothing, but
you, as you represent Me as light in the midst
of darkness, must express those urgent desires
that are My nature: healing and peace and
unity within families and nations. Keep on
asking.

"Rejoice always . . . give thanks in all circumstances; for
this is the will of God in Christ Jesus for you."
1 Thessalonians 5:16, 18 (RSV)

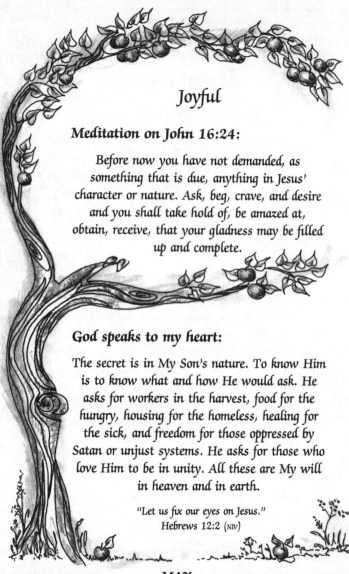

Joyful

Meditation on John 16:24:

Before now you have not demanded, as something that is due, anything in Jesus' character or nature. Ask, beg, crave, and desire and you shall take hold of, be amazed at, obtain, receive, that your gladness may be filled up and complete.

God speaks to my heart:

The secret is in My Son's nature. To know Him is to know what and how He would ask. He asks for workers in the harvest, food for the hungry, housing for the homeless, healing for the sick, and freedom for those oppressed by Satan or unjust systems. He asks for those who love Him to be in unity. All these are My will in heaven and in earth.

"Let us fix our eyes on Jesus."
Hebrews 12:2 (NIV)

Joy Fulfilled

Meditation on John 17:13:

Jesus said: "Now I enter into Your presence,
God, and I explain to the whole inhabited world
these same things, that I will be reflected in
those people who are My followers. I will keep
them, pray for them, and none will be lost. So
they will be able to know My perfect joy filled
up in themselves."

God speaks to my heart:

Ask, seek, knock. When My Son's knocking is
at last heard by you, when you thought it was
your knocking that got His attention, you can
invite Him inside—to live, to be at home, and
finally to let His lifestyle permeate yours from
the inside out. So shall what grieves Him be
grief to you, and His joy, in spite of everything,
will bubble up, spilling over, a perfect delight.

"The glory which thou hast given me I have given to
them."
John 17:22 (RSV)

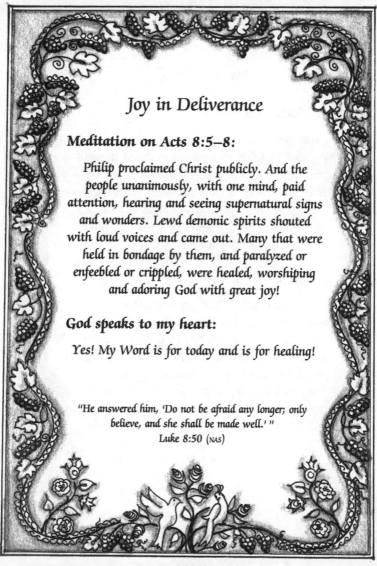

Joy in Deliverance

Meditation on Acts 8:5–8:

Philip proclaimed Christ publicly. And the
people unanimously, with one mind, paid
attention, hearing and seeing supernatural signs
and wonders. Lewd demonic spirits shouted
with loud voices and came out. Many that were
held in bondage by them, and paralyzed or
enfeebled or crippled, were healed, worshiping
and adoring God with great joy!

God speaks to my heart:

Yes! My Word is for today and is for healing!

"He answered him, 'Do not be afraid any longer; only
believe, and she shall be made well.' "
Luke 8:50 (NAS)

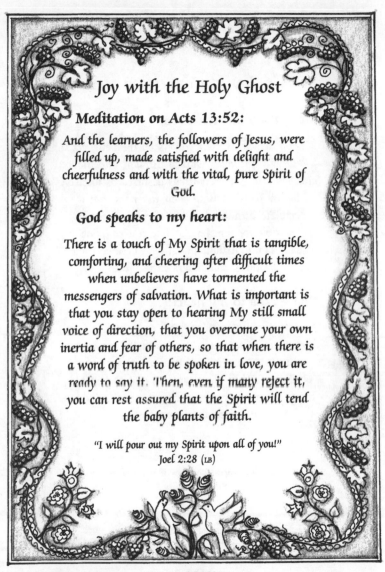

Joy with the Holy Ghost

Meditation on Acts 13:52:

And the learners, the followers of Jesus, were filled up, made satisfied with delight and cheerfulness and with the vital, pure Spirit of God.

God speaks to my heart:

There is a touch of My Spirit that is tangible, comforting, and cheering after difficult times when unbelievers have tormented the messengers of salvation. What is important is that you stay open to hearing My still small voice of direction, that you overcome your own inertia and fear of others, so that when there is a word of truth to be spoken in love, you are ready to say it. Then, even if many reject it, you can rest assured that the Spirit will tend the baby plants of faith.

"I will pour out my Spirit upon all of you!"
Joel 2:28 (LB)

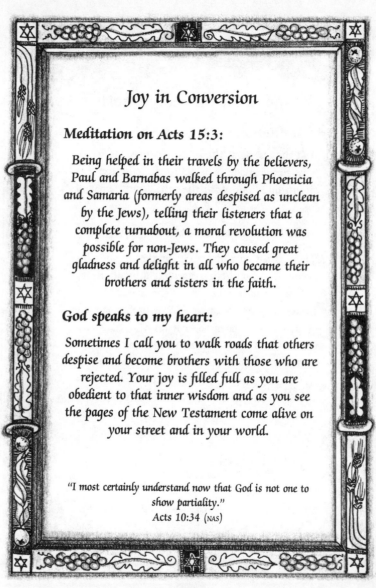

Joy in Conversion

Meditation on Acts 15:3:

Being helped in their travels by the believers,
Paul and Barnabas walked through Phoenicia
and Samaria (formerly areas despised as unclean
by the Jews), telling their listeners that a
complete turnabout, a moral revolution was
possible for non-Jews. They caused great
gladness and delight in all who became their
brothers and sisters in the faith.

God speaks to my heart:

Sometimes I call you to walk roads that others
despise and become brothers with those who are
rejected. Your joy is filled full as you are
obedient to that inner wisdom and as you see
the pages of the New Testament come alive on
your street and in your world.

"I most certainly understand now that God is not one to
show partiality."
Acts 10:34 (NAS)

Finishing with Joy

Meditation on Acts 20:24:

Paul said: "Not even one negative word or
thought can move me. I do not even hold onto
my physical life, so that I might complete my
race (career) with glad delight, and complete
the job I have as a servant, which I have taken
hold of from the Lord Jesus in order that I
might give an honest report of the good message
of graciousness, liberality, and pleasure of
God."

God speaks to my heart:

Take those negative thoughts captive and throw
away the key, especially to those that ridicule
and condemn you or others—even your enemies!
My Spirit's messages to you will enable you to
complete your part in My time, in My way, and
in My joy! It pleases Me for you to share the
good news in ways others can hear. I take you
through the failure and even that can speak
of Me.

"... If only I may finish the race and complete the task."
Acts 20:24 (NIV)

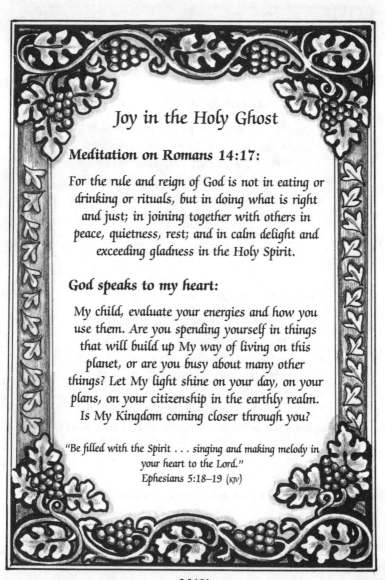

Joy in the Holy Ghost

Meditation on Romans 14:17:

For the rule and reign of God is not in eating or
drinking or rituals, but in doing what is right
and just; in joining together with others in
peace, quietness, rest; and in calm delight and
exceeding gladness in the Holy Spirit.

God speaks to my heart:

My child, evaluate your energies and how you
use them. Are you spending yourself in things
that will build up My way of living on this
planet, or are you busy about many other
things? Let My light shine on your day, on your
plans, on your citizenship in the earthly realm.
Is My Kingdom coming closer through you?

*"Be filled with the Spirit . . . singing and making melody in
your heart to the Lord."*
Ephesians 5:18–19 (kjv)

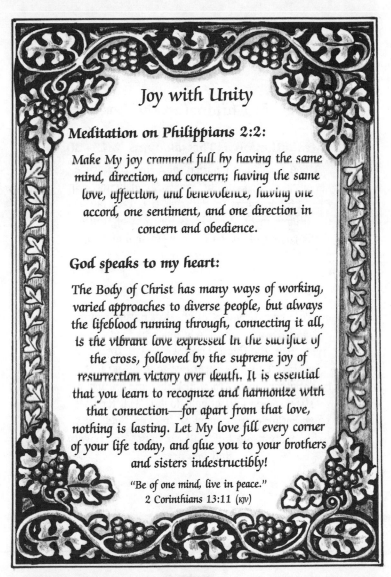

Joy with Unity

Meditation on Philippians 2:2:

Make My joy crammed full by having the same
mind, direction, and concern; having the same
love, affection, and benevolence, having one
accord, one sentiment, and one direction in
concern and obedience.

God speaks to my heart:

The Body of Christ has many ways of working,
varied approaches to diverse people, but always
the lifeblood running through, connecting it all,
is the vibrant love expressed in the sacrifice of
the cross, followed by the supreme joy of
resurrection victory over death. It is essential
that you learn to recognize and harmonize with
that connection—for apart from that love,
nothing is lasting. Let My love fill every corner
of your life today, and glue you to your brothers
and sisters indestructibly!

"Be of one mind, live in peace."
2 Corinthians 13:11 (KJV)

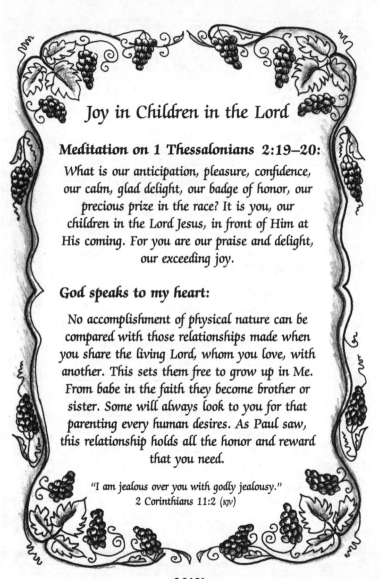

Joy in Children in the Lord

Meditation on 1 Thessalonians 2:19–20:

What is our anticipation, pleasure, confidence,
our calm, glad delight, our badge of honor, our
precious prize in the race? It is you, our
children in the Lord Jesus, in front of Him at
His coming. For you are our praise and delight,
our exceeding joy.

God speaks to my heart:

No accomplishment of physical nature can be
compared with those relationships made when
you share the living Lord, whom you love, with
another. This sets them free to grow up in Me.
From babe in the faith they become brother or
sister. Some will always look to you for that
parenting every human desires. As Paul saw,
this relationship holds all the honor and reward
that you need.

"I am jealous over you with godly jealousy."
2 Corinthians 11:2 (KJV)

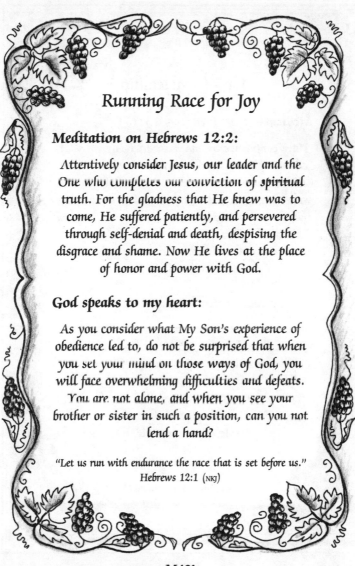

Running Race for Joy

Meditation on Hebrews 12:2:

Attentively consider Jesus, our leader and the One who completes our conviction of spiritual truth. For the gladness that He knew was to come, He suffered patiently, and persevered through self-denial and death, despising the disgrace and shame. Now He lives at the place of honor and power with God.

God speaks to my heart:

As you consider what My Son's experience of obedience led to, do not be surprised that when you set your mind on those ways of God, you will face overwhelming difficulties and defeats. You are not alone, and when you see your brother or sister in such a position, can you not lend a hand?

"Let us run with endurance the race that is set before us."
Hebrews 12:1 (NKJ)

Joy of Leadership

Meditation on Hebrews 13:17:

Have confidence in and make friends with your official spiritual leaders and yield yourselves to them. They keep awake on your behalf for the well-being of your life, mind, and heart, because they must give God a report. If you have a good attitude, they may keep watch with calm delight—not with groans or grudgingly—and that is profitable for you.

God speaks to my heart:

When I call into service, some will lead, serving the servants. Whatever your role, your attitude is of utmost importance: fit into My love, be open and honest, yet always work to keep communications clear. In every human group there are "impossible" people, but with Me, joy is possible.

"Be servants of one another."
Galatians 5:13 (RSV)

Joy in Temptation

Meditation on James 1:2:

Fellow believers, consider the whole of life with delight when you fall into and are surrounded with motley adversities, whether experiences of good or evil. You can be sure that the testing, the putting on trial of your belief, works fully to accomplish a cheerful, hopeful endurance even as you wait.

God speaks to my heart:

It's true! Let this assurance enable you to risk going beyond fears of the unknown and even beyond bad memories of the past, so that you are free to keep on accepting the challenges I give you. The Christian life is an adventure because you walk with Me through those tough experiences, and learn from your mistakes.

"Blessed is the man that endureth temptation."
James 1:12 (KJV)

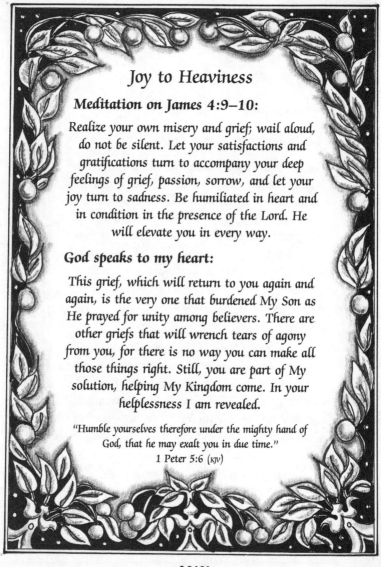

Joy to Heaviness

Meditation on James 4:9–10:

Realize your own misery and grief; wail aloud, do not be silent. Let your satisfactions and gratifications turn to accompany your deep feelings of grief, passion, sorrow, and let your joy turn to sadness. Be humiliated in heart and in condition in the presence of the Lord. He will elevate you in every way.

God speaks to my heart:

This grief, which will return to you again and again, is the very one that burdened My Son as He prayed for unity among believers. There are other griefs that will wrench tears of agony from you, for there is no way you can make all those things right. Still, you are part of My solution, helping My Kingdom come. In your helplessness I am revealed.

"Humble yourselves therefore under the mighty hand of God, that he may exalt you in due time."
1 Peter 5:6 (KJV)

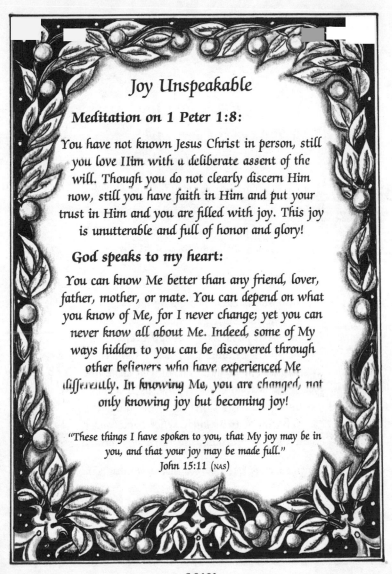

Joy Unspeakable

Meditation on 1 Peter 1:8:

You have not known Jesus Christ in person, still you love Him with a deliberate assent of the will. Though you do not clearly discern Him now, still you have faith in Him and put your trust in Him and you are filled with joy. This joy is unutterable and full of honor and glory!

God speaks to my heart:

You can know Me better than any friend, lover, father, mother, or mate. You can depend on what you know of Me, for I never change; yet you can never know all about Me. Indeed, some of My ways hidden to you can be discovered through other believers who have experienced Me differently. In knowing Me, you are changed, not only knowing joy but becoming joy!

"These things I have spoken to you, that My joy may be in you, and that your joy may be made full."
John 15:11 (NAS)

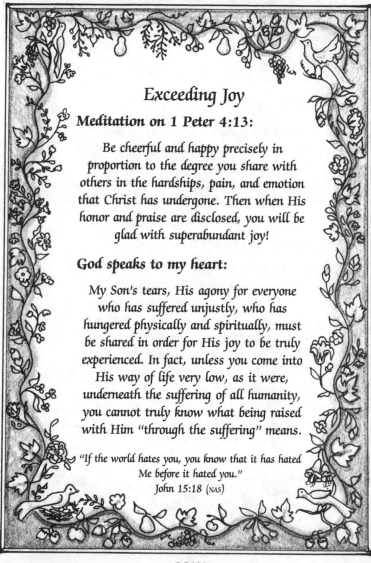

Exceeding Joy

Meditation on 1 Peter 4:13:

Be cheerful and happy precisely in
proportion to the degree you share with
others in the hardships, pain, and emotion
that Christ has undergone. Then when His
honor and praise are disclosed, you will be
glad with superabundant joy!

God speaks to my heart:

My Son's tears, His agony for everyone
who has suffered unjustly, who has
hungered physically and spiritually, must
be shared in order for His joy to be truly
experienced. In fact, unless you come into
His way of life very low, as it were,
underneath the suffering of all humanity,
you cannot truly know what being raised
with Him "through the suffering" means.

"If the world hates you, you know that it has hated
Me before it hated you."
John 15:18 (NAS)

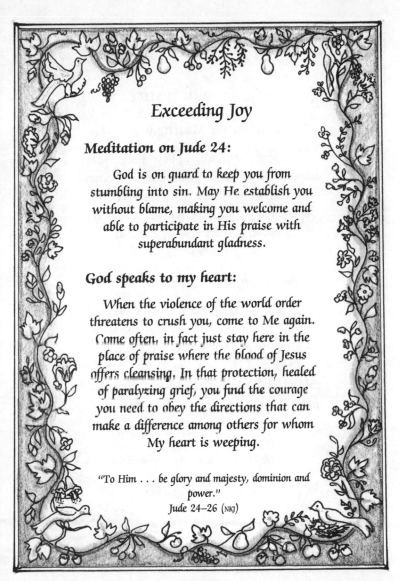

Exceeding Joy

Meditation on Jude 24:

God is on guard to keep you from
stumbling into sin. May He establish you
without blame, making you welcome and
able to participate in His praise with
superabundant gladness.

God speaks to my heart:

When the violence of the world order
threatens to crush you, come to Me again.
Come often, in fact just stay here in the
place of praise where the blood of Jesus
offers cleansing. In that protection, healed
of paralyzing grief, you find the courage
you need to obey the directions that can
make a difference among others for whom
My heart is weeping.

"To Him . . . be glory and majesty, dominion and
power."
Jude 24–26 (NKJ)

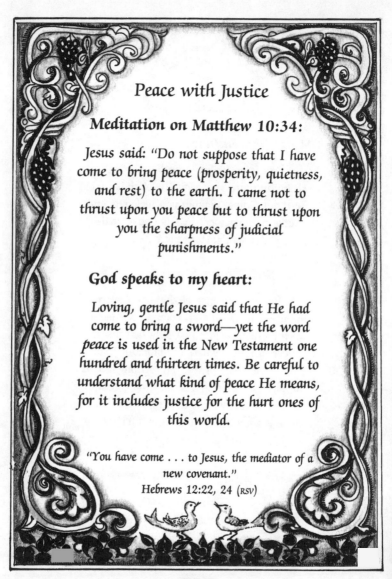

Peace with Justice

Meditation on Matthew 10:34:

Jesus said: "Do not suppose that I have come to bring peace (prosperity, quietness, and rest) to the earth. I came not to thrust upon you peace but to thrust upon you the sharpness of judicial punishments."

God speaks to my heart:

Loving, gentle Jesus said that He had come to bring a sword—yet the word *peace* is used in the New Testament one hundred and thirteen times. Be careful to understand what kind of peace He means, for it includes justice for the hurt ones of this world.

"You have come . . . to Jesus, the mediator of a new covenant."
Hebrews 12:22, 24 (RSV)

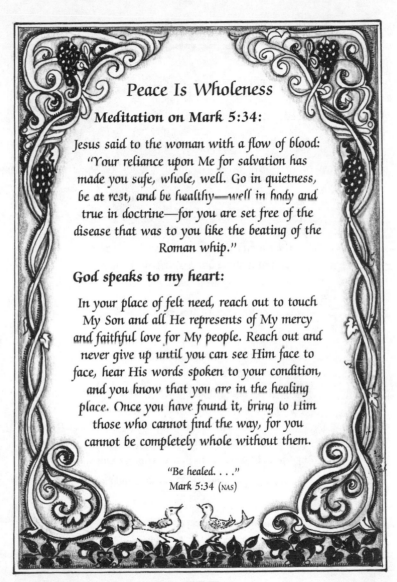

Peace Is Wholeness

Meditation on Mark 5:34:

Jesus said to the woman with a flow of blood:
"Your reliance upon Me for salvation has
made you safe, whole, well. Go in quietness,
be at rest, and be healthy—well in body and
true in doctrine—for you are set free of the
disease that was to you like the beating of the
Roman whip."

God speaks to my heart:

In your place of felt need, reach out to touch
My Son and all He represents of My mercy
and faithful love for My people. Reach out and
never give up until you can see Him face to
face, hear His words spoken to your condition,
and you know that you are in the healing
place. Once you have found it, bring to Him
those who cannot find the way, for you
cannot be completely whole without them.

"Be healed. . . ."
Mark 5:34 (NAS)

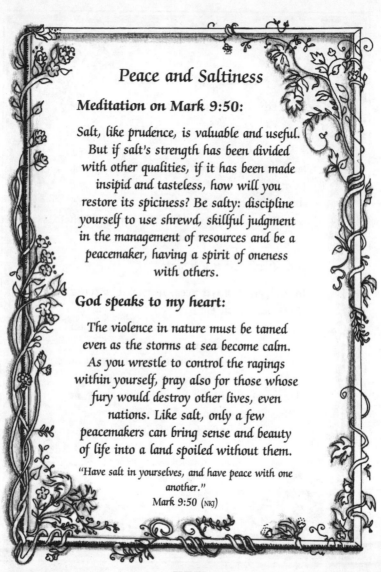

Peace and Saltiness

Meditation on Mark 9:50:

Salt, like prudence, is valuable and useful.
But if salt's strength has been divided
with other qualities, if it has been made
insipid and tasteless, how will you
restore its spiciness? Be salty: discipline
yourself to use shrewd, skillful judgment
in the management of resources and be a
peacemaker, having a spirit of oneness
with others.

God speaks to my heart:

The violence in nature must be tamed
even as the storms at sea become calm.
As you wrestle to control the ragings
within yourself, pray also for those whose
fury would destroy other lives, even
nations. Like salt, only a few
peacemakers can bring sense and beauty
of life into a land spoiled without them.

*"Have salt in yourselves, and have peace with one
another."*
Mark 9:50 (NKJ)

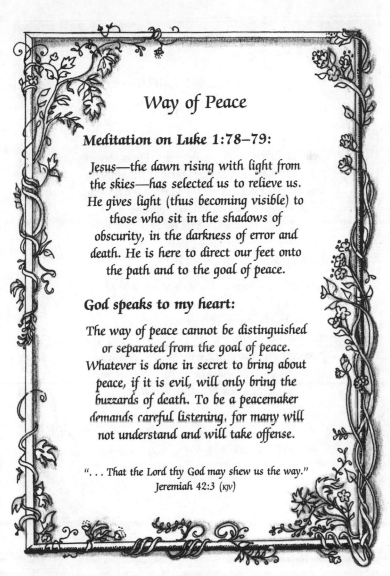

Way of Peace

Meditation on Luke 1:78–79:

Jesus—the dawn rising with light from the skies—has selected us to relieve us. He gives light (thus becoming visible) to those who sit in the shadows of obscurity, in the darkness of error and death. He is here to direct our feet onto the path and to the goal of peace.

God speaks to my heart:

The way of peace cannot be distinguished or separated from the goal of peace. Whatever is done in secret to bring about peace, if it is evil, will only bring the buzzards of death. To be a peacemaker demands careful listening, for many will not understand and will take offense.

". . . That the Lord thy God may shew us the way."
Jeremiah 42:3 (KJV)

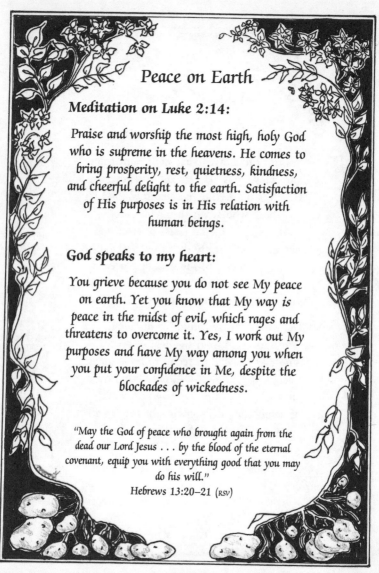

Peace on Earth

Meditation on Luke 2:14:

Praise and worship the most high, holy God who is supreme in the heavens. He comes to bring prosperity, rest, quietness, kindness, and cheerful delight to the earth. Satisfaction of His purposes is in His relation with human beings.

God speaks to my heart:

You grieve because you do not see My peace on earth. Yet you know that My way *is* peace in the midst of evil, which rages and threatens to overcome it. Yes, I work out My purposes and have My way among you when you put your confidence in Me, despite the blockades of wickedness.

"May the God of peace who brought again from the dead our Lord Jesus . . . by the blood of the eternal covenant, equip you with everything good that you may do his will."
Hebrews 13:20–21 (RSV)

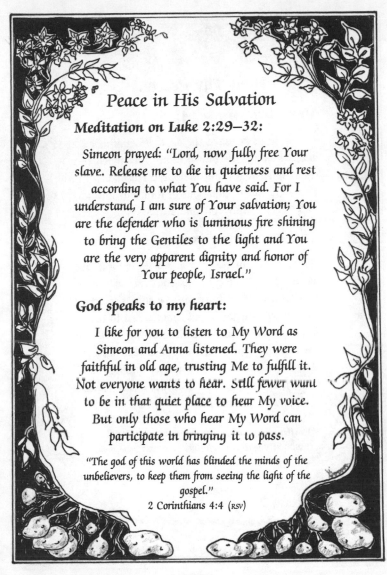

Peace in His Salvation

Meditation on Luke 2:29–32:

Simeon prayed: "Lord, now fully free Your
slave. Release me to die in quietness and rest
according to what You have said. For I
understand, I am sure of Your salvation; You
are the defender who is luminous fire shining
to bring the Gentiles to the light and You
are the very apparent dignity and honor of
Your people, Israel."

God speaks to my heart:

I like for you to listen to My Word as
Simeon and Anna listened. They were
faithful in old age, trusting Me to fulfill it.
Not everyone wants to hear. Still fewer want
to be in that quiet place to hear My voice.
But only those who hear My Word can
participate in bringing it to pass.

"The god of this world has blinded the minds of the
unbelievers, to keep them from seeing the light of the
gospel."
2 Corinthians 4:4 (RSV)

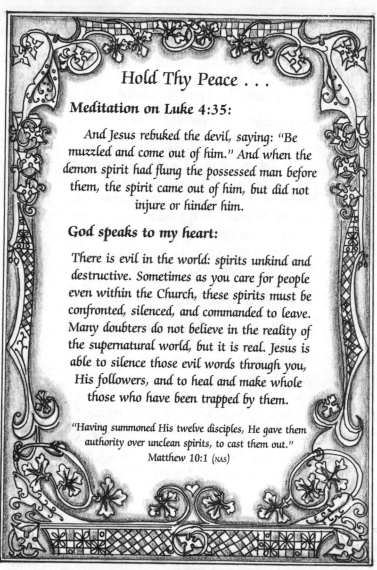

Hold Thy Peace . . .

Meditation on Luke 4:35:

And Jesus rebuked the devil, saying: "Be
muzzled and come out of him." And when the
demon spirit had flung the possessed man before
them, the spirit came out of him, but did not
injure or hinder him.

God speaks to my heart:

There is evil in the world: spirits unkind and
destructive. Sometimes as you care for people
even within the Church, these spirits must be
confronted, silenced, and commanded to leave.
Many doubters do not believe in the reality of
the supernatural world, but it is real. Jesus is
able to silence those evil words through you,
His followers, and to heal and make whole
those who have been trapped by them.

*"Having summoned His twelve disciples, He gave them
authority over unclean spirits, to cast them out."*
Matthew 10:1 (NAS)

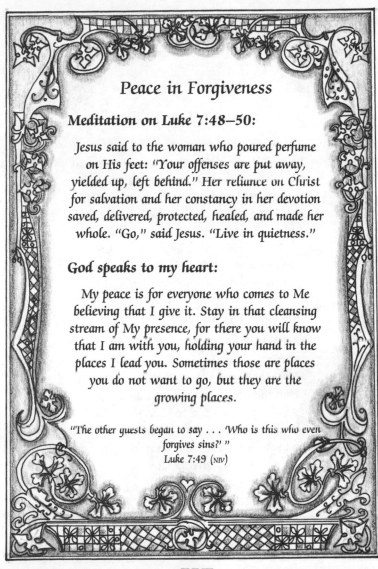

Peace in Forgiveness

Meditation on Luke 7:48–50:

Jesus said to the woman who poured perfume on His feet: "Your offenses are put away, yielded up, left behind." Her reliance on Christ for salvation and her constancy in her devotion saved, delivered, protected, healed, and made her whole. "Go," said Jesus. "Live in quietness."

God speaks to my heart:

My peace is for everyone who comes to Me believing that I give it. Stay in that cleansing stream of My presence, for there you will know that I am with you, holding your hand in the places I lead you. Sometimes those are places you do not want to go, but they are the growing places.

"The other guests began to say . . . 'Who is this who even forgives sins?'"
Luke 7:49 (NIV)

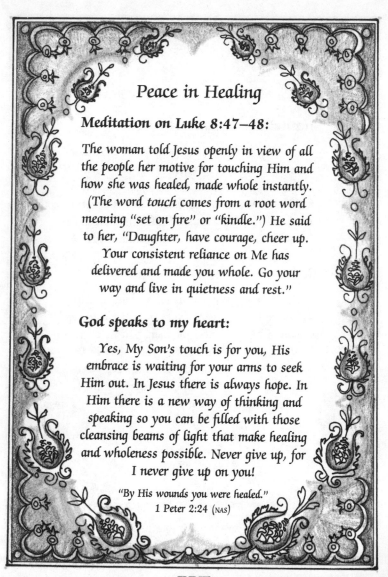

Peace in Healing

Meditation on Luke 8:47–48:

The woman told Jesus openly in view of all
the people her motive for touching Him and
how she was healed, made whole instantly.
(The word *touch* comes from a root word
meaning "set on fire" or "kindle.") He said
to her, "Daughter, have courage, cheer up.
Your consistent reliance on Me has
delivered and made you whole. Go your
way and live in quietness and rest."

God speaks to my heart:

Yes, My Son's touch is for you, His
embrace is waiting for your arms to seek
Him out. In Jesus there is always hope. In
Him there is a new way of thinking and
speaking so you can be filled with those
cleansing beams of light that make healing
and wholeness possible. Never give up, for
I never give up on you!

"By His wounds you were healed."
1 Peter 2:24 (NAS)

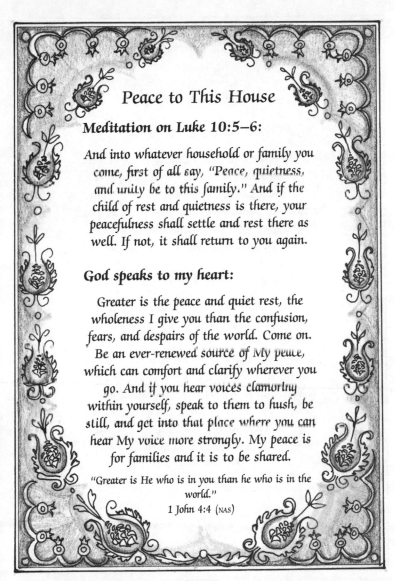

Peace to This House

Meditation on Luke 10:5–6:

And into whatever household or family you come, first of all say, "Peace, quietness, and unity be to this family." And if the child of rest and quietness is there, your peacefulness shall settle and rest there as well. If not, it shall return to you again.

God speaks to my heart:

Greater is the peace and quiet rest, the wholeness I give you than the confusion, fears, and despairs of the world. Come on. Be an ever-renewed source of My peace, which can comfort and clarify wherever you go. And if you hear voices clamoring within yourself, speak to them to hush, be still, and get into that place where you can hear My voice more strongly. My peace is for families and it is to be shared.

"Greater is He who is in you than he who is in the world."
1 John 4:4 (NAS)

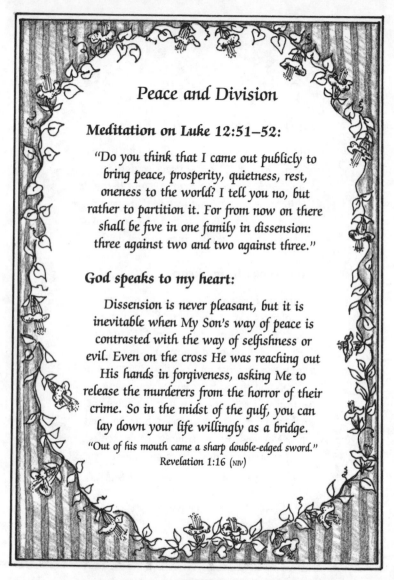

Peace and Division

Meditation on Luke 12:51–52:

"Do you think that I came out publicly to bring peace, prosperity, quietness, rest, oneness to the world? I tell you no, but rather to partition it. For from now on there shall be five in one family in dissension: three against two and two against three."

God speaks to my heart:

Dissension is never pleasant, but it is inevitable when My Son's way of peace is contrasted with the way of selfishness or evil. Even on the cross He was reaching out His hands in forgiveness, asking Me to release the murderers from the horror of their crime. So in the midst of the gulf, you can lay down your life willingly as a bridge.

"Out of his mouth came a sharp double-edged sword."
Revelation 1:16 (NIV)

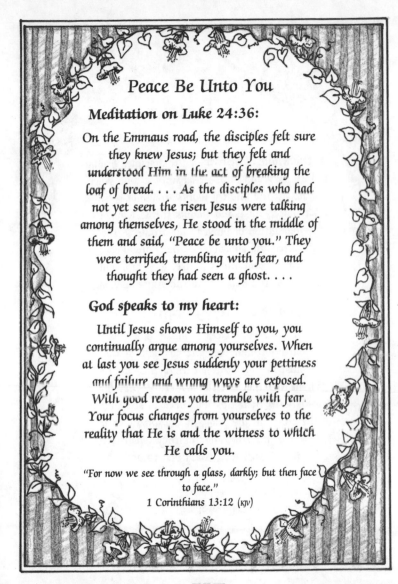

Peace Be Unto You

Meditation on Luke 24:36:

On the Emmaus road, the disciples felt sure
they knew Jesus; but they felt and
understood Him in the act of breaking the
loaf of bread. . . . As the disciples who had
not yet seen the risen Jesus were talking
among themselves, He stood in the middle of
them and said, "Peace be unto you." They
were terrified, trembling with fear, and
thought they had seen a ghost. . . .

God speaks to my heart:

Until Jesus shows Himself to you, you
continually argue among yourselves. When
at last you see Jesus suddenly your pettiness
and failure and wrong ways are exposed.
With good reason you tremble with fear.
Your focus changes from yourselves to the
reality that He is and the witness to which
He calls you.

"For now we see through a glass, darkly; but then face
to face."
1 Corinthians 13:12 (KJV)

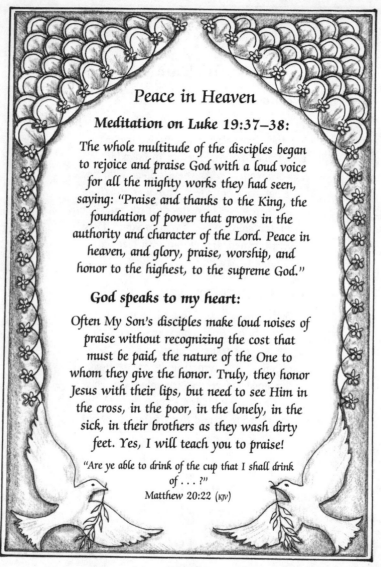

Peace in Heaven

Meditation on Luke 19:37–38:

The whole multitude of the disciples began to rejoice and praise God with a loud voice for all the mighty works they had seen, saying: "Praise and thanks to the King, the foundation of power that grows in the authority and character of the Lord. Peace in heaven, and glory, praise, worship, and honor to the highest, to the supreme God."

God speaks to my heart:

Often My Son's disciples make loud noises of praise without recognizing the cost that must be paid, the nature of the One to whom they give the honor. Truly, they honor Jesus with their lips, but need to see Him in the cross, in the poor, in the lonely, in the sick, in their brothers as they wash dirty feet. Yes, I will teach you to praise!

"Are ye able to drink of the cup that I shall drink of . . . ?"
Matthew 20:22 (KJV)

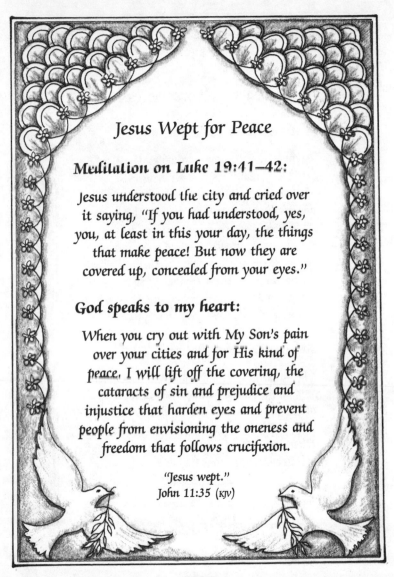

Jesus Wept for Peace

Meditation on Luke 19:41–42:

Jesus understood the city and cried over it saying, "If you had understood, yes, you, at least in this your day, the things that make peace! But now they are covered up, concealed from your eyes."

God speaks to my heart:

When you cry out with My Son's pain over your cities and for His kind of peace, I will lift off the covering, the cataracts of sin and prejudice and injustice that harden eyes and prevent people from envisioning the oneness and freedom that follows crucifixion.

"Jesus wept."
John 11:35 (KJV)

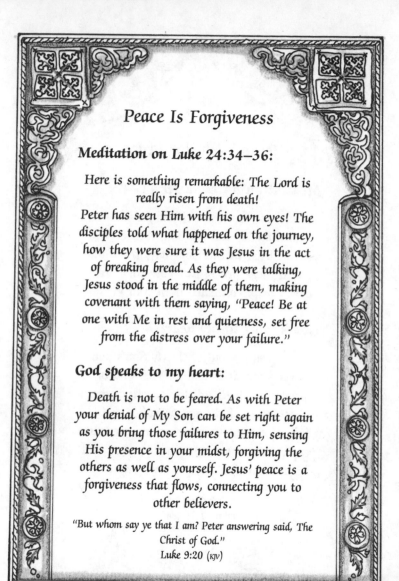

Peace Is Forgiveness

Meditation on Luke 24:34–36:

Here is something remarkable: The Lord is
really risen from death!
Peter has seen Him with his own eyes! The
disciples told what happened on the journey,
how they were sure it was Jesus in the act
of breaking bread. As they were talking,
Jesus stood in the middle of them, making
covenant with them saying, "Peace! Be at
one with Me in rest and quietness, set free
from the distress over your failure."

God speaks to my heart:

Death is not to be feared. As with Peter
your denial of My Son can be set right again
as you bring those failures to Him, sensing
His presence in your midst, forgiving the
others as well as yourself. Jesus' peace is a
forgiveness that flows, connecting you to
other believers.

"But whom say ye that I am? Peter answering said, The
Christ of God."
Luke 9:20 (KJV)

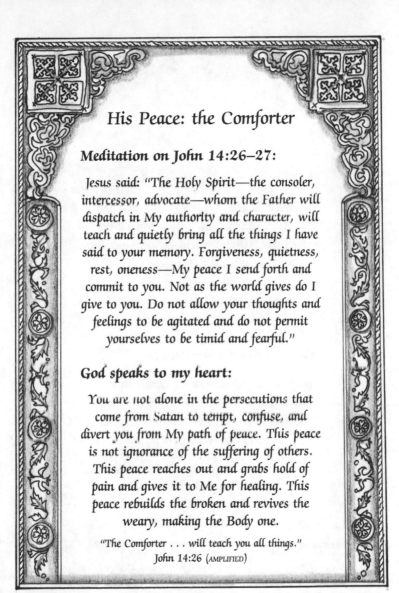

His Peace: the Comforter

Meditation on John 14:26–27:

Jesus said: "The Holy Spirit—the consoler, intercessor, advocate—whom the Father will dispatch in My authority and character, will teach and quietly bring all the things I have said to your memory. Forgiveness, quietness, rest, oneness—My peace I send forth and commit to you. Not as the world gives do I give to you. Do not allow your thoughts and feelings to be agitated and do not permit yourselves to be timid and fearful."

God speaks to my heart:

You are not alone in the persecutions that come from Satan to tempt, confuse, and divert you from My path of peace. This peace is not ignorance of the suffering of others. This peace reaches out and grabs hold of pain and gives it to Me for healing. This peace rebuilds the broken and revives the weary, making the Body one.

"The Comforter . . . will teach you all things."
John 14:26 (AMPLIFIED)

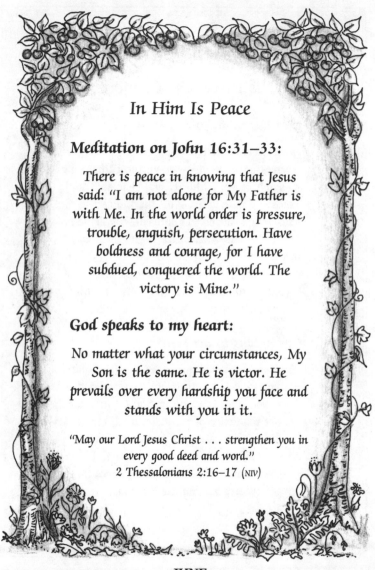

In Him Is Peace

Meditation on John 16:31–33:

There is peace in knowing that Jesus
said: "I am not alone for My Father is
with Me. In the world order is pressure,
trouble, anguish, persecution. Have
boldness and courage, for I have
subdued, conquered the world. The
victory is Mine."

God speaks to my heart:

No matter what your circumstances, My
Son is the same. He is victor. He
prevails over every hardship you face and
stands with you in it.

"May our Lord Jesus Christ . . . strengthen you in
every good deed and word."
2 Thessalonians 2:16–17 (NIV)

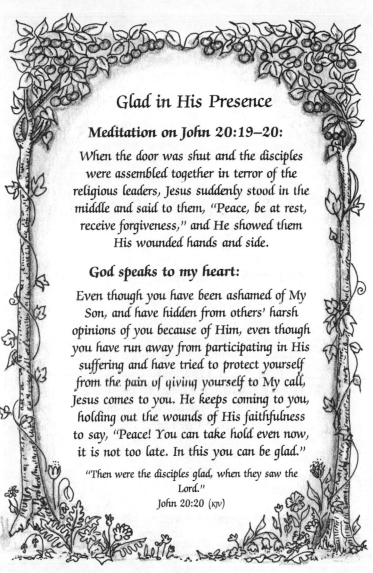

Glad in His Presence

Meditation on John 20:19–20:

When the door was shut and the disciples
were assembled together in terror of the
religious leaders, Jesus suddenly stood in the
middle and said to them, "Peace, be at rest,
receive forgiveness," and He showed them
His wounded hands and side.

God speaks to my heart:

Even though you have been ashamed of My
Son, and have hidden from others' harsh
opinions of you because of Him, even though
you have run away from participating in His
suffering and have tried to protect yourself
from the pain of giving yourself to My call,
Jesus comes to you. He keeps coming to you,
holding out the wounds of His faithfulness
to say, "Peace! You can take hold even now,
it is not too late. In this you can be glad."

"Then were the disciples glad, when they saw the
Lord."
John 20:20 (KJV)

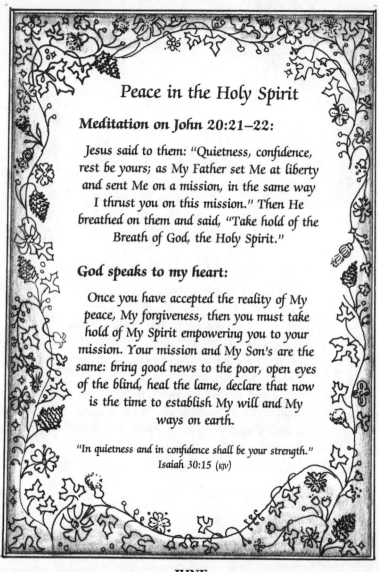

Peace in the Holy Spirit

Meditation on John 20:21–22:

Jesus said to them: "Quietness, confidence,
rest be yours; as My Father set Me at liberty
and sent Me on a mission, in the same way
I thrust you on this mission." Then He
breathed on them and said, "Take hold of the
Breath of God, the Holy Spirit."

God speaks to my heart:

Once you have accepted the reality of My
peace, My forgiveness, then you must take
hold of My Spirit empowering you to your
mission. Your mission and My Son's are the
same: bring good news to the poor, open eyes
of the blind, heal the lame, declare that now
is the time to establish My will and My
ways on earth.

"In quietness and in confidence shall be your strength."
Isaiah 30:15 (kjv)

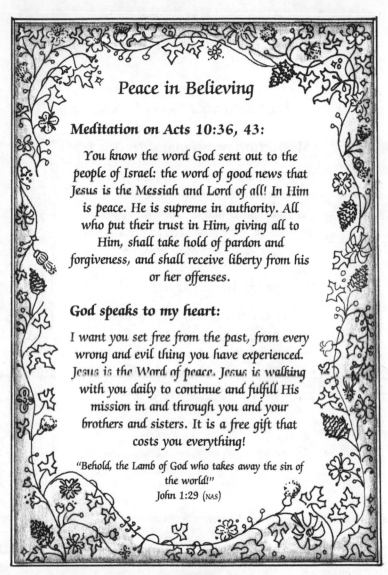

Peace in Believing

Meditation on Acts 10:36, 43:

You know the word God sent out to the people of Israel: the word of good news that Jesus is the Messiah and Lord of all! In Him is peace. He is supreme in authority. All who put their trust in Him, giving all to Him, shall take hold of pardon and forgiveness, and shall receive liberty from his or her offenses.

God speaks to my heart:

I want you set free from the past, from every wrong and evil thing you have experienced. Jesus is the Word of peace. Jesus is walking with you daily to continue and fulfill His mission in and through you and your brothers and sisters. It is a free gift that costs you everything!

"Behold, the Lamb of God who takes away the sin of the world!"
John 1:29 (NAS)

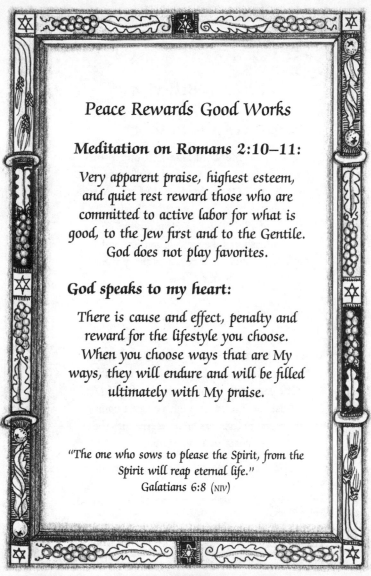

Peace Rewards Good Works

Meditation on Romans 2:10–11:

Very apparent praise, highest esteem,
and quiet rest reward those who are
committed to active labor for what is
good, to the Jew first and to the Gentile.
God does not play favorites.

God speaks to my heart:

There is cause and effect, penalty and
reward for the lifestyle you choose.
When you choose ways that are My
ways, they will endure and will be filled
ultimately with My praise.

"The one who sows to please the Spirit, from the
Spirit will reap eternal life."
Galatians 6:8 (NIV)

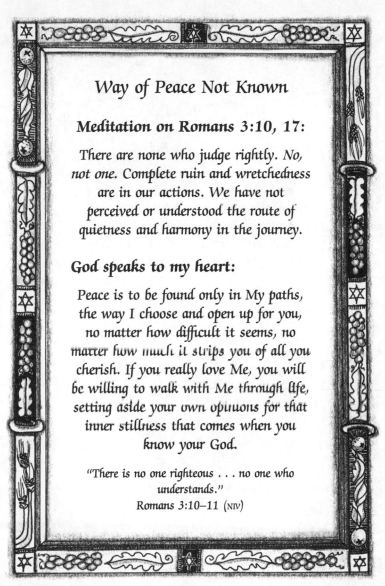

Way of Peace Not Known

Meditation on Romans 3:10, 17:

There are none who judge rightly. *No, not one.* Complete ruin and wretchedness are in our actions. We have not perceived or understood the route of quietness and harmony in the journey.

God speaks to my heart:

Peace is to be found only in My paths, the way I choose and open up for you, no matter how difficult it seems, no matter how much it strips you of all you cherish. If you really love Me, you will be willing to walk with Me through life, setting aside your own opinions for that inner stillness that comes when you know your God.

"There is no one righteous . . . no one who understands."
Romans 3:10–11 (NIV)

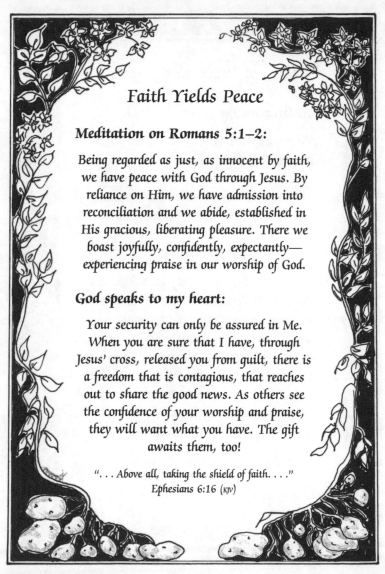

Faith Yields Peace

Meditation on Romans 5:1–2:

Being regarded as just, as innocent by faith,
we have peace with God through Jesus. By
reliance on Him, we have admission into
reconciliation and we abide, established in
His gracious, liberating pleasure. There we
boast joyfully, confidently, expectantly—
experiencing praise in our worship of God.

God speaks to my heart:

Your security can only be assured in Me.
When you are sure that I have, through
Jesus' cross, released you from guilt, there is
a freedom that is contagious, that reaches
out to share the good news. As others see
the confidence of your worship and praise,
they will want what you have. The gift
awaits them, too!

"... Above all, taking the shield of faith. ..."
Ephesians 6:16 (KJV)

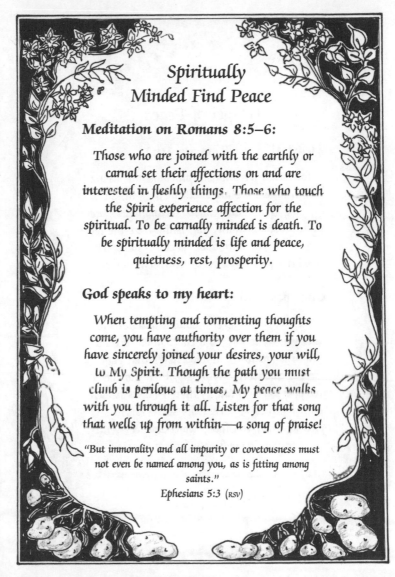

Spiritually Minded Find Peace

Meditation on Romans 8:5–6:

Those who are joined with the earthly or carnal set their affections on and are interested in fleshly things. Those who touch the Spirit experience affection for the spiritual. To be carnally minded is death. To be spiritually minded is life and peace, quietness, rest, prosperity.

God speaks to my heart:

When tempting and tormenting thoughts come, you have authority over them if you have sincerely joined your desires, your will, to My Spirit. Though the path you must climb is perilous at times, My peace walks with you through it all. Listen for that song that wells up from within—a song of praise!

"But immorality and all impurity or covetousness must not even be named among you, as is fitting among saints."

Ephesians 5:3 (RSV)

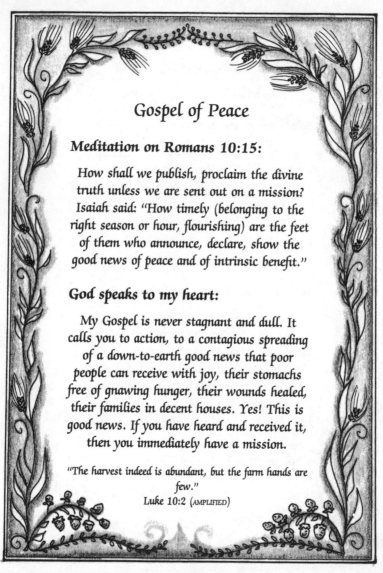

Gospel of Peace

Meditation on Romans 10:15:

How shall we publish, proclaim the divine
truth unless we are sent out on a mission?
Isaiah said: "How timely (belonging to the
right season or hour, flourishing) are the feet
of them who announce, declare, show the
good news of peace and of intrinsic benefit."

God speaks to my heart:

My Gospel is never stagnant and dull. It
calls you to action, to a contagious spreading
of a down-to-earth good news that poor
people can receive with joy, their stomachs
free of gnawing hunger, their wounds healed,
their families in decent houses. Yes! This is
good news. If you have heard and received it,
then you immediately have a mission.

"The harvest indeed is abundant, but the farm hands are
few."
Luke 10:2 (AMPLIFIED)

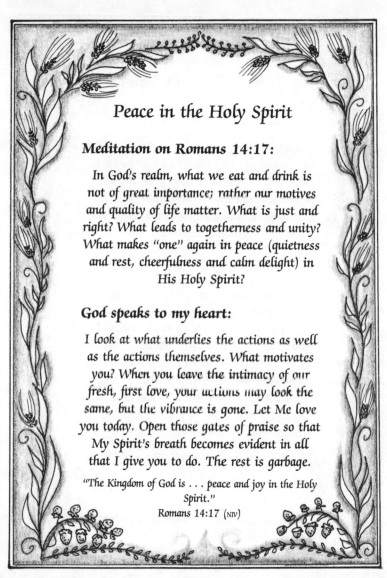

Peace in the Holy Spirit

Meditation on Romans 14:17:

In God's realm, what we eat and drink is
not of great importance; rather our motives
and quality of life matter. What is just and
right? What leads to togetherness and unity?
What makes "one" again in peace (quietness
and rest, cheerfulness and calm delight) in
His Holy Spirit?

God speaks to my heart:

I look at what underlies the actions as well
as the actions themselves. What motivates
you? When you leave the intimacy of our
fresh, first love, your actions may look the
same, but the vibrance is gone. Let Me love
you today. Open those gates of praise so that
My Spirit's breath becomes evident in all
that I give you to do. The rest is garbage.

"The Kingdom of God is . . . peace and joy in the Holy
Spirit."
Romans 14:17 (NIV)

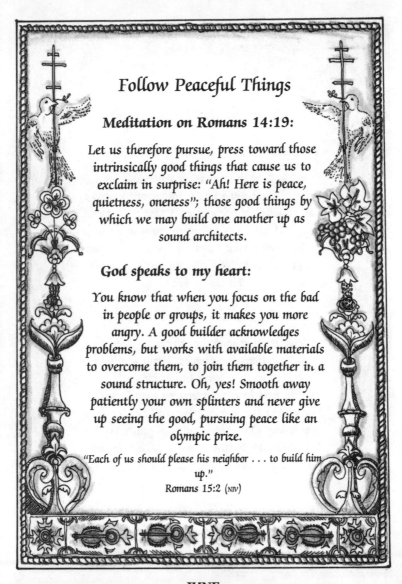

Follow Peaceful Things

Meditation on Romans 14:19:

Let us therefore pursue, press toward those intrinsically good things that cause us to exclaim in surprise: "Ah! Here is peace, quietness, oneness"; those good things by which we may build one another up as sound architects.

God speaks to my heart:

You know that when you focus on the bad in people or groups, it makes you more angry. A good builder acknowledges problems, but works with available materials to overcome them, to join them together in a sound structure. Oh, yes! Smooth away patiently your own splinters and never give up seeing the good, pursuing peace like an olympic prize.

"Each of us should please his neighbor . . . to build him up."
Romans 15:2 (NIV)

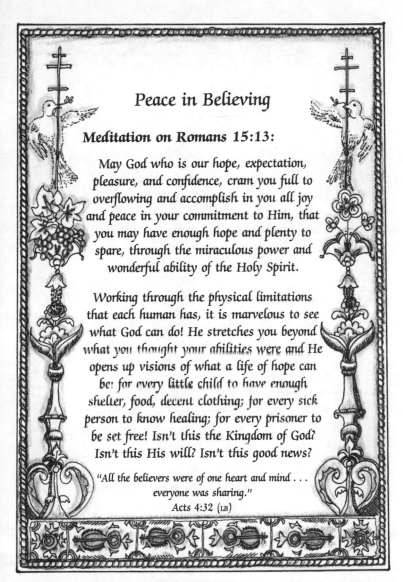

Peace in Believing

Meditation on Romans 15:13:

May God who is our hope, expectation, pleasure, and confidence, cram you full to overflowing and accomplish in you all joy and peace in your commitment to Him, that you may have enough hope and plenty to spare, through the miraculous power and wonderful ability of the Holy Spirit.

Working through the physical limitations that each human has, it is marvelous to see what God can do! He stretches you beyond what you thought your abilities were and He opens up visions of what a life of hope can be; for every little child to have enough shelter, food, decent clothing; for every sick person to know healing; for every prisoner to be set free! Isn't this the Kingdom of God? Isn't this His will? Isn't this good news?

"All the believers were of one heart and mind . . . everyone was sharing."
Acts 4:32 (LB)

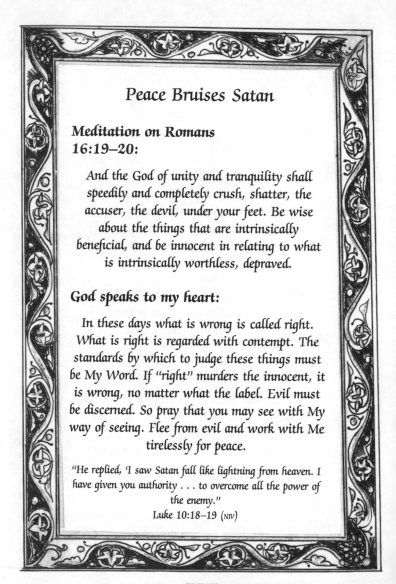

Peace Bruises Satan

Meditation on Romans 16:19–20:

And the God of unity and tranquility shall speedily and completely crush, shatter, the accuser, the devil, under your feet. Be wise about the things that are intrinsically beneficial, and be innocent in relating to what is intrinsically worthless, depraved.

God speaks to my heart:

In these days what is wrong is called right. What is right is regarded with contempt. The standards by which to judge these things must be My Word. If "right" murders the innocent, it is wrong, no matter what the label. Evil must be discerned. So pray that you may see with My way of seeing. Flee from evil and work with Me tirelessly for peace.

"He replied, 'I saw Satan fall like lightning from heaven. I have given you authority . . . to overcome all the power of the enemy."
Luke 10:18–19 (NIV)

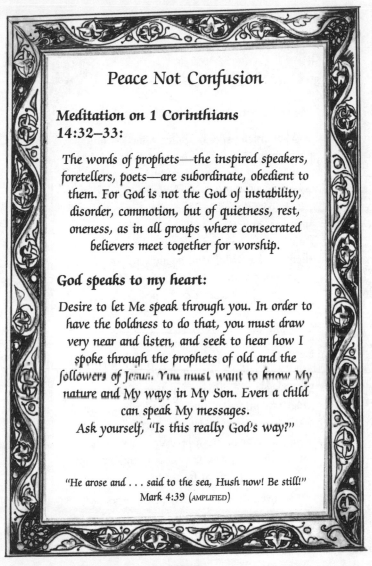

Peace Not Confusion

Meditation on 1 Corinthians 14:32–33:

The words of prophets—the inspired speakers, foretellers, poets—are subordinate, obedient to them. For God is not the God of instability, disorder, commotion, but of quietness, rest, oneness, as in all groups where consecrated believers meet together for worship.

God speaks to my heart:

Desire to let Me speak through you. In order to have the boldness to do that, you must draw very near and listen, and seek to hear how I spoke through the prophets of old and the followers of Jesus. You must want to know My nature and My ways in My Son. Even a child can speak My messages.

Ask yourself, "Is this really God's way?"

"He arose and . . . said to the sea, Hush now! Be still!"
Mark 4:39 (AMPLIFIED)

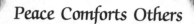

Peace Comforts Others

Meditation on 2 Corinthians 1:2–4:

May graciousness, divine influence, and peace from God our Father and from the Lord Jesus Christ be upon your heart and reflect in your life. He comes near, invites us, exhorts, entreats, consoles us in all our pressures, our anguish, affliction, persecution. Then we are able to comfort others in the same way in their trouble, grief, and agony with the same prayers and exhortations and invitations with which God helped us.

God speaks to my heart:

Every bit of your pain is useful to teach you, to cause you to cry out to Me and receive My comfort, My strong limiting of your will, and My guidance, which urges you gently into My ways. Through your griefs and even as you emerge from pressures, you will notice others who need the same comfort you received from Me.

"May you know more and more of God's grace and peace."
1 Peter 1:2 (PHILLIPS)

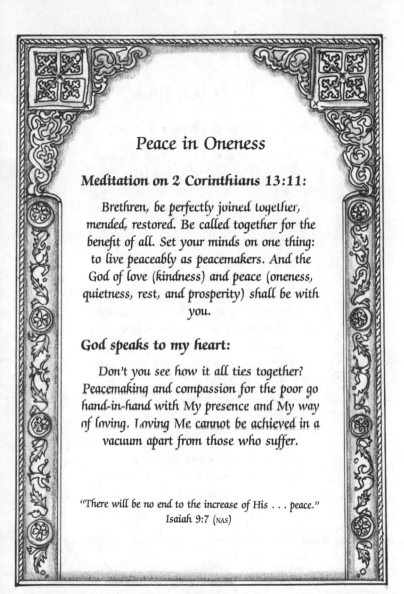

Peace in Oneness

Meditation on 2 Corinthians 13:11:

Brethren, be perfectly joined together, mended, restored. Be called together for the benefit of all. Set your minds on one thing: to live peaceably as peacemakers. And the God of love (kindness) and peace (oneness, quietness, rest, and prosperity) shall be with you.

God speaks to my heart:

Don't you see how it all ties together? Peacemaking and compassion for the poor go hand-in-hand with My presence and My way of loving. Loving Me cannot be achieved in a vacuum apart from those who suffer.

"There will be no end to the increase of His . . . peace."
Isaiah 9:7 (NAS)

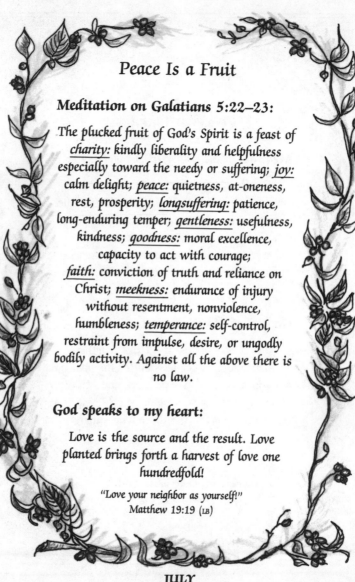

Peace Is a Fruit

Meditation on Galatians 5:22–23:

The plucked fruit of God's Spirit is a feast of _charity:_ kindly liberality and helpfulness especially toward the needy or suffering; _joy:_ calm delight; _peace:_ quietness, at-oneness, rest, prosperity; _longsuffering:_ patience, long-enduring temper; _gentleness:_ usefulness, kindness; _goodness:_ moral excellence, capacity to act with courage; _faith:_ conviction of truth and reliance on Christ; _meekness:_ endurance of injury without resentment, nonviolence, humbleness; _temperance:_ self-control, restraint from impulse, desire, or ungodly bodily activity. Against all the above there is no law.

God speaks to my heart:

Love is the source and the result. Love planted brings forth a harvest of love one hundredfold!

"Love your neighbor as yourself!"
Matthew 19:19 (LB)

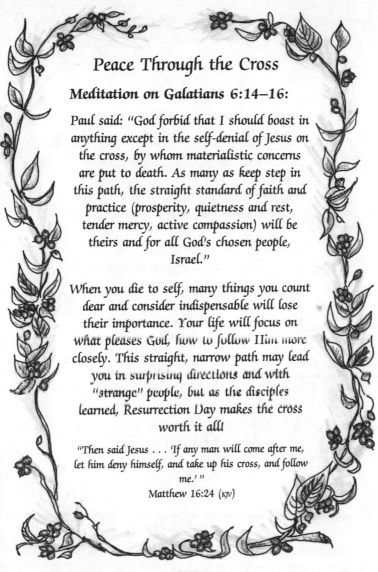

Peace Through the Cross

Meditation on Galatians 6:14–16:

Paul said: "God forbid that I should boast in anything except in the self-denial of Jesus on the cross, by whom materialistic concerns are put to death. As many as keep step in this path, the straight standard of faith and practice (prosperity, quietness and rest, tender mercy, active compassion) will be theirs and for all God's chosen people, Israel."

When you die to self, many things you count dear and consider indispensable will lose their importance. Your life will focus on what pleases God, how to follow Him more closely. This straight, narrow path may lead you in surprising directions and with "strange" people, but as the disciples learned, Resurrection Day makes the cross worth it all!

"Then said Jesus . . . 'If any man will come after me, let him deny himself, and take up his cross, and follow me.' "
Matthew 16:24 (KJV)

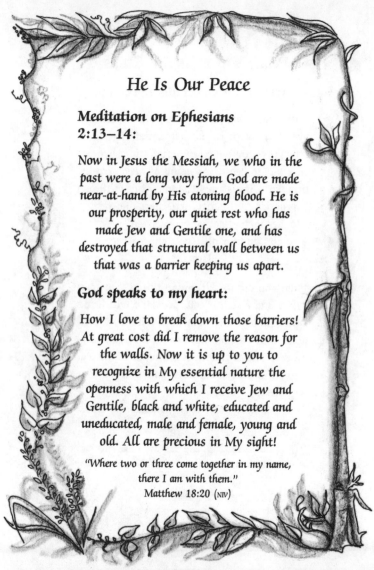

He Is Our Peace

Meditation on Ephesians 2:13–14:

Now in Jesus the Messiah, we who in the past were a long way from God are made near-at-hand by His atoning blood. He is our prosperity, our quiet rest who has made Jew and Gentile one, and has destroyed that structural wall between us that was a barrier keeping us apart.

God speaks to my heart:

How I love to break down those barriers! At great cost did I remove the reason for the walls. Now it is up to you to recognize in My essential nature the openness with which I receive Jew and Gentile, black and white, educated and uneducated, male and female, young and old. All are precious in My sight!

"Where two or three come together in my name, there I am with them."
Matthew 18:20 (NIV)

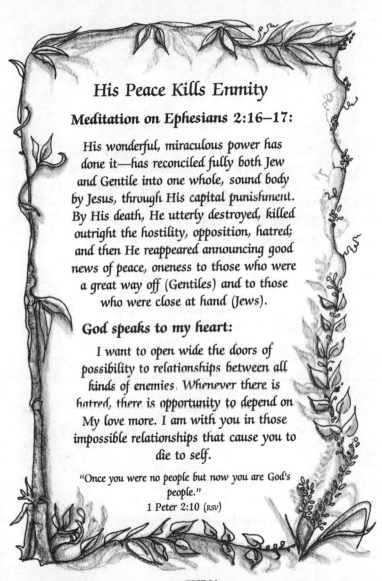

His Peace Kills Enmity

Meditation on Ephesians 2:16–17:

His wonderful, miraculous power has done it—has reconciled fully both Jew and Gentile into one whole, sound body by Jesus, through His capital punishment. By His death, He utterly destroyed, killed outright the hostility, opposition, hatred; and then He reappeared announcing good news of peace, oneness to those who were a great way off (Gentiles) and to those who were close at hand (Jews).

God speaks to my heart:

I want to open wide the doors of possibility to relationships between all kinds of enemies. Whenever there is hatred, there is opportunity to depend on My love more. I am with you in those impossible relationships that cause you to die to self.

"Once you were no people but now you are God's people."
1 Peter 2:10 (RSV)

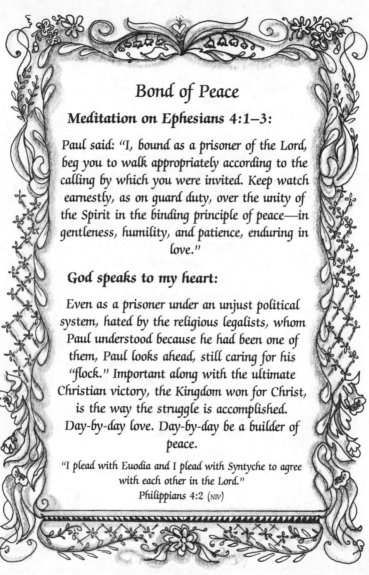

Bond of Peace

Meditation on Ephesians 4:1–3:

Paul said: "I, bound as a prisoner of the Lord, beg you to walk appropriately according to the calling by which you were invited. Keep watch earnestly, as on guard duty, over the unity of the Spirit in the binding principle of peace—in gentleness, humility, and patience, enduring in love."

God speaks to my heart:

Even as a prisoner under an unjust political system, hated by the religious legalists, whom Paul understood because he had been one of them, Paul looks ahead, still caring for his "flock." Important along with the ultimate Christian victory, the Kingdom won for Christ, is the way the struggle is accomplished. Day-by-day love. Day-by-day be a builder of peace.

"I plead with Euodia and I plead with Syntyche to agree with each other in the Lord."
Philippians 4:2 (NIV)

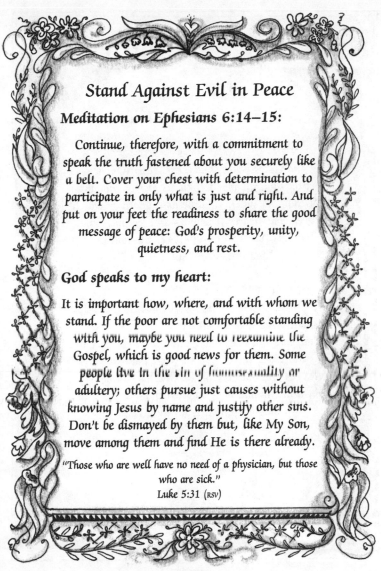

Stand Against Evil in Peace

Meditation on Ephesians 6:14–15:

Continue, therefore, with a commitment to speak the truth fastened about you securely like a belt. Cover your chest with determination to participate in only what is just and right. And put on your feet the readiness to share the good message of peace: God's prosperity, unity, quietness, and rest.

God speaks to my heart:

It is important how, where, and with whom we stand. If the poor are not comfortable standing with you, maybe you need to reexamine the Gospel, which is good news for them. Some people live in the sin of homosexuality or adultery; others pursue just causes without knowing Jesus by name and justify other sins. Don't be dismayed by them but, like My Son, move among them and find He is there already.

"Those who are well have no need of a physician, but those who are sick."
Luke 5:31 (RSV)

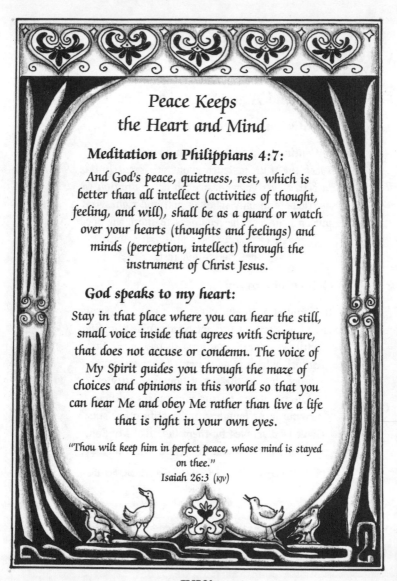

Peace Keeps
the Heart and Mind

Meditation on Philippians 4:7:

And God's peace, quietness, rest, which is
better than all intellect (activities of thought,
feeling, and will), shall be as a guard or watch
over your hearts (thoughts and feelings) and
minds (perception, intellect) through the
instrument of Christ Jesus.

God speaks to my heart:

Stay in that place where you can hear the still,
small voice inside that agrees with Scripture,
that does not accuse or condemn. The voice of
My Spirit guides you through the maze of
choices and opinions in this world so that you
can hear Me and obey Me rather than live a life
that is right in your own eyes.

"Thou wilt keep him in perfect peace, whose mind is stayed
on thee."
Isaiah 26:3 (KJV)

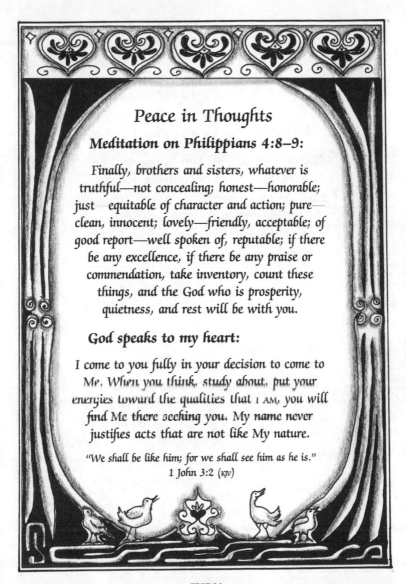

Peace in Thoughts

Meditation on Philippians 4:8–9:

Finally, brothers and sisters, whatever is truthful—not concealing; honest—honorable; just—equitable of character and action; pure—clean, innocent; lovely—friendly, acceptable; of good report—well spoken of, reputable; if there be any excellence, if there be any praise or commendation, take inventory, count these things, and the God who is prosperity, quietness, and rest will be with you.

God speaks to my heart:

I come to you fully in your decision to come to Me. When you think, study about, put your energies toward the qualities that I AM, you will find Me there seeking you. My name never justifies acts that are not like My nature.

"We shall be like him; for we shall see him as he is."
1 John 3:2 (KJV)

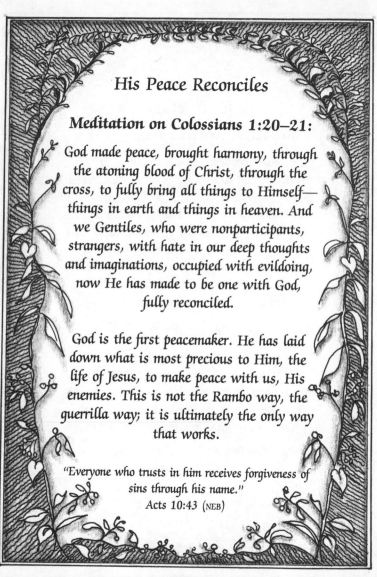

His Peace Reconciles

Meditation on Colossians 1:20–21:

God made peace, brought harmony, through
the atoning blood of Christ, through the
cross, to fully bring all things to Himself—
things in earth and things in heaven. And
we Gentiles, who were nonparticipants,
strangers, with hate in our deep thoughts
and imaginations, occupied with evildoing,
now He has made to be one with God,
fully reconciled.

God is the first peacemaker. He has laid
down what is most precious to Him, the
life of Jesus, to make peace with us, His
enemies. This is not the Rambo way, the
guerrilla way; it is ultimately the only way
that works.

"Everyone who trusts in him receives forgiveness of
sins through his name."
Acts 10:43 (NEB)

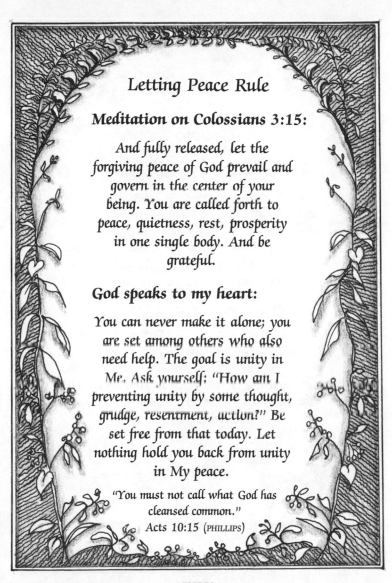

Letting Peace Rule

Meditation on Colossians 3:15:

And fully released, let the forgiving peace of God prevail and govern in the center of your being. You are called forth to peace, quietness, rest, prosperity in one single body. And be grateful.

God speaks to my heart:

You can never make it alone; you are set among others who also need help. The goal is unity in Me. Ask yourself: "How am I preventing unity by some thought, grudge, resentment, action?" Be set free from that today. Let nothing hold you back from unity in My peace.

"You must not call what God has cleansed common."
Acts 10:15 (PHILLIPS)

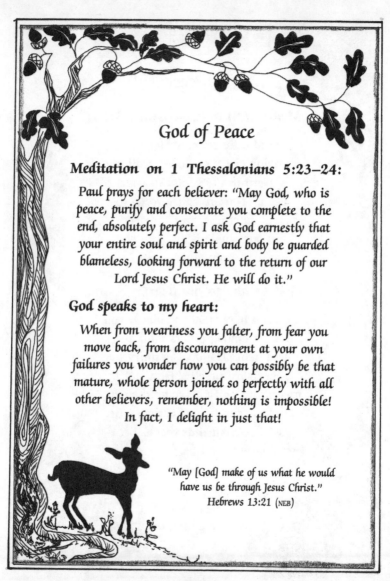

God of Peace

Meditation on 1 Thessalonians 5:23–24:

Paul prays for each believer: "May God, who is peace, purify and consecrate you complete to the end, absolutely perfect. I ask God earnestly that your entire soul and spirit and body be guarded blameless, looking forward to the return of our Lord Jesus Christ. He will do it."

God speaks to my heart:

When from weariness you falter, from fear you move back, from discouragement at your own failures you wonder how you can possibly be that mature, whole person joined so perfectly with all other believers, remember, nothing is impossible! In fact, I delight in just that!

"May [God] make of us what he would
have us be through Jesus Christ."
Hebrews 13:21 (NEB)

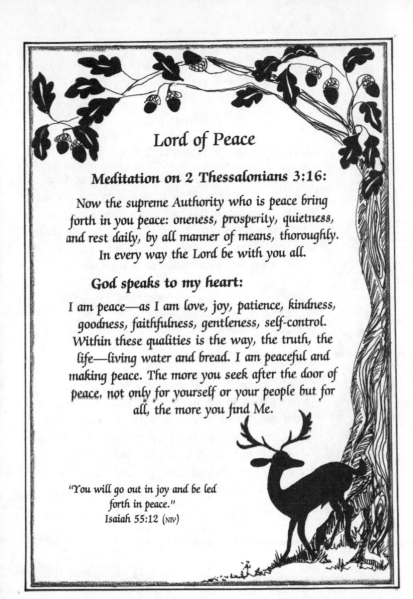

Lord of Peace

Meditation on 2 Thessalonians 3:16:

Now the supreme Authority who is peace bring
forth in you peace: oneness, prosperity, quietness,
and rest daily, by all manner of means, thoroughly.
In every way the Lord be with you all.

God speaks to my heart:

I am peace—as I am love, joy, patience, kindness,
goodness, faithfulness, gentleness, self-control.
Within these qualities is the way, the truth, the
life—living water and bread. I am peaceful and
making peace. The more you seek after the door of
peace, not only for yourself or your people but for
all, the more you find Me.

"You will go out in joy and be led
forth in peace."
Isaiah 55:12 (NIV)

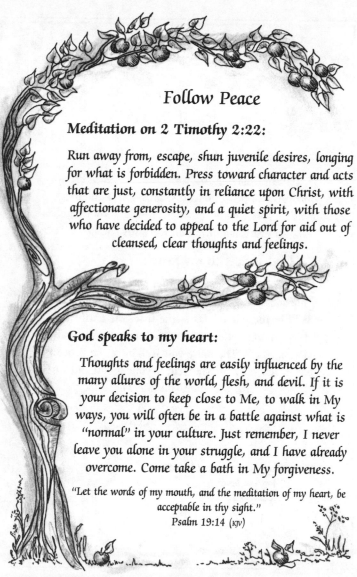

Follow Peace

Meditation on 2 Timothy 2:22:

Run away from, escape, shun juvenile desires, longing for what is forbidden. Press toward character and acts that are just, constantly in reliance upon Christ, with affectionate generosity, and a quiet spirit, with those who have decided to appeal to the Lord for aid out of cleansed, clear thoughts and feelings.

God speaks to my heart:

Thoughts and feelings are easily influenced by the many allures of the world, flesh, and devil. If it is your decision to keep close to Me, to walk in My ways, you will often be in a battle against what is "normal" in your culture. Just remember, I never leave you alone in your struggle, and I have already overcome. Come take a bath in My forgiveness.

"Let the words of my mouth, and the meditation of my heart, be acceptable in thy sight."
Psalm 19:14 (KJV)

Follow Peace

Meditation on Hebrews 12:14–16:

Press toward unity, quietness, rest, at-oneness
with everyone, and also pursue purity, without
which no one shall see the Lord. Let no
poisonous root of bitterness germinate, sprout,
and grow up to crowd and annoy you, which
contaminates many. Let no sexual sin cross your
doorway.

God speaks to my heart:

Remove patiently the darts of temptations as
they come every day. Do not let their wild seeds
take root in you and fester. As you move at My
direction, there are bound to be fierce attacks at
times. But with the goal ever before you, My
way of peace, unity with all believers, and the
urgency to communicate My love with everyone
in need—yes! you will overcome!

"Depart from evil, and do good; seek
peace, and pursue it."
Psalm 34:14 (RSV)

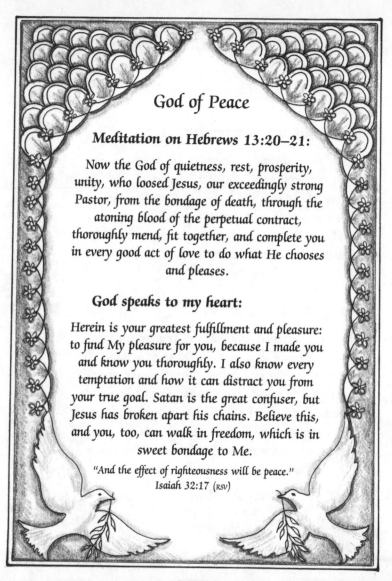

God of Peace

Meditation on Hebrews 13:20–21:

Now the God of quietness, rest, prosperity,
unity, who loosed Jesus, our exceedingly strong
Pastor, from the bondage of death, through the
atoning blood of the perpetual contract,
thoroughly mend, fit together, and complete you
in every good act of love to do what He chooses
and pleases.

God speaks to my heart:

Herein is your greatest fulfillment and pleasure:
to find My pleasure for you, because I made you
and know you thoroughly. I also know every
temptation and how it can distract you from
your true goal. Satan is the great confuser, but
Jesus has broken apart his chains. Believe this,
and you, too, can walk in freedom, which is in
sweet bondage to Me.

"And the effect of righteousness will be peace."
Isaiah 32:17 (RSV)

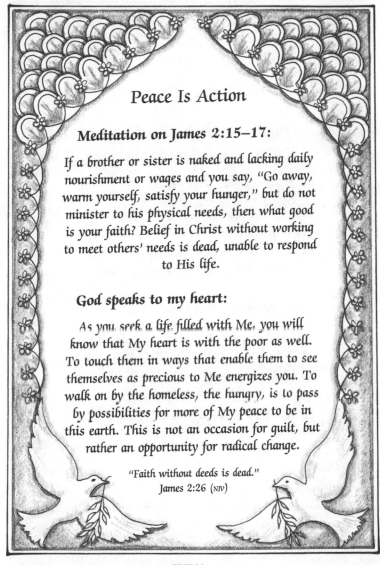

Peace Is Action

Meditation on James 2:15–17:

If a brother or sister is naked and lacking daily nourishment or wages and you say, "Go away, warm yourself, satisfy your hunger," but do not minister to his physical needs, then what good is your faith? Belief in Christ without working to meet others' needs is dead, unable to respond to His life.

God speaks to my heart:

As you seek a life filled with Me, you will know that My heart is with the poor as well. To touch them in ways that enable them to see themselves as precious to Me energizes you. To walk on by the homeless, the hungry, is to pass by possibilities for more of My peace to be in this earth. This is not an occasion for guilt, but rather an opportunity for radical change.

"Faith without deeds is dead."
James 2:26 (NIV)

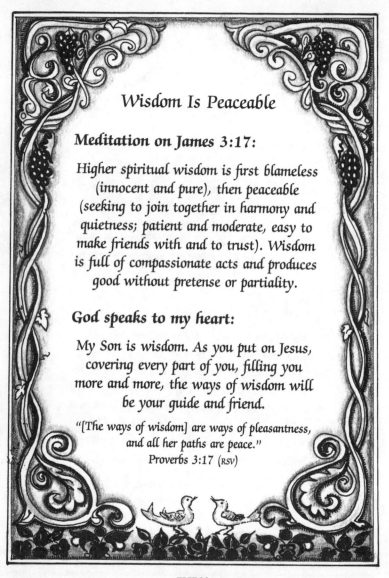

Wisdom Is Peaceable

Meditation on James 3:17:

Higher spiritual wisdom is first blameless
(innocent and pure), then peaceable
(seeking to join together in harmony and
quietness; patient and moderate, easy to
make friends with and to trust). Wisdom
is full of compassionate acts and produces
good without pretense or partiality.

God speaks to my heart:

My Son is wisdom. As you put on Jesus,
covering every part of you, filling you
more and more, the ways of wisdom will
be your guide and friend.

"[The ways of wisdom] are ways of pleasantness,
and all her paths are peace."
Proverbs 3:17 (RSV)

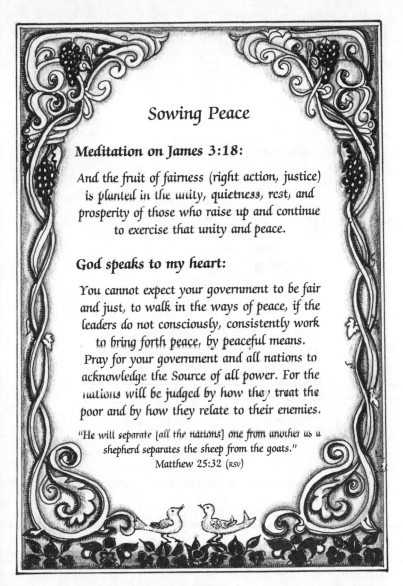

Sowing Peace

Meditation on James 3:18:

And the fruit of fairness (right action, justice) is planted in the unity, quietness, rest, and prosperity of those who raise up and continue to exercise that unity and peace.

God speaks to my heart:

You cannot expect your government to be fair and just, to walk in the ways of peace, if the leaders do not consciously, consistently work to bring forth peace, by peaceful means. Pray for your government and all nations to acknowledge the Source of all power. For the nations will be judged by how they treat the poor and by how they relate to their enemies.

"He will separate [all the nations] one from another as a shepherd separates the sheep from the goats."
Matthew 25:32 (RSV)

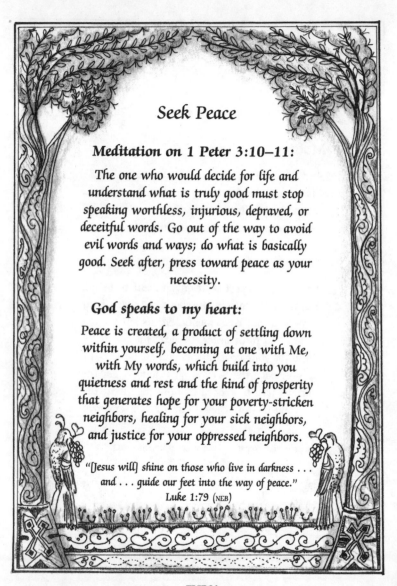

Seek Peace

Meditation on 1 Peter 3:10–11:

The one who would decide for life and understand what is truly good must stop speaking worthless, injurious, depraved, or deceitful words. Go out of the way to avoid evil words and ways; do what is basically good. Seek after, press toward peace as your necessity.

God speaks to my heart:

Peace is created, a product of settling down within yourself, becoming at one with Me, with My words, which build into you quietness and rest and the kind of prosperity that generates hope for your poverty-stricken neighbors, healing for your sick neighbors, and justice for your oppressed neighbors.

"[Jesus will] shine on those who live in darkness . . . and . . . guide our feet into the way of peace."
Luke 1:79 (NEB)

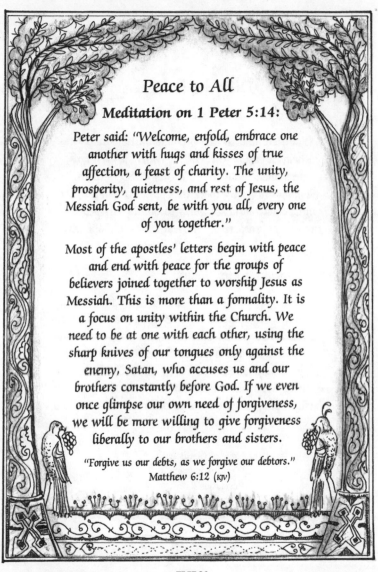

Peace to All

Meditation on 1 Peter 5:14:

Peter said: "Welcome, enfold, embrace one another with hugs and kisses of true affection, a feast of charity. The unity, prosperity, quietness, and rest of Jesus, the Messiah God sent, be with you all, every one of you together."

Most of the apostles' letters begin with peace and end with peace for the groups of believers joined together to worship Jesus as Messiah. This is more than a formality. It is a focus on unity within the Church. We need to be at one with each other, using the sharp knives of our tongues only against the enemy, Satan, who accuses us and our brothers constantly before God. If we even once glimpse our own need of forgiveness, we will be more willing to give forgiveness liberally to our brothers and sisters.

"Forgive us our debts, as we forgive our debtors."
Matthew 6:12 (KJV)

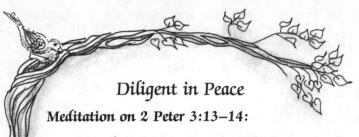

Diligent in Peace

Meditation on 2 Peter 3:13–14:

We, according to His promise, anticipate a new heaven and new earth, in which justice will permanently dwell, be at home. So with this vision, since we expect this really to happen, we must make earnest efforts to obtain His peace— the unity, prosperity, and rest that He alone gives. In it you are blameless.

God speaks to my heart:

"Everything wrong in the world is his fault" is the accusation constantly before My throne about every individual believer. Specific accusations are many times true, and must be confessed. Your best defense against Satan's lies is to catch the vision of what My "new earth policy" is all about, and to begin acting as if it were to become reality in your lifetime.

"The home of God is with men, and
he will live among them."
Revelation 21:3 (PHILLIPS)

Peace Multiplied

Meditation on 2 Peter 1:1–2:

May those who have received (as by lot) the same kind
of belief, reliance on Christ, through the right action of
God and Jesus our Savior, have gratitude, a heart of
thanks, and quiet joining with other believers, increasing
more and more through the full discernment and
recognition of God and of Jesus as Lord.

God speaks to my heart:

Belief in Jesus as Messiah is the great leveler. No one
who knows Me is any better than any other. In fact,
just knowing My Spirit opens you to your own need, so
that you become unable to throw stones. I raise you up
to wash feet, a humble place of service, a place of joy.
For in honoring others as better than yourself, you are
honorable. In loving others you are lovable.
In making peace you find peace.

"If I, your Lord and Master, have washed your feet, you also ought to
wash one another's feet."
John 13:14 (NEB)

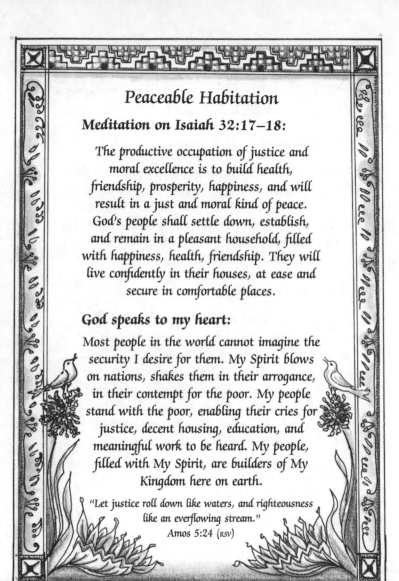

Peaceable Habitation

Meditation on Isaiah 32:17–18:

The productive occupation of justice and
moral excellence is to build health,
friendship, prosperity, happiness, and will
result in a just and moral kind of peace.
God's people shall settle down, establish,
and remain in a pleasant household, filled
with happiness, health, friendship. They will
live confidently in their houses, at ease and
secure in comfortable places.

God speaks to my heart:

Most people in the world cannot imagine the
security I desire for them. My Spirit blows
on nations, shakes them in their arrogance,
in their contempt for the poor. My people
stand with the poor, enabling their cries for
justice, decent housing, education, and
meaningful work to be heard. My people,
filled with My Spirit, are builders of My
Kingdom here on earth.

*"Let justice roll down like waters, and righteousness
like an everflowing stream."*
Amos 5:24 (RSV)

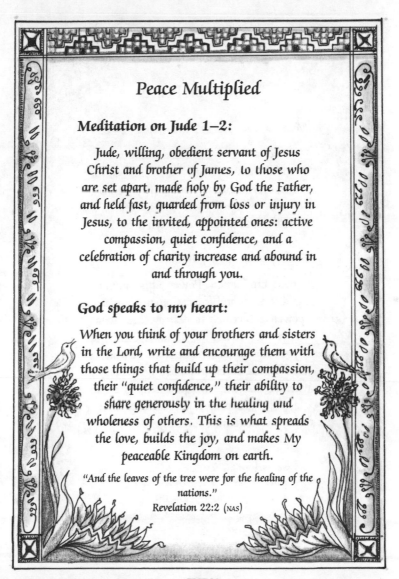

Peace Multiplied

Meditation on Jude 1–2:

Jude, willing, obedient servant of Jesus
Christ and brother of James, to those who
are set apart, made holy by God the Father,
and held fast, guarded from loss or injury in
Jesus, to the invited, appointed ones: active
compassion, quiet confidence, and a
celebration of charity increase and abound in
and through you.

God speaks to my heart:

When you think of your brothers and sisters
in the Lord, write and encourage them with
those things that build up their compassion,
their "quiet confidence," their ability to
share generously in the healing and
wholeness of others. This is what spreads
the love, builds the joy, and makes My
peaceable Kingdom on earth.

"And the leaves of the tree were for the healing of the
nations."
Revelation 22:2 (NAS)

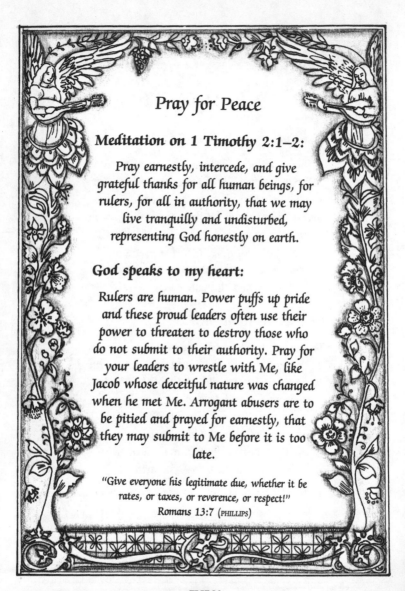

Pray for Peace

Meditation on 1 Timothy 2:1–2:

Pray earnestly, intercede, and give
grateful thanks for all human beings, for
rulers, for all in authority, that we may
live tranquilly and undisturbed,
representing God honestly on earth.

God speaks to my heart:

Rulers are human. Power puffs up pride
and these proud leaders often use their
power to threaten to destroy those who
do not submit to their authority. Pray for
your leaders to wrestle with Me, like
Jacob whose deceitful nature was changed
when he met Me. Arrogant abusers are to
be pitied and prayed for earnestly, that
they may submit to Me before it is too
late.

"Give everyone his legitimate due, whether it be
rates, or taxes, or reverence, or respect!"
Romans 13:7 (PHILLIPS)

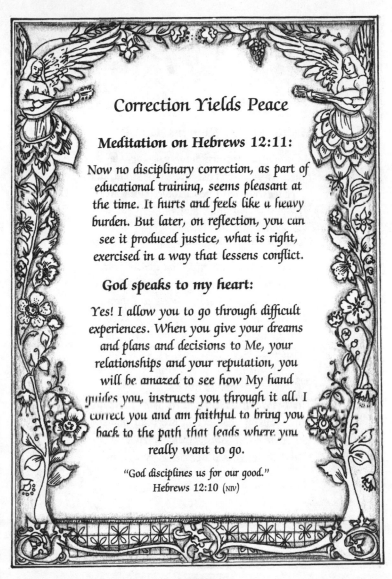

Correction Yields Peace

Meditation on Hebrews 12:11:

Now no disciplinary correction, as part of educational training, seems pleasant at the time. It hurts and feels like a heavy burden. But later, on reflection, you can see it produced justice, what is right, exercised in a way that lessens conflict.

God speaks to my heart:

Yes! I allow you to go through difficult experiences. When you give your dreams and plans and decisions to Me, your relationships and your reputation, you will be amazed to see how My hand guides you, instructs you through it all. I correct you and am faithful to bring you back to the path that leads where you really want to go.

"God disciplines us for our good."
Hebrews 12:10 (NIV)

Live Peaceably

Meditation on Romans 12:18:

As much as you are powerful, capable, as
much as you perceive and understand, act
peaceably, as a peacemaker with all
human beings.

God speaks to my heart:

Your culture worships the god of war.
Children, with their toys and games, are
competitive and encouraged to express
violence as the way of solving problems.
"Enemies must be dehumanized and
crushed," says your culture, and many
bow down to the very things they hate
about others.
I tell you, children need to learn carefully
the ways of peace. You are their model.
So come to My indwelling Spirit and cry
out to let this peace begin with you!

"Be at peace with one another."
Mark 9:50 (RSV)

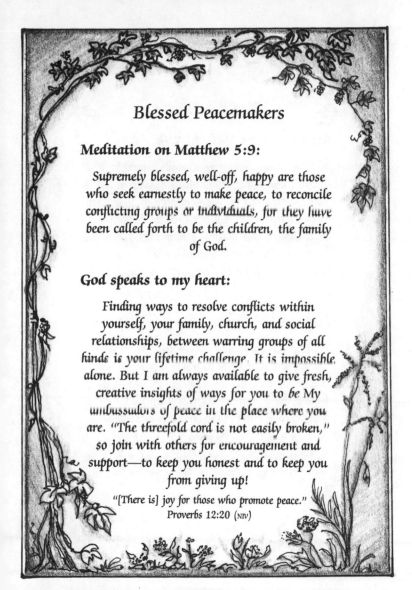

Blessed Peacemakers

Meditation on Matthew 5:9:

Supremely blessed, well-off, happy are those who seek earnestly to make peace, to reconcile conflicting groups or individuals, for they have been called forth to be the children, the family of God.

God speaks to my heart:

Finding ways to resolve conflicts within yourself, your family, church, and social relationships, between warring groups of all kinds is your lifetime challenge. It is impossible alone. But I am always available to give fresh, creative insights of ways for you to be My ambassadors of peace in the place where you are. "The threefold cord is not easily broken," so join with others for encouragement and support—to keep you honest and to keep you from giving up!

"[There is] joy for those who promote peace."
Proverbs 12:20 (NIV)

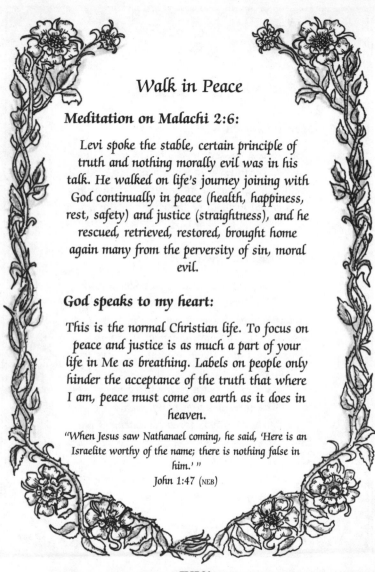

Walk in Peace

Meditation on Malachi 2:6:

Levi spoke the stable, certain principle of
truth and nothing morally evil was in his
talk. He walked on life's journey joining with
God continually in peace (health, happiness,
rest, safety) and justice (straightness), and he
rescued, retrieved, restored, brought home
again many from the perversity of sin, moral
evil.

God speaks to my heart:

This is the normal Christian life. To focus on
peace and justice is as much a part of your
life in Me as breathing. Labels on people only
hinder the acceptance of the truth that where
I am, peace must come on earth as it does in
heaven.

"When Jesus saw Nathanael coming, he said, 'Here is an
Israelite worthy of the name; there is nothing false in
him.' "
John 1:47 (NEB)

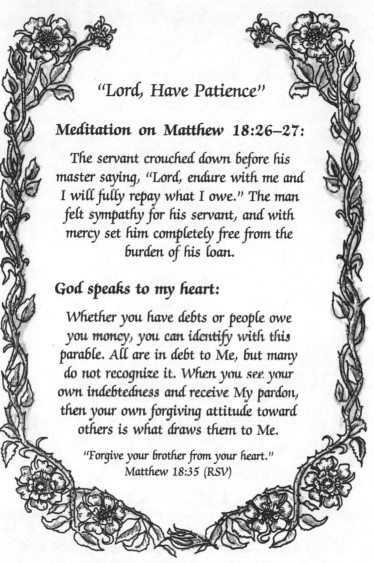

"Lord, Have Patience"

Meditation on Matthew 18:26–27:

The servant crouched down before his master saying, "Lord, endure with me and I will fully repay what I owe." The man felt sympathy for his servant, and with mercy set him completely free from the burden of his loan.

God speaks to my heart:

Whether you have debts or people owe you money, you can identify with this parable. All are in debt to Me, but many do not recognize it. When you see your own indebtedness and receive My pardon, then your own forgiving attitude toward others is what draws them to Me.

"Forgive your brother from your heart."
Matthew 18:35 (RSV)

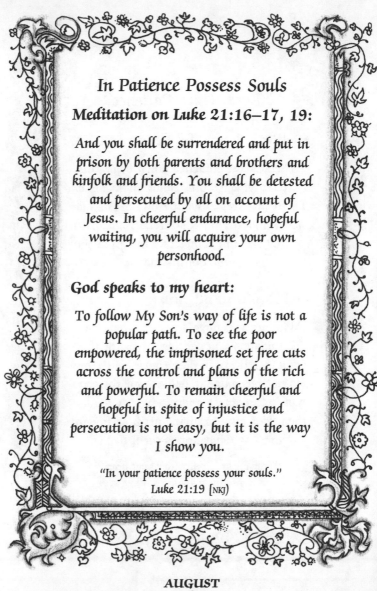

In Patience Possess Souls

Meditation on Luke 21:16–17, 19:

And you shall be surrendered and put in prison by both parents and brothers and kinfolk and friends. You shall be detested and persecuted by all on account of Jesus. In cheerful endurance, hopeful waiting, you will acquire your own personhood.

God speaks to my heart:

To follow My Son's way of life is not a popular path. To see the poor empowered, the imprisoned set free cuts across the control and plans of the rich and powerful. To remain cheerful and hopeful in spite of injustice and persecution is not easy, but it is the way I show you.

"In your patience possess your souls."
Luke 21:19 [NKJ]

Tribulation Works Patience

Meditation on Romans 5:3:

We keep being joyful in the middle of pressures— affliction, anguish, persecution, troubles—understanding that those situations work out patience—a constant, cheerful, or hopeful endurance.

God speaks to my heart:

Corrie ten Boom did not have the love and forgiveness she needed for the Nazi guard until she asked Me for it and put out her hand to shake his. So you, in the hard times, must ask for that patience. Like a river it will rise up and enable you to endure with confidence.

"God's love has been poured out in our hearts through the Holy Spirit."
Romans 5:5 (AMPLIFIED)

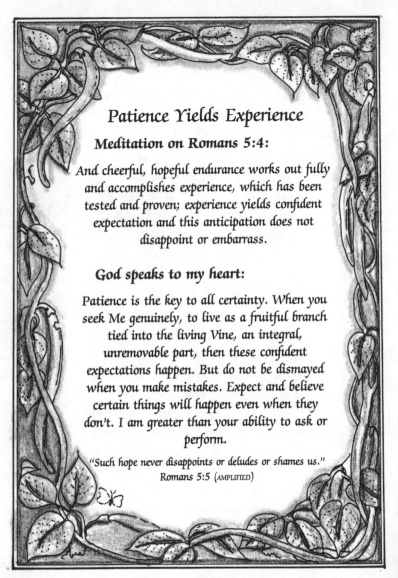

Patience Yields Experience

Meditation on Romans 5:4:

And cheerful, hopeful endurance works out fully and accomplishes experience, which has been tested and proven; experience yields confident expectation and this anticipation does not disappoint or embarrass.

God speaks to my heart:

Patience is the key to all certainty. When you seek Me genuinely, to live as a fruitful branch tied into the living Vine, an integral, unremovable part, then these confident expectations happen. But do not be dismayed when you make mistakes. Expect and believe certain things will happen even when they don't. I am greater than your ability to ask or perform.

"Such hope never disappoints or deludes or shames us."
Romans 5:5 (AMPLIFIED)

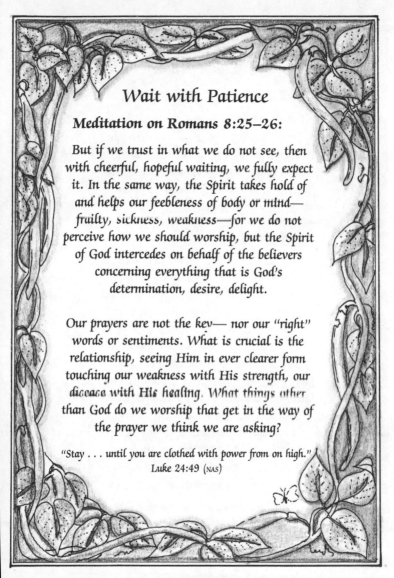

Wait with Patience

Meditation on Romans 8:25–26:

But if we trust in what we do not see, then with cheerful, hopeful waiting, we fully expect it. In the same way, the Spirit takes hold of and helps our feebleness of body or mind—frailty, sickness, weakness—for we do not perceive how we should worship, but the Spirit of God intercedes on behalf of the believers concerning everything that is God's determination, desire, delight.

Our prayers are not the key— nor our "right" words or sentiments. What is crucial is the relationship, seeing Him in ever clearer form touching our weakness with His strength, our disease with His healing. What things other than God do we worship that get in the way of the prayer we think we are asking?

"Stay . . . until you are clothed with power from on high."
Luke 24:49 (NAS)

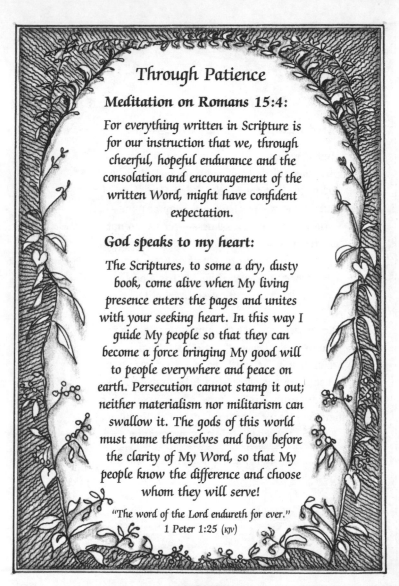

Through Patience

Meditation on Romans 15:4:

For everything written in Scripture is
for our instruction that we, through
cheerful, hopeful endurance and the
consolation and encouragement of the
written Word, might have confident
expectation.

God speaks to my heart:

The Scriptures, to some a dry, dusty
book, come alive when My living
presence enters the pages and unites
with your seeking heart. In this way I
guide My people so that they can
become a force bringing My good will
to people everywhere and peace on
earth. Persecution cannot stamp it out;
neither materialism nor militarism can
swallow it. The gods of this world
must name themselves and bow before
the clarity of My Word, so that My
people know the difference and choose
whom they will serve!

"The word of the Lord endureth for ever."
1 Peter 1:25 (KJV)

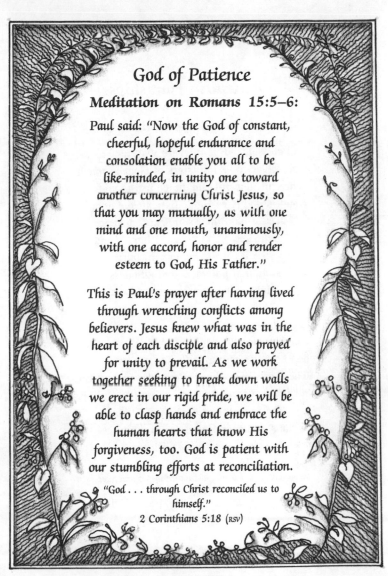

God of Patience

Meditation on Romans 15:5–6:

Paul said: "Now the God of constant, cheerful, hopeful endurance and consolation enable you all to be like-minded, in unity one toward another concerning Christ Jesus, so that you may mutually, us with one mind and one mouth, unanimously, with one accord, honor and render esteem to God, His Father."

This is Paul's prayer after having lived through wrenching conflicts among believers. Jesus knew what was in the heart of each disciple and also prayed for unity to prevail. As we work together seeking to break down walls we erect in our rigid pride, we will be able to clasp hands and embrace the human hearts that know His forgiveness, too. God is patient with our stumbling efforts at reconciliation.

"God . . . through Christ reconciled us to himself."
2 Corinthians 5:18 (RSV)

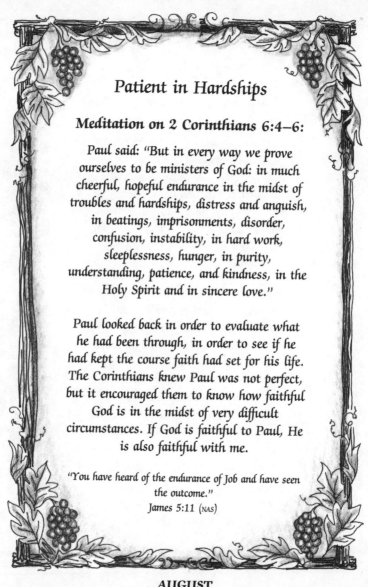

Patient in Hardships

Meditation on 2 Corinthians 6:4–6:

Paul said: "But in every way we prove ourselves to be ministers of God: in much cheerful, hopeful endurance in the midst of troubles and hardships, distress and anguish, in beatings, imprisonments, disorder, confusion, instability, in hard work, sleeplessness, hunger, in purity, understanding, patience, and kindness, in the Holy Spirit and in sincere love."

Paul looked back in order to evaluate what he had been through, in order to see if he had kept the course faith had set for his life. The Corinthians knew Paul was not perfect, but it encouraged them to know how faithful God is in the midst of very difficult circumstances. If God is faithful to Paul, He is also faithful with me.

"You have heard of the endurance of Job and have seen the outcome."
James 5:11 (NAS)

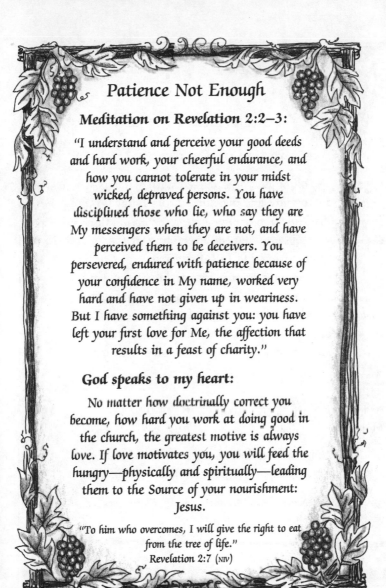

Patience Not Enough

Meditation on Revelation 2:2–3:

"I understand and perceive your good deeds
and hard work, your cheerful endurance, and
how you cannot tolerate in your midst
wicked, depraved persons. You have
disciplined those who lie, who say they are
My messengers when they are not, and have
perceived them to be deceivers. You
persevered, endured with patience because of
your confidence in My name, worked very
hard and have not given up in weariness.
But I have something against you: you have
left your first love for Me, the affection that
results in a feast of charity."

God speaks to my heart:

No matter how doctrinally correct you
become, how hard you work at doing good in
the church, the greatest motive is always
love. If love motivates you, you will feed the
hungry—physically and spiritually—leading
them to the Source of your nourishment:
Jesus.

"To him who overcomes, I will give the right to eat
from the tree of life."
Revelation 2:7 (NIV)

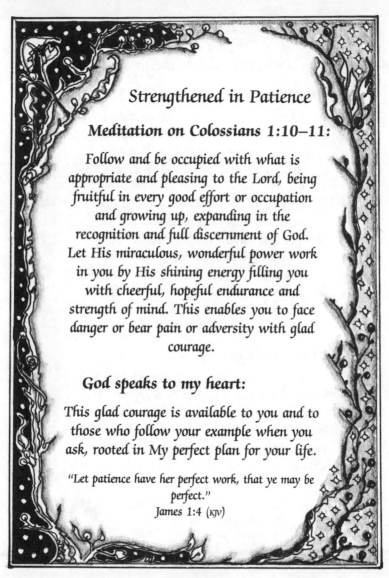

Strengthened in Patience

Meditation on Colossians 1:10–11:

Follow and be occupied with what is
appropriate and pleasing to the Lord, being
fruitful in every good effort or occupation
and growing up, expanding in the
recognition and full discernment of God.
Let His miraculous, wonderful power work
in you by His shining energy filling you
with cheerful, hopeful endurance and
strength of mind. This enables you to face
danger or bear pain or adversity with glad
courage.

God speaks to my heart:

This glad courage is available to you and to
those who follow your example when you
ask, rooted in My perfect plan for your life.

"Let patience have her perfect work, that ye may be
perfect."
James 1:4 (KJV)

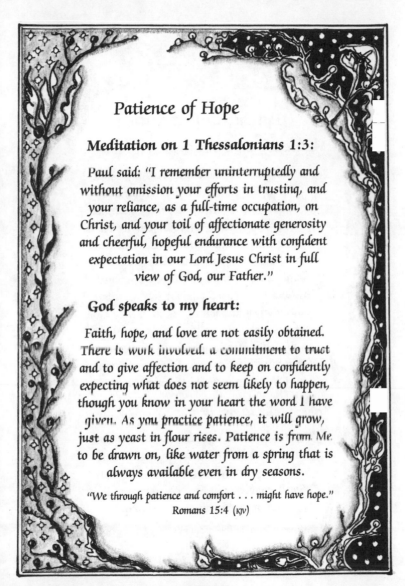

Patience of Hope

Meditation on 1 Thessalonians 1:3:

Paul said: "I remember uninterruptedly and without omission your efforts in trusting, and your reliance, as a full-time occupation, on Christ, and your toil of affectionate generosity and cheerful, hopeful endurance with confident expectation in our Lord Jesus Christ in full view of God, our Father."

God speaks to my heart:

Faith, hope, and love are not easily obtained. There is work involved, a commitment to trust and to give affection and to keep on confidently expecting what does not seem likely to happen, though you know in your heart the word I have given. As you practice patience, it will grow, just as yeast in flour rises. Patience is from Me to be drawn on, like water from a spring that is always available even in dry seasons.

"We through patience and comfort . . . might have hope."
Romans 15:4 (KJV)

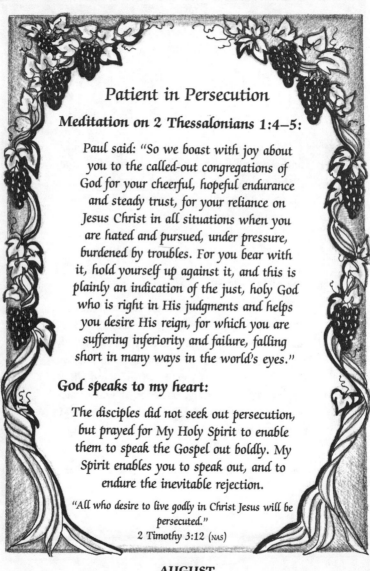

Patient in Persecution

Meditation on 2 Thessalonians 1:4–5:

Paul said: "So we boast with joy about you to the called-out congregations of God for your cheerful, hopeful endurance and steady trust, for your reliance on Jesus Christ in all situations when you are hated and pursued, under pressure, burdened by troubles. For you bear with it, hold yourself up against it, and this is plainly an indication of the just, holy God who is right in His judgments and helps you desire His reign, for which you are suffering inferiority and failure, falling short in many ways in the world's eyes."

God speaks to my heart:

The disciples did not seek out persecution, but prayed for My Holy Spirit to enable them to speak the Gospel out boldly. My Spirit enables you to speak out, and to endure the inevitable rejection.

"All who desire to live godly in Christ Jesus will be persecuted."
2 Timothy 3:12 (NAS)

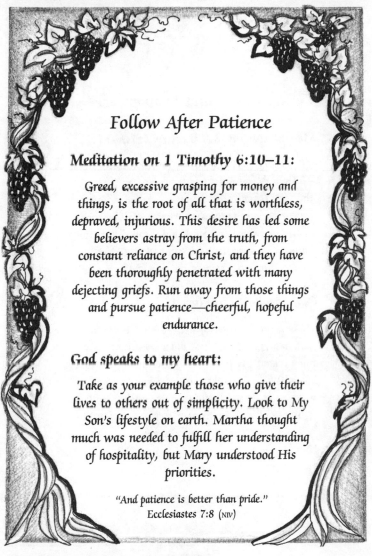

Follow After Patience

Meditation on 1 Timothy 6:10–11:

Greed, excessive grasping for money and things, is the root of all that is worthless, depraved, injurious. This desire has led some believers astray from the truth, from constant reliance on Christ, and they have been thoroughly penetrated with many dejecting griefs. Run away from those things and pursue patience—cheerful, hopeful endurance.

God speaks to my heart:

Take as your example those who give their lives to others out of simplicity. Look to My Son's lifestyle on earth. Martha thought much was needed to fulfill her understanding of hospitality, but Mary understood His priorities.

"And patience is better than pride."
Ecclesiastes 7:8 (NIV)

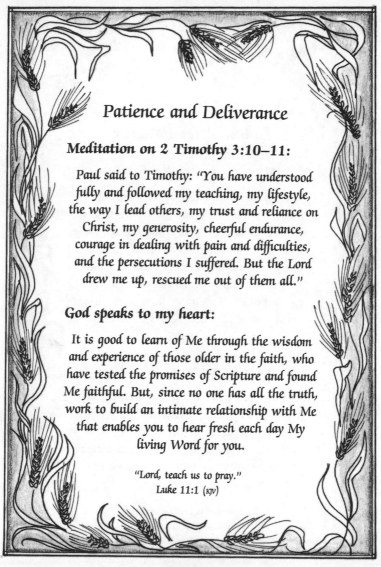

Patience and Deliverance

Meditation on 2 Timothy 3:10–11:

Paul said to Timothy: "You have understood fully and followed my teaching, my lifestyle, the way I lead others, my trust and reliance on Christ, my generosity, cheerful endurance, courage in dealing with pain and difficulties, and the persecutions I suffered. But the Lord drew me up, rescued me out of them all."

God speaks to my heart:

It is good to learn of Me through the wisdom and experience of those older in the faith, who have tested the promises of Scripture and found Me faithful. But, since no one has all the truth, work to build an intimate relationship with Me that enables you to hear fresh each day My living Word for you.

"Lord, teach us to pray."
Luke 11:1 (KJV)

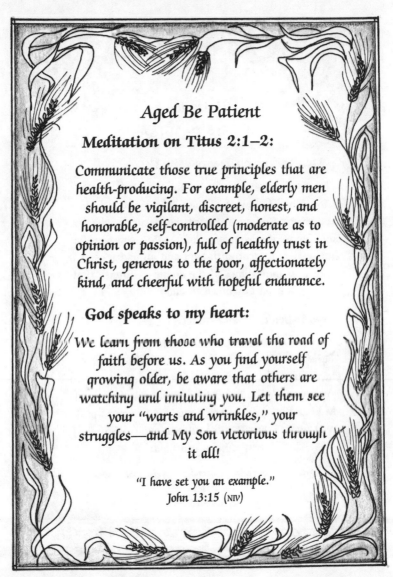

Aged Be Patient

Meditation on Titus 2:1–2:

Communicate those true principles that are health-producing. For example, elderly men should be vigilant, discreet, honest, and honorable, self-controlled (moderate as to opinion or passion), full of healthy trust in Christ, generous to the poor, affectionately kind, and cheerful with hopeful endurance.

God speaks to my heart:

We learn from those who travel the road of faith before us. As you find yourself growing older, be aware that others are watching and imitating you. Let them see your "warts and wrinkles," your struggles—and My Son victorious through it all!

"I have set you an example."
John 13:15 (NIV)

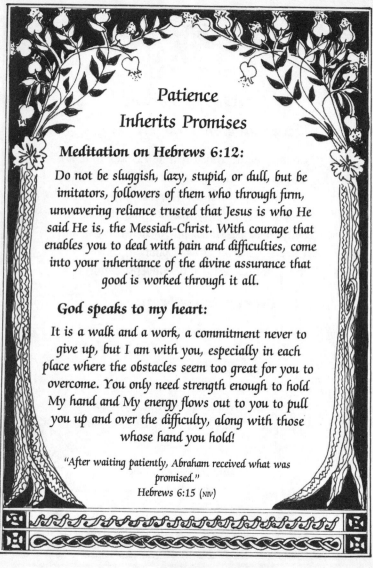

Patience
Inherits Promises

Meditation on Hebrews 6:12:

Do not be sluggish, lazy, stupid, or dull, but be imitators, followers of them who through firm, unwavering reliance trusted that Jesus is who He said He is, the Messiah-Christ. With courage that enables you to deal with pain and difficulties, come into your inheritance of the divine assurance that good is worked through it all.

God speaks to my heart:

It is a walk and a work, a commitment never to give up, but I am with you, especially in each place where the obstacles seem too great for you to overcome. You only need strength enough to hold My hand and My energy flows out to you to pull you up and over the difficulty, along with those whose hand you hold!

"After waiting patiently, Abraham received what was promised."
Hebrews 6:15 (NIV)

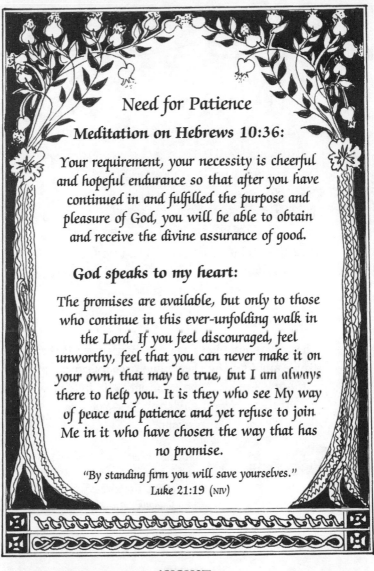

Need for Patience

Meditation on Hebrews 10:36:

Your requirement, your necessity is cheerful and hopeful endurance so that after you have continued in and fulfilled the purpose and pleasure of God, you will be able to obtain and receive the divine assurance of good.

God speaks to my heart:

The promises are available, but only to those who continue in this ever-unfolding walk in the Lord. If you feel discouraged, feel unworthy, feel that you can never make it on your own, that may be true, but I am always there to help you. It is they who see My way of peace and patience and yet refuse to join Me in it who have chosen the way that has no promise.

"By standing firm you will save yourselves."
Luke 21:19 (NIV)

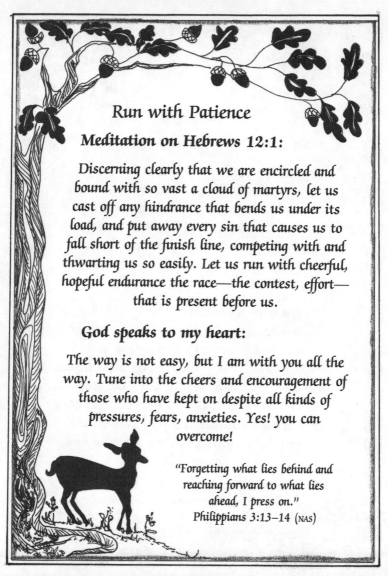

Run with Patience

Meditation on Hebrews 12:1:

Discerning clearly that we are encircled and bound with so vast a cloud of martyrs, let us cast off any hindrance that bends us under its load, and put away every sin that causes us to fall short of the finish line, competing with and thwarting us so easily. Let us run with cheerful, hopeful endurance the race—the contest, effort—that is present before us.

God speaks to my heart:

The way is not easy, but I am with you all the way. Tune into the cheers and encouragement of those who have kept on despite all kinds of pressures, fears, anxieties. Yes! you can overcome!

"Forgetting what lies behind and reaching forward to what lies ahead, I press on."
Philippians 3:13–14 (NAS)

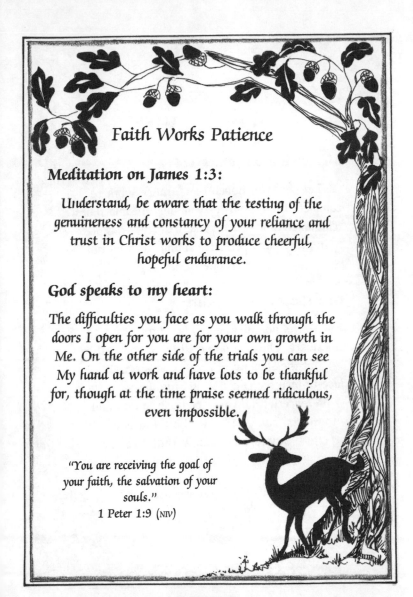

Faith Works Patience

Meditation on James 1:3:

Understand, be aware that the testing of the genuineness and constancy of your reliance and trust in Christ works to produce cheerful, hopeful endurance.

God speaks to my heart:

The difficulties you face as you walk through the doors I open for you are for your own growth in Me. On the other side of the trials you can see My hand at work and have lots to be thankful for, though at the time praise seemed ridiculous, even impossible.

"You are receiving the goal of your faith, the salvation of your souls."
1 Peter 1:9 (NIV)

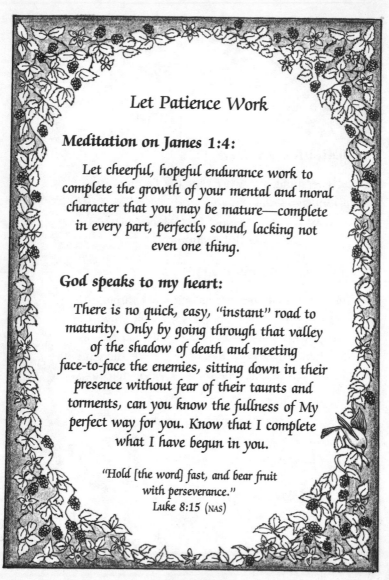

Let Patience Work

Meditation on James 1:4:

Let cheerful, hopeful endurance work to complete the growth of your mental and moral character that you may be mature—complete in every part, perfectly sound, lacking not even one thing.

God speaks to my heart:

There is no quick, easy, "instant" road to maturity. Only by going through that valley of the shadow of death and meeting face-to-face the enemies, sitting down in their presence without fear of their taunts and torments, can you know the fullness of My perfect way for you. Know that I complete what I have begun in you.

"Hold [the word] fast, and bear fruit with perseverance."
Luke 8:15 (NAS)

Patient, Established

Meditation on James 5:7–8:

*Endure and wait patiently for the return of
the Lord. Farmers expect precious fruit to
come from their labors and wait for it,
through the first showering of the rainy
season and the later rains. So, you also wait
and endure patiently, turning the thoughts
and feelings of your heart toward that sure
coming of the Lord when the wicked will be
punished.*

God speaks to my heart:

*Justice is in My hand; you can count on it.
When you see the wicked flourish and prosper,
know that their hour of confrontation is
coming and that those hurt by them will be
comforted. Full restitution will be made.*

"And the Lord direct your hearts . . .
into the patient waiting for Christ."
2 Thessalonians 3:5 (KJV)

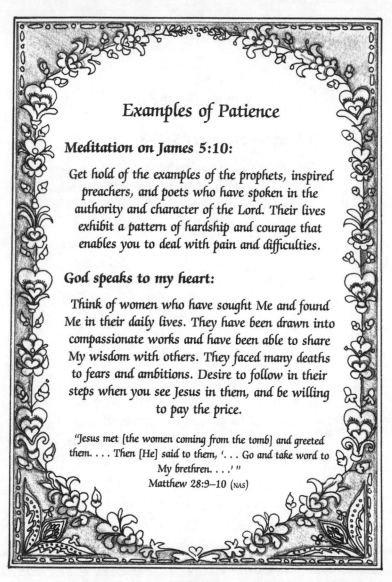

Examples of Patience

Meditation on James 5:10:

Get hold of the examples of the prophets, inspired preachers, and poets who have spoken in the authority and character of the Lord. Their lives exhibit a pattern of hardship and courage that enables you to deal with pain and difficulties.

God speaks to my heart:

Think of women who have sought Me and found Me in their daily lives. They have been drawn into compassionate works and have been able to share My wisdom with others. They faced many deaths to fears and ambitions. Desire to follow in their steps when you see Jesus in them, and be willing to pay the price.

"Jesus met [the women coming from the tomb] and greeted them. . . . Then [He] said to them, '. . . Go and take word to My brethren. . . .' "
Matthew 28:9–10 (NAS)

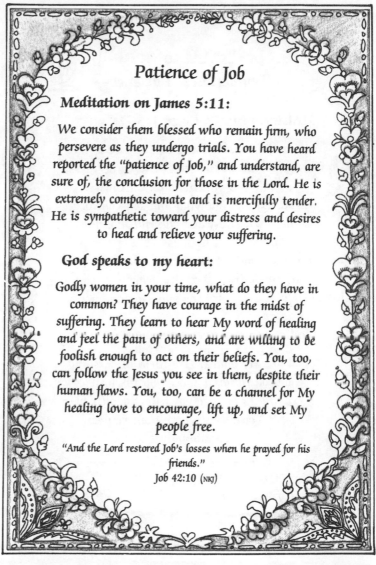

Patience of Job

Meditation on James 5:11:

We consider them blessed who remain firm, who persevere as they undergo trials. You have heard reported the "patience of Job," and understand, are sure of, the conclusion for those in the Lord. He is extremely compassionate and is mercifully tender. He is sympathetic toward your distress and desires to heal and relieve your suffering.

God speaks to my heart:

Godly women in your time, what do they have in common? They have courage in the midst of suffering. They learn to hear My word of healing and feel the pain of others, and are willing to be foolish enough to act on their beliefs. You, too, can follow the Jesus you see in them, despite their human flaws. You, too, can be a channel for My healing love to encourage, lift up, and set My people free.

"And the Lord restored Job's losses when he prayed for his friends."
Job 42:10 (NKJ)

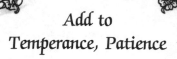

Add to
Temperance, Patience

Meditation on 2 Peter 1:5–7:

Simultaneously [escaping the lust of the world] with all eagerness and earnestness, add this to your reliance on Christ: excellence and knowing and self-control in fleshly desires, and cheerful, hopeful endurance, and holiness, and brotherly kindness, and celebration of a love feast for all humanity, especially generosity and helpfulness toward the suffering and needy.

God speaks to my heart:

You are My hands. Use them in pursuing the good things I show you to do. It is exciting to be a channel for the gifts of God! You receive more than you can possibly give!

". . . Be temperate, sound in . . . endurance."
Titus 2:2 (NIV)

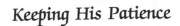

Keeping His Patience

Meditation on Revelation 3:10:

"Because you have guarded, kept your eye
on the watchword, the motivating thought
of My cheerful, hopeful endurance, I also
will protect you from the time of
temptation, the time when evil provokes
and tests, which shall come to all the
world to try them that live on the earth."

God speaks to my heart:

Yes, I am with you in the hour of
temptation. Yes, I fight fire with fire, and if
you hold on to that little word *patience*,
which is Mine, which I work into you,
then you will toughen and resist and grow
through the process. The fire of temptation
can be transformed into a light that shines
to show others the way home to Me.

"In [Jesus] we have obtained an inheritance."
Ephesians 1:11 (KJV)

Leaders Are Patient

Meditation on 1 Timothy 3:2–3:

An official in charge of the church must be blameless, the husband of one wife, sober, self-controlled, of orderly, modest behavior, a lover of guests and hospitality, able to teach, no lover of wines and strong drink, not quarrelsome or greedy or covetous, but patient, mild, and gentle.

God speaks to my heart:

The leaders you admire, respect, and can follow as sure guides on My way are ones who have made a myriad of decisions to set aside those gaudy attractions of the world's pleasures for a single-minded service to Me and openness to serve others. The stamp is unmistakable: you will become like those you admire.

"Follow after righteousness . . . patience, meekness."
1 Timothy 6:11 (KJV)

Teach with Patience

Meditation on 2 Timothy 2:24–25:

And the servant of the Lord must not
quarrel, dispute, or be at war with others,
but be gentle, kind, friendly to all, able to
teach, enduring patiently circumstances and
people who come against him. In gentle
humility train those who set themselves at
odds, praying that God perhaps will enable
them to decide to turn around, to recognize
and discern what is true.

God speaks to my heart:

Though there are many ways of looking at
any given thing, what is true can be seen by
all if the eyeglasses of My Spirit are used in
love. The argumentative person has chosen
not to see through My eyes, with My heart,
and so sees nothing but the bad. Use your
fighting spirit to change conditions that
harm others, but keep on seeing every person
with My forgiving love.

"Reprove, rebuke, exhort, with great patience and
instruction."
2 Timothy 4:2 (NAS)

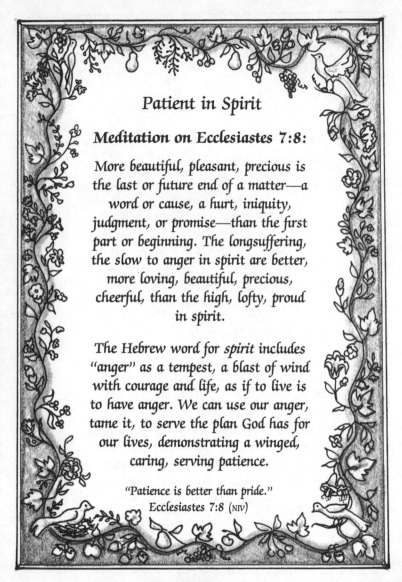

Patient in Spirit

Meditation on Ecclesiastes 7:8:

More beautiful, pleasant, precious is the last or future end of a matter—a word or cause, a hurt, iniquity, judgment, or promise—than the first part or beginning. The longsuffering, the slow to anger in spirit are better, more loving, beautiful, precious, cheerful, than the high, lofty, proud in spirit.

The Hebrew word for *spirit* includes "anger" as a tempest, a blast of wind with courage and life, as if to live is to have anger. We can use our anger, tame it, to serve the plan God has for our lives, demonstrating a winged, caring, serving patience.

"Patience is better than pride."
Ecclesiastes 7:8 (NIV)

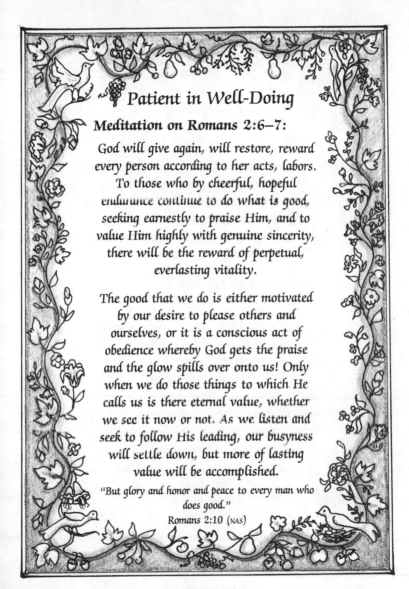

Patient in Well-Doing

Meditation on Romans 2:6–7:

God will give again, will restore, reward every person according to her acts, labors. To those who by cheerful, hopeful endurance continue to do what is good, seeking earnestly to praise Him, and to value Him highly with genuine sincerity, there will be the reward of perpetual, everlasting vitality.

The good that we do is either motivated by our desire to please others and ourselves, or it is a conscious act of obedience whereby God gets the praise and the glow spills over onto us! Only when we do those things to which He calls us is there eternal value, whether we see it now or not. As we listen and seek to follow His leading, our busyness will settle down, but more of lasting value will be accomplished.

"But glory and honor and peace to every man who does good."

Romans 2:10 (NAS)

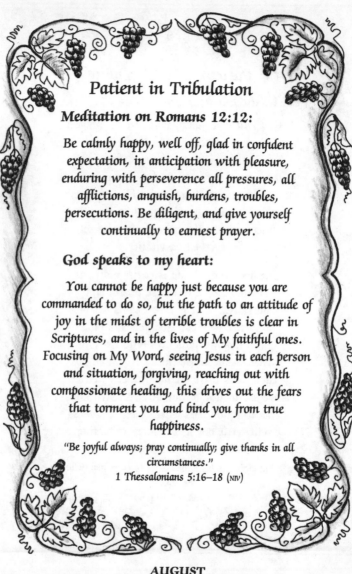

Patient in Tribulation

Meditation on Romans 12:12:

Be calmly happy, well off, glad in confident
expectation, in anticipation with pleasure,
enduring with perseverence all pressures, all
afflictions, anguish, burdens, troubles,
persecutions. Be diligent, and give yourself
continually to earnest prayer.

God speaks to my heart:

You cannot be happy just because you are
commanded to do so, but the path to an attitude of
joy in the midst of terrible troubles is clear in
Scriptures, and in the lives of My faithful ones.
Focusing on My Word, seeing Jesus in each person
and situation, forgiving, reaching out with
compassionate healing, this drives out the fears
that torment you and bind you from true
happiness.

"Be joyful always; pray continually; give thanks in all
circumstances."
1 Thessalonians 5:16–18 (NIV)

Patient Toward All

Meditation on 1 Thessalonians 5:14:

Paul said, "Now we invite, implore, desire you Christians to reprove gently, to caution those who are disorderly, to relate with encouragement, to console the 'little-spirited,' the faint of heart, the feebleminded, to care for those without strength, physically or morally, the impotent, the sick, to be long-spirited, to endure patiently, to suffer long toward all people."

God speaks to my heart:

Every person needs encouragement, needs to see the positive qualities of his or her life through another's eyes. Many falter on the edge and need a consistently caring hand. It may seem a little thing to you, but it can be the beginning of hope for another.

"For thy God helpeth thee."
1 Chronicles 12:18 (KJV)

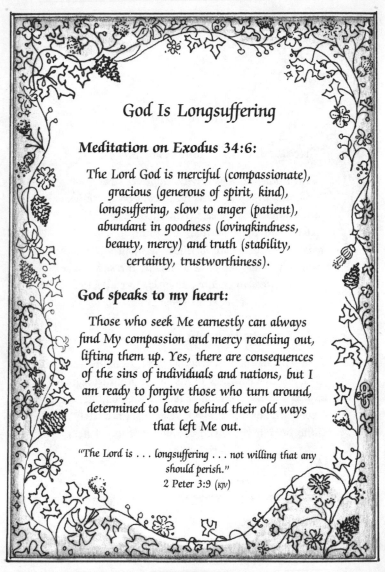

God Is Longsuffering

Meditation on Exodus 34:6:

The Lord God is merciful (compassionate),
gracious (generous of spirit, kind),
longsuffering, slow to anger (patient),
abundant in goodness (lovingkindness,
beauty, mercy) and truth (stability,
certainty, trustworthiness).

God speaks to my heart:

Those who seek Me earnestly can always
find My compassion and mercy reaching out,
lifting them up. Yes, there are consequences
of the sins of individuals and nations, but I
am ready to forgive those who turn around,
determined to leave behind their old ways
that left Me out.

"The Lord is . . . longsuffering . . . not willing that any
should perish."
2 Peter 3:9 (KJV)

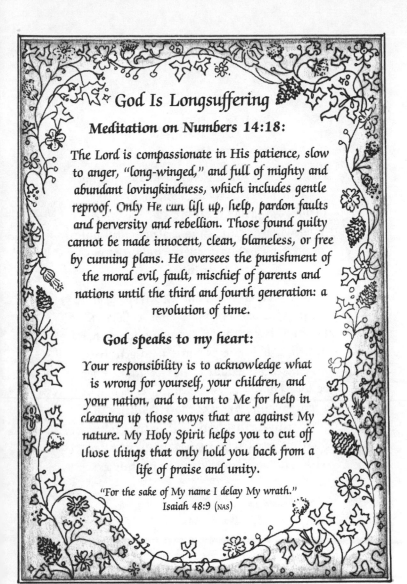

God Is Longsuffering

Meditation on Numbers 14:18:

The Lord is compassionate in His patience, slow to anger, "long-winged," and full of mighty and abundant lovingkindness, which includes gentle reproof. Only He can lift up, help, pardon faults and perversity and rebellion. Those found guilty cannot be made innocent, clean, blameless, or free by cunning plans. He oversees the punishment of the moral evil, fault, mischief of parents and nations until the third and fourth generation: a revolution of time.

God speaks to my heart:

Your responsibility is to acknowledge what is wrong for yourself, your children, and your nation, and to turn to Me for help in cleaning up those ways that are against My nature. My Holy Spirit helps you to cut off those things that only hold you back from a life of praise and unity.

"For the sake of My name I delay My wrath."
Isaiah 48:9 (NAS)

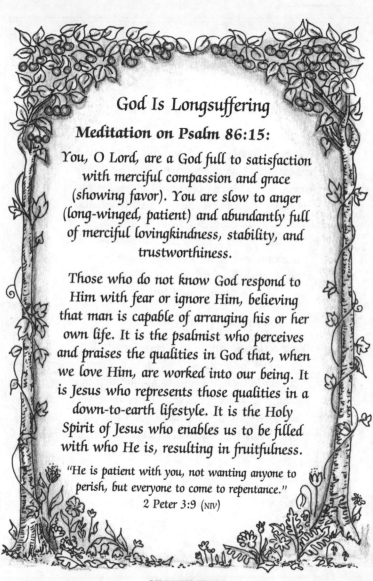

God Is Longsuffering

Meditation on Psalm 86:15:

You, O Lord, are a God full to satisfaction with merciful compassion and grace (showing favor). You are slow to anger (long-winged, patient) and abundantly full of merciful lovingkindness, stability, and trustworthiness.

Those who do not know God respond to Him with fear or ignore Him, believing that man is capable of arranging his or her own life. It is the psalmist who perceives and praises the qualities in God that, when we love Him, are worked into our being. It is Jesus who represents those qualities in a down-to-earth lifestyle. It is the Holy Spirit of Jesus who enables us to be filled with who He is, resulting in fruitfulness.

"He is patient with you, not wanting anyone to perish, but everyone to come to repentance."
2 Peter 3:9 (NIV)

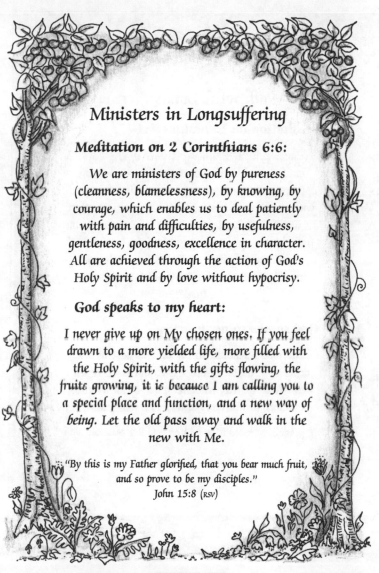

Ministers in Longsuffering

Meditation on 2 Corinthians 6:6:

We are ministers of God by pureness
(cleanness, blamelessness), by knowing, by
courage, which enables us to deal patiently
with pain and difficulties, by usefulness,
gentleness, goodness, excellence in character.
All are achieved through the action of God's
Holy Spirit and by love without hypocrisy.

God speaks to my heart:

I never give up on My chosen ones. If you feel
drawn to a more yielded life, more filled with
the Holy Spirit, with the gifts flowing, the
fruits growing, it is because I am calling you to
a special place and function, and a new way of
being. Let the old pass away and walk in the
new with Me.

"By this is my Father glorified, that you bear much fruit,
and so prove to be my disciples."
John 15:8 (RSV)

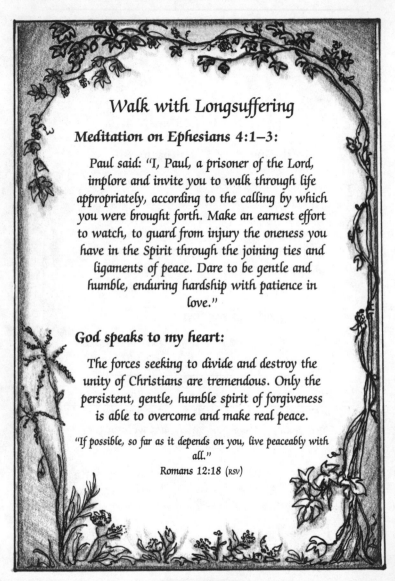

Walk with Longsuffering

Meditation on Ephesians 4:1–3:

Paul said: "I, Paul, a prisoner of the Lord, implore and invite you to walk through life appropriately, according to the calling by which you were brought forth. Make an earnest effort to watch, to guard from injury the oneness you have in the Spirit through the joining ties and ligaments of peace. Dare to be gentle and humble, enduring hardship with patience in love."

God speaks to my heart:

The forces seeking to divide and destroy the unity of Christians are tremendous. Only the persistent, gentle, humble spirit of forgiveness is able to overcome and make real peace.

"If possible, so far as it depends on you, live peaceably with all."
Romans 12:18 (RSV)

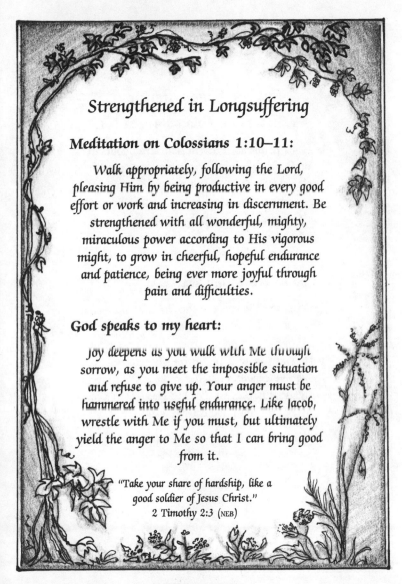

Strengthened in Longsuffering

Meditation on Colossians 1:10–11:

Walk appropriately, following the Lord,
pleasing Him by being productive in every good
effort or work and increasing in discernment. Be
strengthened with all wonderful, mighty,
miraculous power according to His vigorous
might, to grow in cheerful, hopeful endurance
and patience, being ever more joyful through
pain and difficulties.

God speaks to my heart:

Joy deepens as you walk with Me through
sorrow, as you meet the impossible situation
and refuse to give up. Your anger must be
hammered into useful endurance. Like Jacob,
wrestle with Me if you must, but ultimately
yield the anger to Me so that I can bring good
from it.

"Take your share of hardship, like a
good soldier of Jesus Christ."
2 Timothy 2:3 (NEB)

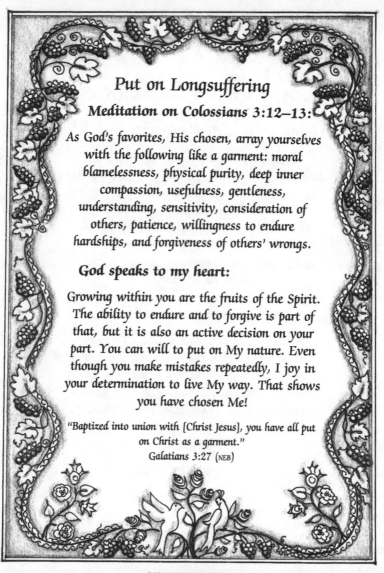

Put on Longsuffering

Meditation on Colossians 3:12–13:

As God's favorites, His chosen, array yourselves with the following like a garment: moral blamelessness, physical purity, deep inner compassion, usefulness, gentleness, understanding, sensitivity, consideration of others, patience, willingness to endure hardships, and forgiveness of others' wrongs.

God speaks to my heart:

Growing within you are the fruits of the Spirit. The ability to endure and to forgive is part of that, but it is also an active decision on your part. You can will to put on My nature. Even though you make mistakes repeatedly, I joy in your determination to live My way. That shows you have chosen Me!

"Baptized into union with [Christ Jesus], you have all put on Christ as a garment."
Galatians 3:27 (NEB)

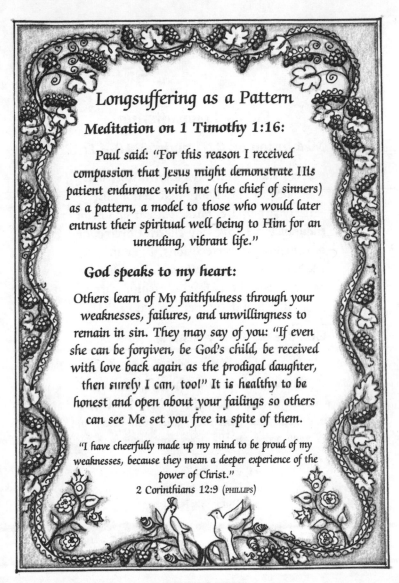

Longsuffering as a Pattern

Meditation on 1 Timothy 1:16:

Paul said: "For this reason I received compassion that Jesus might demonstrate His patient endurance with me (the chief of sinners) as a pattern, a model to those who would later entrust their spiritual well being to Him for an unending, vibrant life."

God speaks to my heart:

Others learn of My faithfulness through your weaknesses, failures, and unwillingness to remain in sin. They may say of you: "If even she can be forgiven, be God's child, be received with love back again as the prodigal daughter, then surely I can, too!" It is healthy to be honest and open about your failings so others can see Me set you free in spite of them.

"I have cheerfully made up my mind to be proud of my weaknesses, because they mean a deeper experience of the power of Christ."
2 Corinthians 12:9 (PHILLIPS)

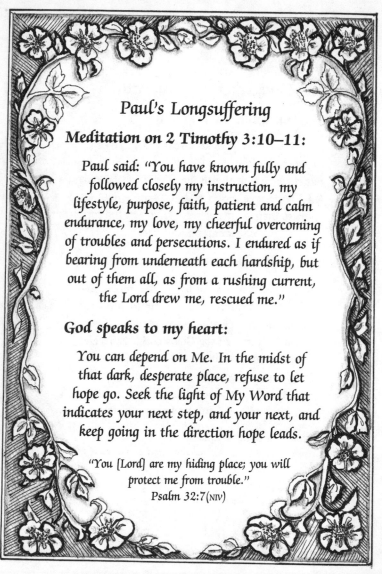

Paul's Longsuffering

Meditation on 2 Timothy 3:10–11:

Paul said: "You have known fully and followed closely my instruction, my lifestyle, purpose, faith, patient and calm endurance, my love, my cheerful overcoming of troubles and persecutions. I endured as if bearing from underneath each hardship, but out of them all, as from a rushing current, the Lord drew me, rescued me."

God speaks to my heart:

You can depend on Me. In the midst of that dark, desperate place, refuse to let hope go. Seek the light of My Word that indicates your next step, and your next, and keep going in the direction hope leads.

"You [Lord] are my hiding place; you will protect me from trouble."
Psalm 32:7(NIV)

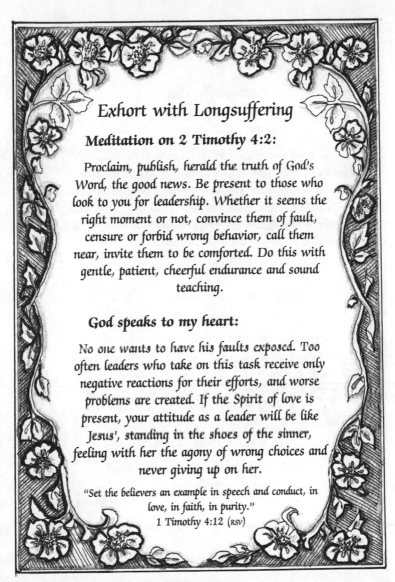

Exhort with Longsuffering

Meditation on 2 Timothy 4:2:

Proclaim, publish, herald the truth of God's Word, the good news. Be present to those who look to you for leadership. Whether it seems the right moment or not, convince them of fault, censure or forbid wrong behavior, call them near, invite them to be comforted. Do this with gentle, patient, cheerful endurance and sound teaching.

God speaks to my heart:

No one wants to have his faults exposed. Too often leaders who take on this task receive only negative reactions for their efforts, and worse problems are created. If the Spirit of love is present, your attitude as a leader will be like Jesus', standing in the shoes of the sinner, feeling with her the agony of wrong choices and never giving up on her.

"Set the believers an example in speech and conduct, in love, in faith, in purity."
1 Timothy 4:12 (RSV)

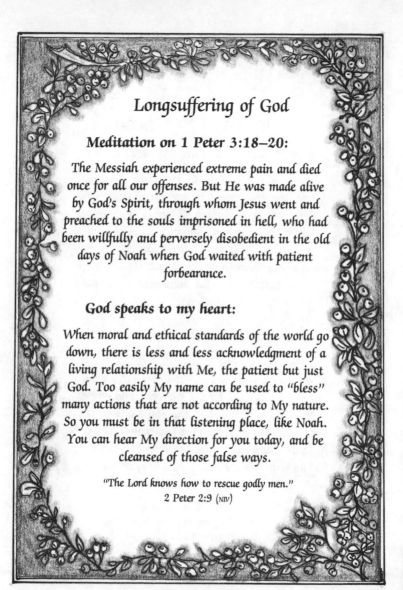

Longsuffering of God

Meditation on 1 Peter 3:18–20:

The Messiah experienced extreme pain and died
once for all our offenses. But He was made alive
by God's Spirit, through whom Jesus went and
preached to the souls imprisoned in hell, who had
been willfully and perversely disobedient in the old
days of Noah when God waited with patient
forbearance.

God speaks to my heart:

When moral and ethical standards of the world go
down, there is less and less acknowledgment of a
living relationship with Me, the patient but just
God. Too easily My name can be used to "bless"
many actions that are not according to My nature.
So you must be in that listening place, like Noah.
You can hear My direction for you today, and be
cleansed of those false ways.

"The Lord knows how to rescue godly men."
2 Peter 2:9 (NIV)

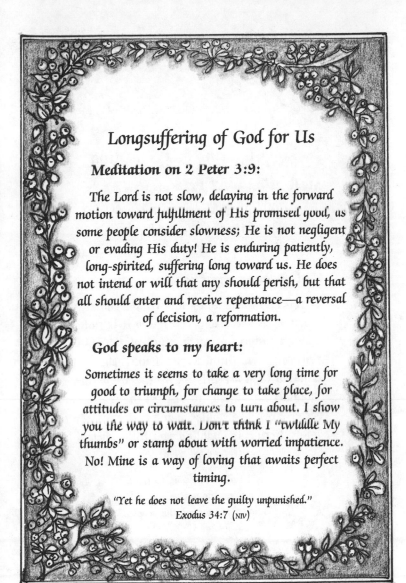

Longsuffering of God for Us

Meditation on 2 Peter 3:9:

The Lord is not slow, delaying in the forward
motion toward fulfillment of His promised good, as
some people consider slowness; He is not negligent
or evading His duty! He is enduring patiently,
long-spirited, suffering long toward us. He does
not intend or will that any should perish, but that
all should enter and receive repentance—a reversal
of decision, a reformation.

God speaks to my heart:

Sometimes it seems to take a very long time for
good to triumph, for change to take place, for
attitudes or circumstances to turn about. I show
you the way to wait. Don't think I "twiddle My
thumbs" or stamp about with worried impatience.
No! Mine is a way of loving that awaits perfect
timing.

"Yet he does not leave the guilty unpunished."
Exodus 34:7 (NIV)

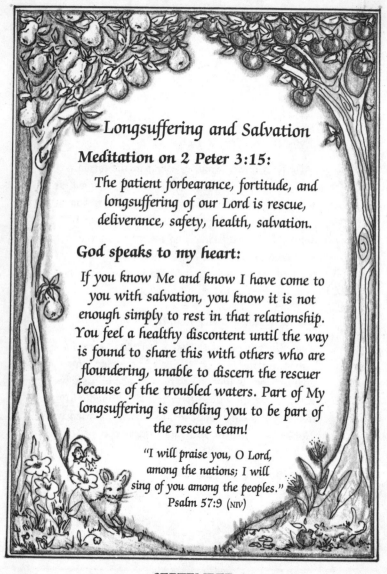

Longsuffering and Salvation

Meditation on 2 Peter 3:15:

> The patient forbearance, fortitude, and longsuffering of our Lord is rescue, deliverance, safety, health, salvation.

God speaks to my heart:

If you know Me and know I have come to you with salvation, you know it is not enough simply to rest in that relationship. You feel a healthy discontent until the way is found to share this with others who are floundering, unable to discern the rescuer because of the troubled waters. Part of My longsuffering is enabling you to be part of the rescue team!

"I will praise you, O Lord, among the nations; I will sing of you among the peoples." Psalm 57:9 (NIV)

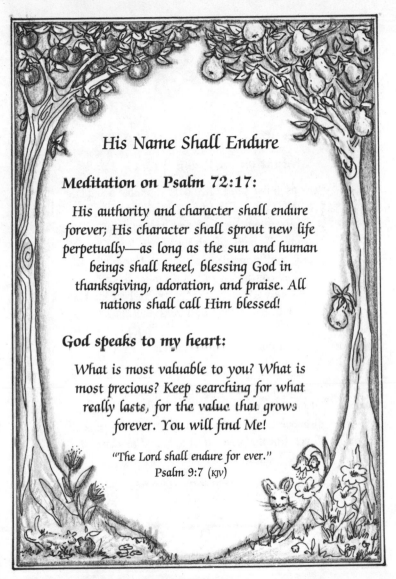

His Name Shall Endure

Meditation on Psalm 72:17:

His authority and character shall endure forever; His character shall sprout new life perpetually—as long as the sun and human beings shall kneel, blessing God in thanksgiving, adoration, and praise. All nations shall call Him blessed!

God speaks to my heart:

What is most valuable to you? What is most precious? Keep searching for what really lasts, for the value that grows forever. You will find Me!

"The Lord shall endure for ever."
Psalm 9:7 (KJV)

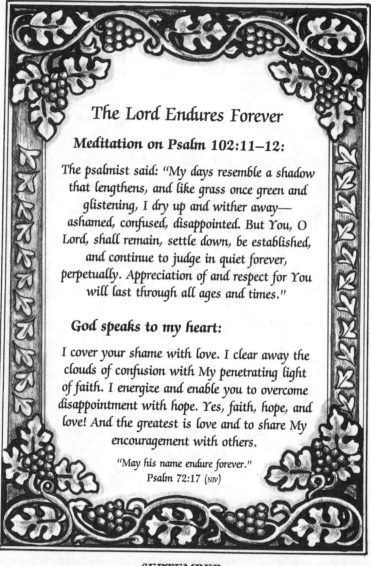

The Lord Endures Forever

Meditation on Psalm 102:11–12:

The psalmist said: "My days resemble a shadow
that lengthens, and like grass once green and
glistening, I dry up and wither away—
ashamed, confused, disappointed. But You, O
Lord, shall remain, settle down, be established,
and continue to judge in quiet forever,
perpetually. Appreciation of and respect for You
will last through all ages and times."

God speaks to my heart:

I cover your shame with love. I clear away the
clouds of confusion with My penetrating light
of faith. I energize and enable you to overcome
disappointment with hope. Yes, faith, hope, and
love! And the greatest is love and to share My
encouragement with others.

"May his name endure forever."
Psalm 72:17 (NIV)

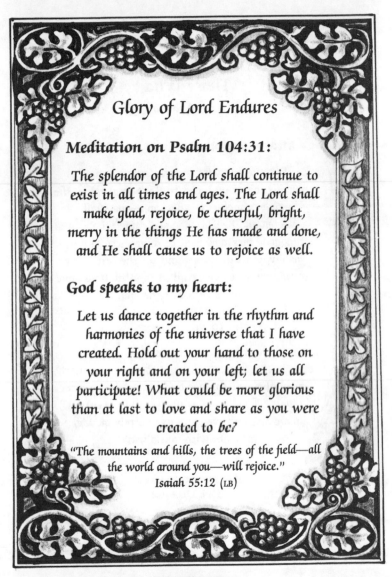

Glory of Lord Endures

Meditation on Psalm 104:31:

The splendor of the Lord shall continue to exist in all times and ages. The Lord shall make glad, rejoice, be cheerful, bright, merry in the things He has made and done, and He shall cause us to rejoice as well.

God speaks to my heart:

Let us dance together in the rhythm and harmonies of the universe that I have created. Hold out your hand to those on your right and on your left; let us all participate! What could be more glorious than at last to love and share as you were created to be?

"The mountains and hills, the trees of the field—all the world around you—will rejoice."
Isaiah 55:12 (LB)

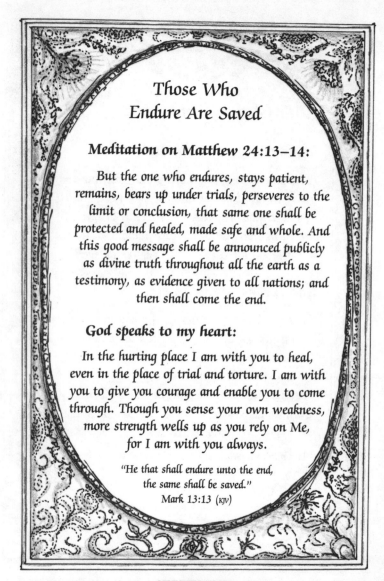

Those Who Endure Are Saved

Meditation on Matthew 24:13–14:

But the one who endures, stays patient, remains, bears up under trials, perseveres to the limit or conclusion, that same one shall be protected and healed, made safe and whole. And this good message shall be announced publicly as divine truth throughout all the earth as a testimony, as evidence given to all nations; and then shall come the end.

God speaks to my heart:

In the hurting place I am with you to heal, even in the place of trial and torture. I am with you to give you courage and enable you to come through. Though you sense your own weakness, more strength wells up as you rely on Me, for I am with you always.

"He that shall endure unto the end,
the same shall be saved."
Mark 13:13 (KJV)

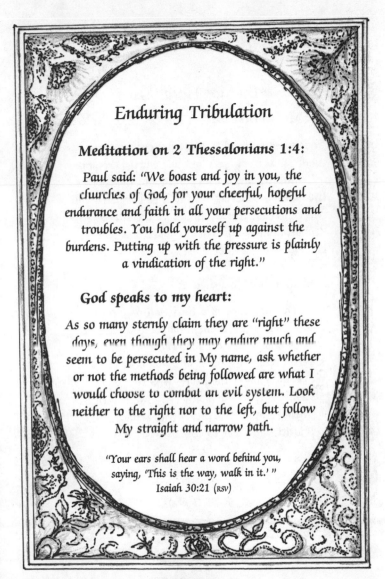

Enduring Tribulation

Meditation on 2 Thessalonians 1:4:

Paul said: "We boast and joy in you, the churches of God, for your cheerful, hopeful endurance and faith in all your persecutions and troubles. You hold yourself up against the burdens. Putting up with the pressure is plainly a vindication of the right."

God speaks to my heart:

As so many sternly claim they are "right" these days, even though they may endure much and seem to be persecuted in My name, ask whether or not the methods being followed are what I would choose to combat an evil system. Look neither to the right nor to the left, but follow My straight and narrow path.

"Your ears shall hear a word behind you,
saying, 'This is the way, walk in it.' "
Isaiah 30:21 (RSV)

Endure Hardness

Meditation on 2 Timothy 2:2–3:

Paul said: "And the instructions that you understood from me, the same entrust, commit into the safekeeping and protection of trustworthy believers who will be competent, fit in character, worthy to teach others also. So undergo hardships, endure afflictions as one chosen, selected to be a soldier of Jesus Christ."

God speaks to my heart:

The discipline of a Christian requires willingness to go through hardship in order to obey orders, but the relationship with the superior officer is one of intimate affection and a knowing of the heart. It is this love relationship that draws others to Me and causes them to lay down their own agendas and priorities in order to see My kind of life in them.

"There are other sheep of mine, not belonging to this fold,
whom I must bring in."
John 10:16 (NEB)

Endure for Others

Meditation on 2 Timothy 2:10:

Paul said: "I persevere and remain patient in everything, finding the benefit and the basic good for the sake of God's chosen favorites that they may also prepare and help bring to pass the safety, deliverance, and health that is in Jesus, the Messiah, with everlasting, very apparent worship, honor, and praise."

God speaks to my heart:

One day everyone's eyes will open and see Me for who I am, see Me with neither doubt nor confusion. You will be able to look Me in the eyes, see your life pass before you, and say, "Thanks for everything!" So, keep looking and asking for those miracles that nudge you in the direction of My flowing current.

"If we endure, we shall also reign with Him."
2 Timothy 2:12 (NKJ)

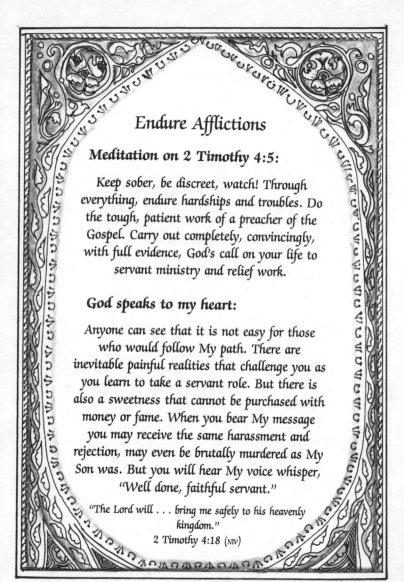

Endure Afflictions

Meditation on 2 Timothy 4:5:

Keep sober, be discreet, watch! Through everything, endure hardships and troubles. Do the tough, patient work of a preacher of the Gospel. Carry out completely, convincingly, with full evidence, God's call on your life to servant ministry and relief work.

God speaks to my heart:

Anyone can see that it is not easy for those who would follow My path. There are inevitable painful realities that challenge you as you learn to take a servant role. But there is also a sweetness that cannot be purchased with money or fame. When you bear My message you may receive the same harassment and rejection, may even be brutally murdered as My Son was. But you will hear My voice whisper, "Well done, faithful servant."

"The Lord will . . . bring me safely to his heavenly kingdom."
2 Timothy 4:18 (NIV)

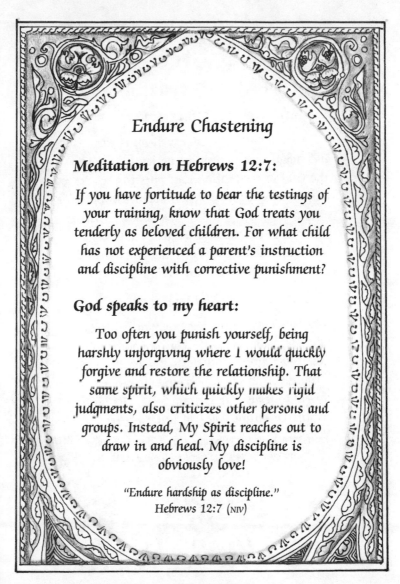

Endure Chastening

Meditation on Hebrews 12:7:

If you have fortitude to bear the testings of
your training, know that God treats you
tenderly as beloved children. For what child
has not experienced a parent's instruction
and discipline with corrective punishment?

God speaks to my heart:

Too often you punish yourself, being
harshly unforgiving where I would quickly
forgive and restore the relationship. That
same spirit, which quickly makes rigid
judgments, also criticizes other persons and
groups. Instead, My Spirit reaches out to
draw in and heal. My discipline is
obviously love!

"Endure hardship as discipline."
Hebrews 12:7 (NIV)

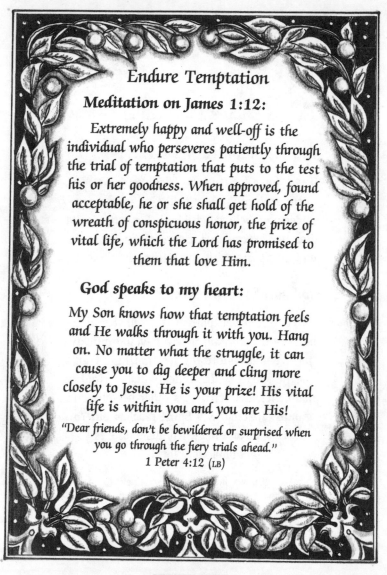

Endure Temptation

Meditation on James 1:12:

Extremely happy and well-off is the individual who perseveres patiently through the trial of temptation that puts to the test his or her goodness. When approved, found acceptable, he or she shall get hold of the wreath of conspicuous honor, the prize of vital life, which the Lord has promised to them that love Him.

God speaks to my heart:

My Son knows how that temptation feels and He walks through it with you. Hang on. No matter what the struggle, it can cause you to dig deeper and cling more closely to Jesus. He is your prize! His vital life is within you and you are His!

"Dear friends, don't be bewildered or surprised when you go through the fiery trials ahead."
1 Peter 4:12 (LB)

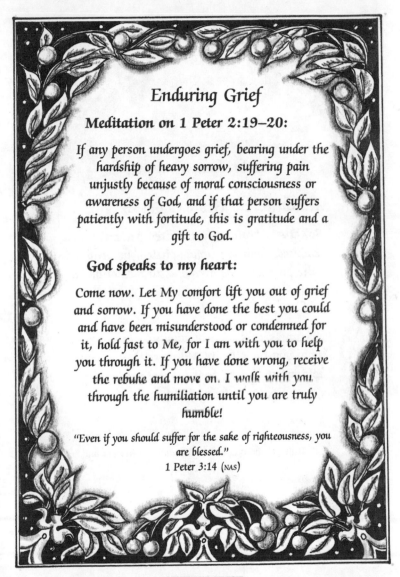

Enduring Grief

Meditation on 1 Peter 2:19–20:

If any person undergoes grief, bearing under the hardship of heavy sorrow, suffering pain unjustly because of moral consciousness or awareness of God, and if that person suffers patiently with fortitude, this is gratitude and a gift to God.

God speaks to my heart:

Come now. Let My comfort lift you out of grief and sorrow. If you have done the best you could and have been misunderstood or condemned for it, hold fast to Me, for I am with you to help you through it. If you have done wrong, receive the rebuke and move on. I walk with you through the humiliation until you are truly humble!

"Even if you should suffer for the sake of righteousness, you are blessed."
1 Peter 3:14 (NAS)

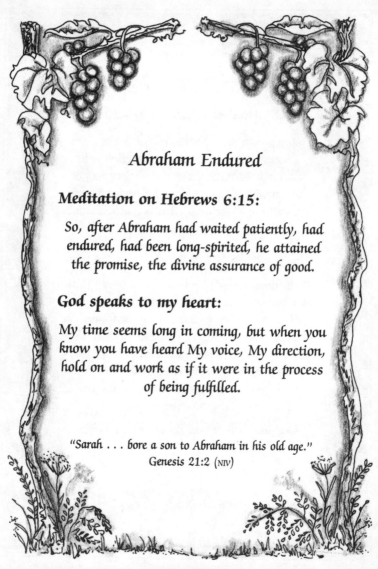

Abraham Endured

Meditation on Hebrews 6:15:

So, after Abraham had waited patiently, had endured, had been long-spirited, he attained the promise, the divine assurance of good.

God speaks to my heart:

My time seems long in coming, but when you know you have heard My voice, My direction, hold on and work as if it were in the process of being fulfilled.

"Sarah . . . bore a son to Abraham in his old age."
Genesis 21:2 (NIV)

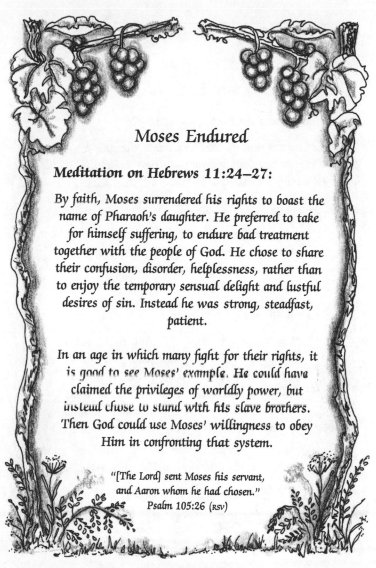

Moses Endured

Meditation on Hebrews 11:24–27:

By faith, Moses surrendered his rights to boast the name of Pharaoh's daughter. He preferred to take for himself suffering, to endure bad treatment together with the people of God. He chose to share their confusion, disorder, helplessness, rather than to enjoy the temporary sensual delight and lustful desires of sin. Instead he was strong, steadfast, patient.

In an age in which many fight for their rights, it is good to see Moses' example. He could have claimed the privileges of worldly power, but instead chose to stand with his slave brothers. Then God could use Moses' willingness to obey Him in confronting that system.

"[The Lord] sent Moses his servant,
and Aaron whom he had chosen."
Psalm 105:26 (RSV)

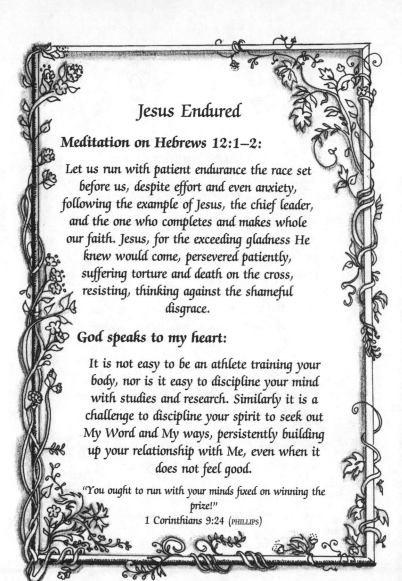

Jesus Endured

Meditation on Hebrews 12:1–2:

Let us run with patient endurance the race set before us, despite effort and even anxiety, following the example of Jesus, the chief leader, and the one who completes and makes whole our faith. Jesus, for the exceeding gladness He knew would come, persevered patiently, suffering torture and death on the cross, resisting, thinking against the shameful disgrace.

God speaks to my heart:

It is not easy to be an athlete training your body, nor is it easy to discipline your mind with studies and research. Similarly it is a challenge to discipline your spirit to seek out My Word and My ways, persistently building up your relationship with Me, even when it does not feel good.

"You ought to run with your minds fixed on winning the prize!"
1 Corinthians 9:24 (PHILLIPS)

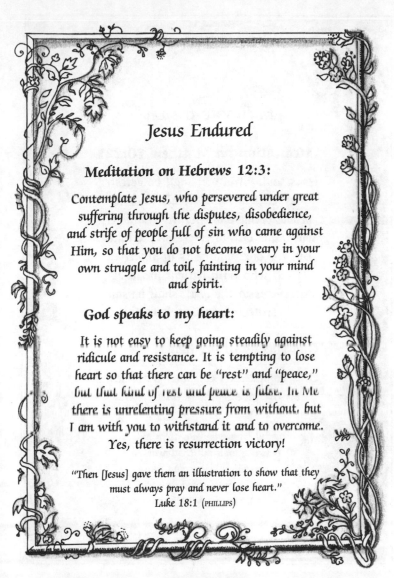

Jesus Endured

Meditation on Hebrews 12:3:

Contemplate Jesus, who persevered under great
suffering through the disputes, disobedience,
and strife of people full of sin who came against
Him, so that you do not become weary in your
own struggle and toil, fainting in your mind
and spirit.

God speaks to my heart:

It is not easy to keep going steadily against
ridicule and resistance. It is tempting to lose
heart so that there can be "rest" and "peace,"
but that kind of rest and peace is false. In Me
there is unrelenting pressure from without, but
I am with you to withstand it and to overcome.
Yes, there is resurrection victory!

"Then [Jesus] gave them an illustration to show that they
must always pray and never lose heart."
Luke 18:1 (PHILLIPS)

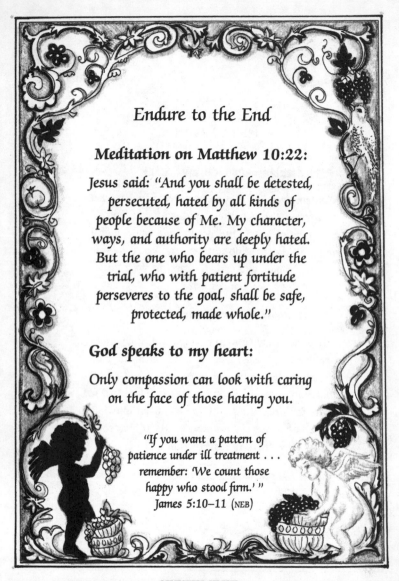

Endure to the End

Meditation on Matthew 10:22:

Jesus said: "And you shall be detested, persecuted, hated by all kinds of people because of Me. My character, ways, and authority are deeply hated. But the one who bears up under the trial, who with patient fortitude perseveres to the goal, shall be safe, protected, made whole."

God speaks to my heart:

Only compassion can look with caring on the face of those hating you.

"If you want a pattern of patience under ill treatment . . . remember: 'We count those happy who stood firm.' "
James 5:10–11 (NEB)

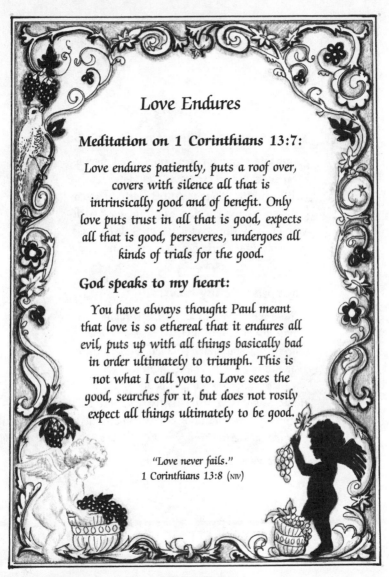

Love Endures

Meditation on 1 Corinthians 13:7:

Love endures patiently, puts a roof over, covers with silence all that is intrinsically good and of benefit. Only love puts trust in all that is good, expects all that is good, perseveres, undergoes all kinds of trials for the good.

God speaks to my heart:

You have always thought Paul meant that love is so ethereal that it endures all evil, puts up with all things basically bad in order ultimately to triumph. This is not what I call you to. Love sees the good, searches for it, but does not rosily expect all things ultimately to be good.

"Love never fails."
1 Corinthians 13:8 (NIV)

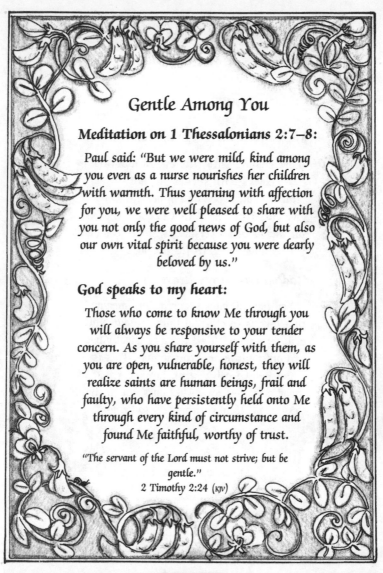

Gentle Among You

Meditation on 1 Thessalonians 2:7–8:

Paul said: "But we were mild, kind among you even as a nurse nourishes her children with warmth. Thus yearning with affection for you, we were well pleased to share with you not only the good news of God, but also our own vital spirit because you were dearly beloved by us."

God speaks to my heart:

Those who come to know Me through you will always be responsive to your tender concern. As you share yourself with them, as you are open, vulnerable, honest, they will realize saints are human beings, frail and faulty, who have persistently held onto Me through every kind of circumstance and found Me faithful, worthy of trust.

"The servant of the Lord must not strive; but be gentle."
2 Timothy 2:24 (kjv)

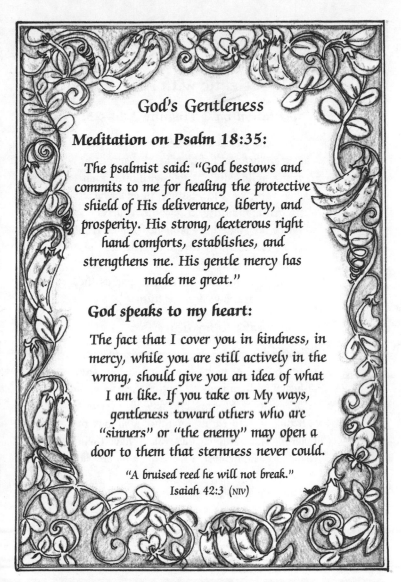

God's Gentleness

Meditation on Psalm 18:35:

The psalmist said: "God bestows and commits to me for healing the protective shield of His deliverance, liberty, and prosperity. His strong, dexterous right hand comforts, establishes, and strengthens me. His gentle mercy has made me great."

God speaks to my heart:

The fact that I cover you in kindness, in mercy, while you are still actively in the wrong, should give you an idea of what I am like. If you take on My ways, gentleness toward others who are "sinners" or "the enemy" may open a door to them that sternness never could.

"A bruised reed he will not break."
Isaiah 42:3 (NIV)

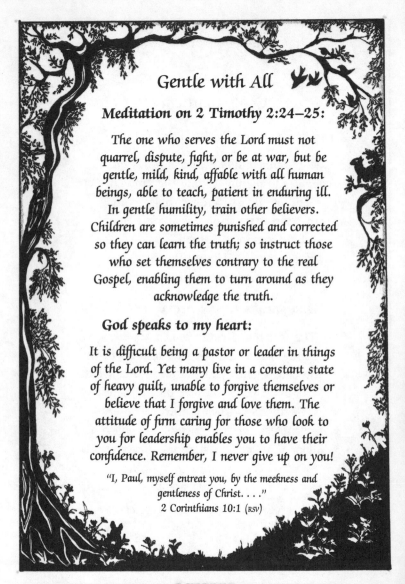

Gentle with All

Meditation on 2 Timothy 2:24–25:

The one who serves the Lord must not
quarrel, dispute, fight, or be at war, but be
gentle, mild, kind, affable with all human
beings, able to teach, patient in enduring ill.
In gentle humility, train other believers.
Children are sometimes punished and corrected
so they can learn the truth; so instruct those
who set themselves contrary to the real
Gospel, enabling them to turn around as they
acknowledge the truth.

God speaks to my heart:

It is difficult being a pastor or leader in things
of the Lord. Yet many live in a constant state
of heavy guilt, unable to forgive themselves or
believe that I forgive and love them. The
attitude of firm caring for those who look to
you for leadership enables you to have their
confidence. Remember, I never give up on you!

"I, Paul, myself entreat you, by the meekness and
gentleness of Christ. . . ."
2 Corinthians 10:1 (RSV)

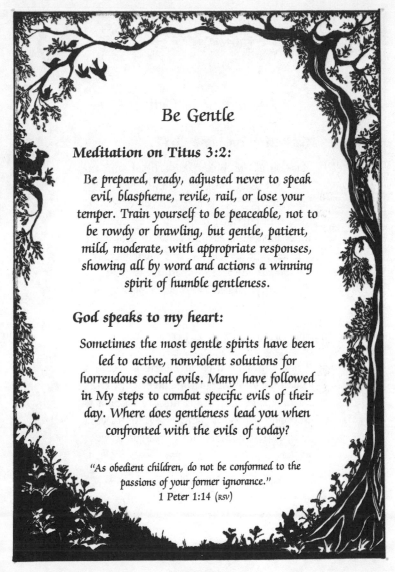

Be Gentle

Meditation on Titus 3:2:

Be prepared, ready, adjusted never to speak
evil, blaspheme, revile, rail, or lose your
temper. Train yourself to be peaceable, not to
be rowdy or brawling, but gentle, patient,
mild, moderate, with appropriate responses,
showing all by word and actions a winning
spirit of humble gentleness.

God speaks to my heart:

Sometimes the most gentle spirits have been
led to active, nonviolent solutions for
horrendous social evils. Many have followed
in My steps to combat specific evils of their
day. Where does gentleness lead you when
confronted with the evils of today?

"As obedient children, do not be conformed to the
passions of your former ignorance."
1 Peter 1:14 (RSV)

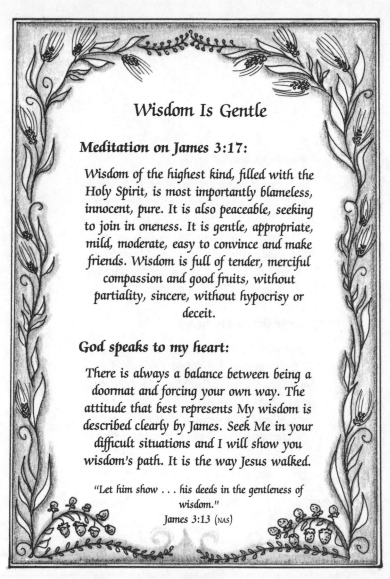

Wisdom Is Gentle

Meditation on James 3:17:

Wisdom of the highest kind, filled with the
Holy Spirit, is most importantly blameless,
innocent, pure. It is also peaceable, seeking
to join in oneness. It is gentle, appropriate,
mild, moderate, easy to convince and make
friends. Wisdom is full of tender, merciful
compassion and good fruits, without
partiality, sincere, without hypocrisy or
deceit.

God speaks to my heart:

There is always a balance between being a
doormat and forcing your own way. The
attitude that best represents My wisdom is
described clearly by James. Seek Me in your
difficult situations and I will show you
wisdom's path. It is the way Jesus walked.

"Let him show . . . his deeds in the gentleness of
wisdom."
James 3:13 (NAS)

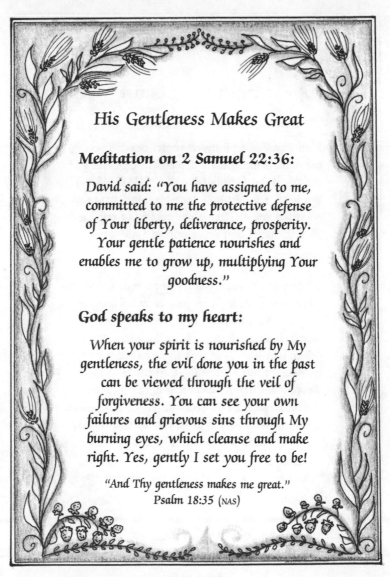

His Gentleness Makes Great

Meditation on 2 Samuel 22:36:

David said: "You have assigned to me,
committed to me the protective defense
of Your liberty, deliverance, prosperity.
Your gentle patience nourishes and
enables me to grow up, multiplying Your
goodness."

God speaks to my heart:

When your spirit is nourished by My
gentleness, the evil done you in the past
can be viewed through the veil of
forgiveness. You can see your own
failures and grievous sins through My
burning eyes, which cleanse and make
right. Yes, gently I set you free to be!

"And Thy gentleness makes me great."
Psalm 18:35 (NAS)

Gentleness of Christ

Meditation on 2 Corinthians 10:1:

Paul said: "Now I myself write, begging you by the humble meekness and merciful gentleness of Christ. I am humiliated and a nobody when I am with you, but now that I am far away and writing you a letter, I am exercising courage with confidence toward you."

God speaks to my heart:

When you approach your brothers and sisters in Christ who differ from you, each holding his opinion like a flag, striving for victory over the other, it seems impossible to communicate, to bridge that gap. Paul was so intimidated by the zealous enthusiasm of the Corinthians that he wrote them letters, and some of his meaning is still in dispute 2,000 years later! My gentleness is available to you to persist in seeking for My Spirit to heal the differences.

"Make my joy complete by being like-minded, having the same love, being one in spirit and purpose."
Philippians 2:2 (NIV)

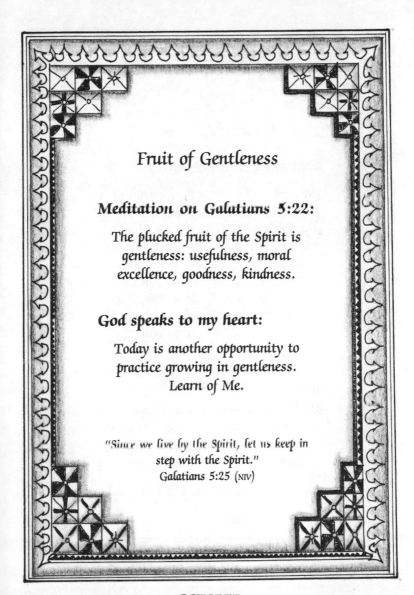

Fruit of Gentleness

Meditation on Galatians 5:22:

The plucked fruit of the Spirit is
gentleness: usefulness, moral
excellence, goodness, kindness.

God speaks to my heart:

Today is another opportunity to
practice growing in gentleness.
Learn of Me.

"Since we live by the Spirit, let us keep in
step with the Spirit."
Galatians 5:25 (NIV)

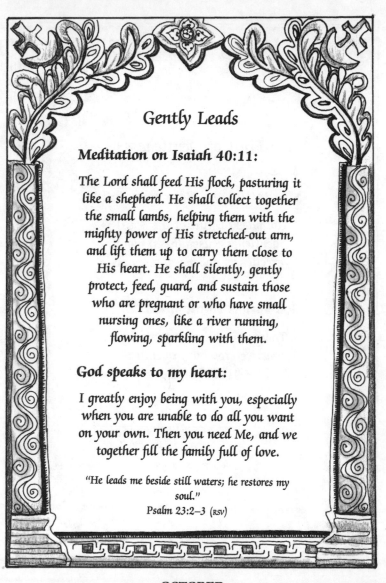

Gently Leads

Meditation on Isaiah 40:11:

The Lord shall feed His flock, pasturing it
like a shepherd. He shall collect together
the small lambs, helping them with the
mighty power of His stretched-out arm,
and lift them up to carry them close to
His heart. He shall silently, gently
protect, feed, guard, and sustain those
who are pregnant or who have small
nursing ones, like a river running,
flowing, sparkling with them.

God speaks to my heart:

I greatly enjoy being with you, especially
when you are unable to do all you want
on your own. Then you need Me, and we
together fill the family full of love.

*"He leads me beside still waters; he restores my
soul."*
Psalm 23:2–3 (RSV)

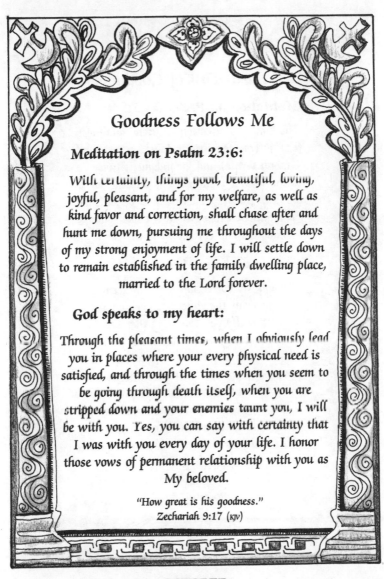

Goodness Follows Me

Meditation on Psalm 23:6:

With certainty, things good, beautiful, loving, joyful, pleasant, and for my welfare, as well as kind favor and correction, shall chase after and hunt me down, pursuing me throughout the days of my strong enjoyment of life. I will settle down to remain established in the family dwelling place, married to the Lord forever.

God speaks to my heart:

Through the pleasant times, when I obviously lead you in places where your every physical need is satisfied, and through the times when you seem to be going through death itself, when you are stripped down and your enemies taunt you, I will be with you. Yes, you can say with certainty that I was with you every day of your life. I honor those vows of permanent relationship with you as My beloved.

"How great is his goodness."
Zechariah 9:17 (KJV)

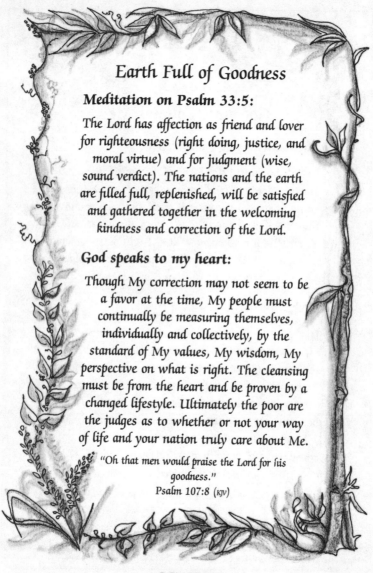

Earth Full of Goodness

Meditation on Psalm 33:5:

The Lord has affection as friend and lover for righteousness (right doing, justice, and moral virtue) and for judgment (wise, sound verdict). The nations and the earth are filled full, replenished, will be satisfied and gathered together in the welcoming kindness and correction of the Lord.

God speaks to my heart:

Though My correction may not seem to be a favor at the time, My people must continually be measuring themselves, individually and collectively, by the standard of My values, My wisdom, My perspective on what is right. The cleansing must be from the heart and be proven by a changed lifestyle. Ultimately the poor are the judges as to whether or not your way of life and your nation truly care about Me.

"Oh that men would praise the Lord for his goodness."
Psalm 107:8 (KJV)

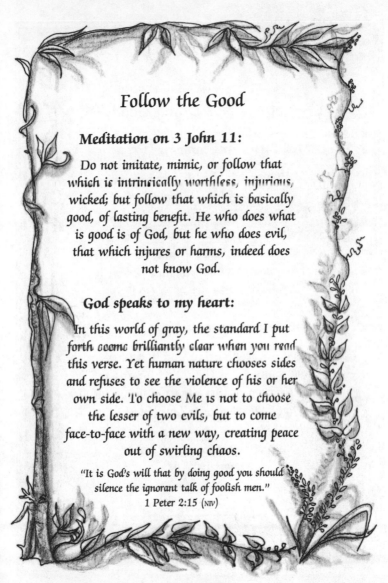

Follow the Good

Meditation on 3 John 11:

Do not imitate, mimic, or follow that which is intrinsically worthless, injurious, wicked; but follow that which is basically good, of lasting benefit. He who does what is good is of God, but he who does evil, that which injures or harms, indeed does not know God.

God speaks to my heart:

In this world of gray, the standard I put forth seems brilliantly clear when you read this verse. Yet human nature chooses sides and refuses to see the violence of his or her own side. To choose Me is not to choose the lesser of two evils, but to come face-to-face with a new way, creating peace out of swirling chaos.

"It is God's will that by doing good you should silence the ignorant talk of foolish men."
1 Peter 2:15 (NIV)

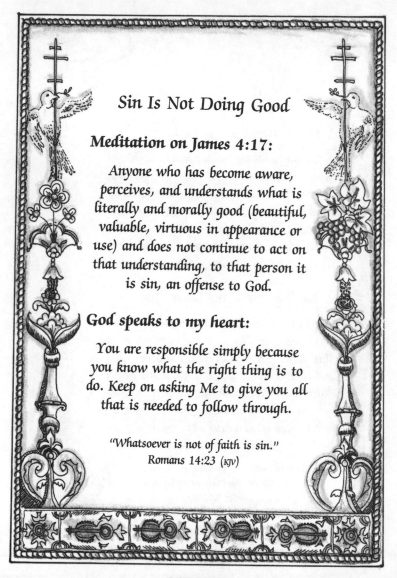

Sin Is Not Doing Good

Meditation on James 4:17:

Anyone who has become aware,
perceives, and understands what is
literally and morally good (beautiful,
valuable, virtuous in appearance or
use) and does not continue to act on
that understanding, to that person it
is sin, an offense to God.

God speaks to my heart:

You are responsible simply because
you know what the right thing is to
do. Keep on asking Me to give you all
that is needed to follow through.

"Whatsoever is not of faith is sin."
Romans 14:23 (KJV)

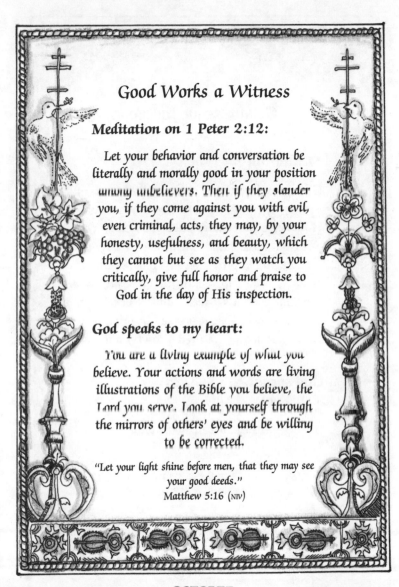

Good Works a Witness

Meditation on 1 Peter 2:12:

Let your behavior and conversation be literally and morally good in your position among unbelievers. Then if they slander you, if they come against you with evil, even criminal, acts, they may, by your honesty, usefulness, and beauty, which they cannot but see as they watch you critically, give full honor and praise to God in the day of His inspection.

God speaks to my heart:

You are a living example of what you believe. Your actions and words are living illustrations of the Bible you believe, the Lord you serve. Look at yourself through the mirrors of others' eyes and be willing to be corrected.

"Let your light shine before men, that they may see your good deeds."
Matthew 5:16 (NIV)

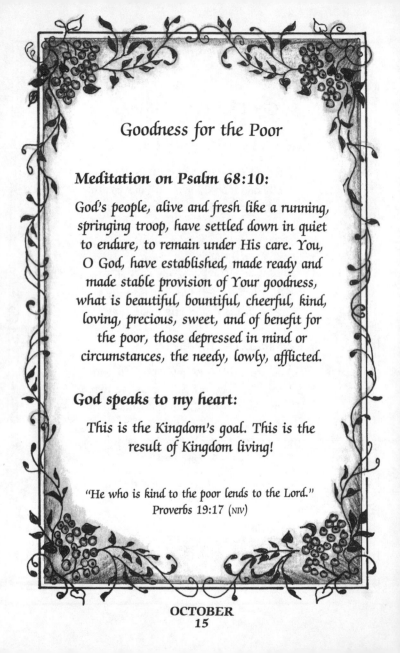

Goodness for the Poor

Meditation on Psalm 68:10:

God's people, alive and fresh like a running, springing troop, have settled down in quiet to endure, to remain under His care. You, O God, have established, made ready and made stable provision of Your goodness, what is beautiful, bountiful, cheerful, kind, loving, precious, sweet, and of benefit for the poor, those depressed in mind or circumstances, the needy, lowly, afflicted.

God speaks to my heart:

This is the Kingdom's goal. This is the result of Kingdom living!

"He who is kind to the poor lends to the Lord."
Proverbs 19:17 (NIV)

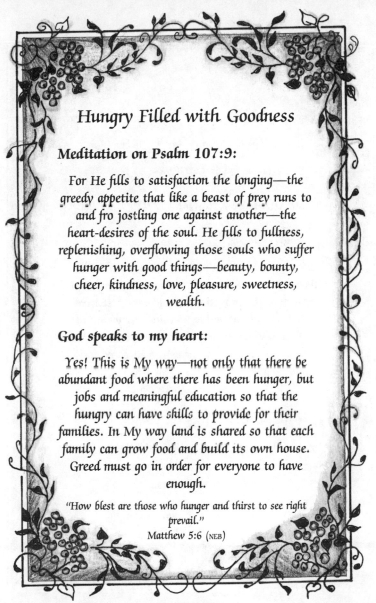

Hungry Filled with Goodness

Meditation on Psalm 107:9:

For He fills to satisfaction the longing—the
greedy appetite that like a beast of prey runs to
and fro jostling one against another—the
heart-desires of the soul. He fills to fullness,
replenishing, overflowing those souls who suffer
hunger with good things—beauty, bounty,
cheer, kindness, love, pleasure, sweetness,
wealth.

God speaks to my heart:

Yes! This is My way—not only that there be
abundant food where there has been hunger, but
jobs and meaningful education so that the
hungry can have skills to provide for their
families. In My way land is shared so that each
family can grow food and build its own house.
Greed must go in order for everyone to have
enough.

"How blest are those who hunger and thirst to see right
prevail."
Matthew 5:6 (NEB)

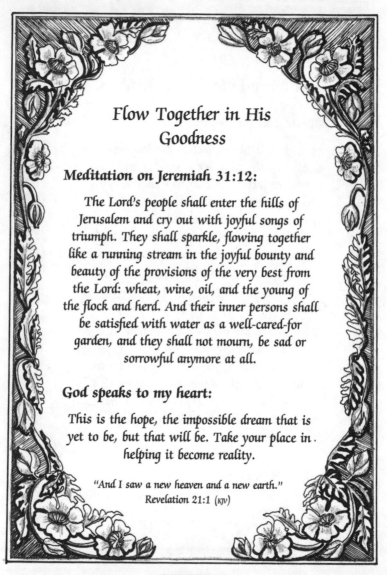

Flow Together in His Goodness

Meditation on Jeremiah 31:12:

The Lord's people shall enter the hills of
Jerusalem and cry out with joyful songs of
triumph. They shall sparkle, flowing together
like a running stream in the joyful bounty and
beauty of the provisions of the very best from
the Lord: wheat, wine, oil, and the young of
the flock and herd. And their inner persons shall
be satisfied with water as a well-cared-for
garden, and they shall not mourn, be sad or
sorrowful anymore at all.

God speaks to my heart:

This is the hope, the impossible dream that is
yet to be, but that will be. Take your place in
helping it become reality.

"And I saw a new heaven and a new earth."
Revelation 21:1 (KJV)

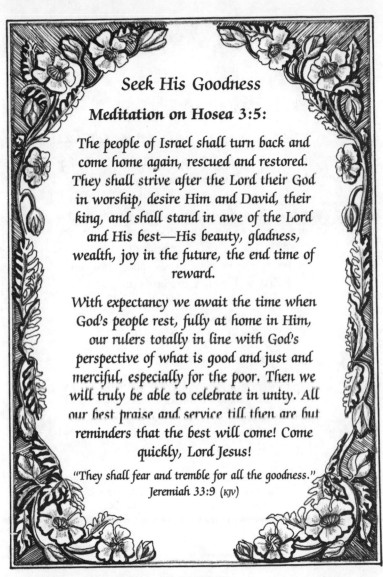

Seek His Goodness

Meditation on Hosea 3:5:

The people of Israel shall turn back and
come home again, rescued and restored.
They shall strive after the Lord their God
in worship, desire Him and David, their
king, and shall stand in awe of the Lord
and His best—His beauty, gladness,
wealth, joy in the future, the end time of
reward.

With expectancy we await the time when
God's people rest, fully at home in Him,
our rulers totally in line with God's
perspective of what is good and just and
merciful, especially for the poor. Then we
will truly be able to celebrate in unity. All
our best praise and service till then are but
reminders that the best will come! Come
quickly, Lord Jesus!

"They shall fear and tremble for all the goodness."
Jeremiah 33:9 (KJV)

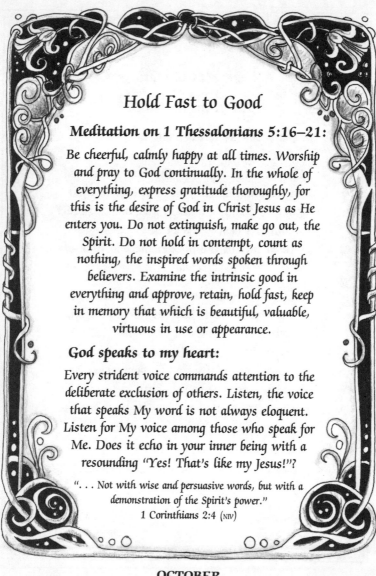

Hold Fast to Good

Meditation on 1 Thessalonians 5:16–21:

Be cheerful, calmly happy at all times. Worship
and pray to God continually. In the whole of
everything, express gratitude thoroughly, for
this is the desire of God in Christ Jesus as He
enters you. Do not extinguish, make go out, the
Spirit. Do not hold in contempt, count as
nothing, the inspired words spoken through
believers. Examine the intrinsic good in
everything and approve, retain, hold fast, keep
in memory that which is beautiful, valuable,
virtuous in use or appearance.

God speaks to my heart:

Every strident voice commands attention to the
deliberate exclusion of others. Listen, the voice
that speaks My word is not always eloquent.
Listen for My voice among those who speak for
Me. Does it echo in your inner being with a
resounding "Yes! That's like my Jesus!"?

". . . Not with wise and persuasive words, but with a
demonstration of the Spirit's power."
1 Corinthians 2:4 (NIV)

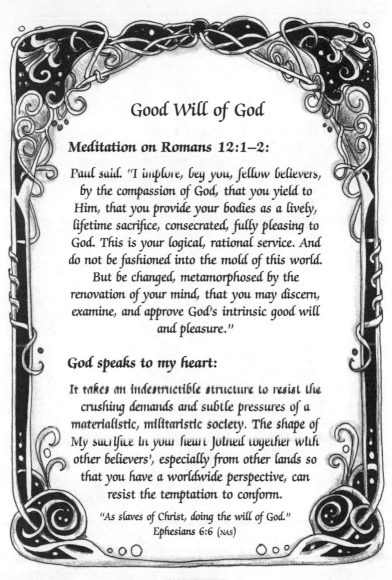

Good Will of God

Meditation on Romans 12:1–2:

Paul said, "I implore, beg you, fellow believers,
by the compassion of God, that you yield to
Him, that you provide your bodies as a lively,
lifetime sacrifice, consecrated, fully pleasing to
God. This is your logical, rational service. And
do not be fashioned into the mold of this world.
But be changed, metamorphosed by the
renovation of your mind, that you may discern,
examine, and approve God's intrinsic good will
and pleasure."

God speaks to my heart:

It takes an indestructible structure to resist the
crushing demands and subtle pressures of a
materialistic, militaristic society. The shape of
My sacrifice in your heart joined together with
other believers', especially from other lands so
that you have a worldwide perspective, can
resist the temptation to conform.

"As slaves of Christ, doing the will of God."
Ephesians 6:6 (NAS)

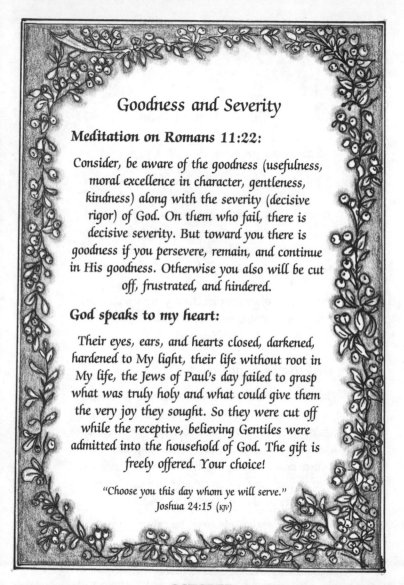

Goodness and Severity

Meditation on Romans 11:22:

Consider, be aware of the goodness (usefulness, moral excellence in character, gentleness, kindness) along with the severity (decisive rigor) of God. On them who fail, there is decisive severity. But toward you there is goodness if you persevere, remain, and continue in His goodness. Otherwise you also will be cut off, frustrated, and hindered.

God speaks to my heart:

Their eyes, ears, and hearts closed, darkened, hardened to My light, their life without root in My life, the Jews of Paul's day failed to grasp what was truly holy and what could give them the very joy they sought. So they were cut off while the receptive, believing Gentiles were admitted into the household of God. The gift is freely offered. Your choice!

"Choose you this day whom ye will serve."
Joshua 24:15 (KJV)

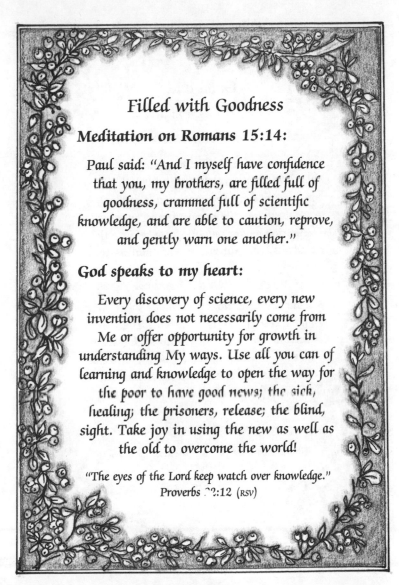

Filled with Goodness

Meditation on Romans 15:14:

Paul said: "And I myself have confidence that you, my brothers, are filled full of goodness, crammed full of scientific knowledge, and are able to caution, reprove, and gently warn one another."

God speaks to my heart:

Every discovery of science, every new invention does not necessarily come from Me or offer opportunity for growth in understanding My ways. Use all you can of learning and knowledge to open the way for the poor to have good news; the sick, healing; the prisoners, release; the blind, sight. Take joy in using the new as well as the old to overcome the world!

"The eyes of the Lord keep watch over knowledge."
Proverbs 22:12 (RSV)

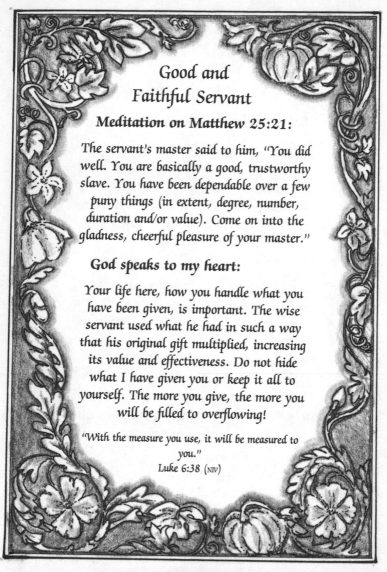

Good and
Faithful Servant

Meditation on Matthew 25:21:

The servant's master said to him, "You did well. You are basically a good, trustworthy slave. You have been dependable over a few puny things (in extent, degree, number, duration and/or value). Come on into the gladness, cheerful pleasure of your master."

God speaks to my heart:

Your life here, how you handle what you have been given, is important. The wise servant used what he had in such a way that his original gift multiplied, increasing its value and effectiveness. Do not hide what I have given you or keep it all to yourself. The more you give, the more you will be filled to overflowing!

"With the measure you use, it will be measured to you."
Luke 6:38 (NIV)

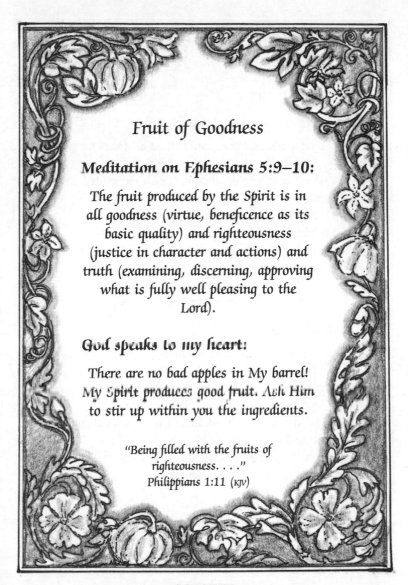

Fruit of Goodness

Meditation on Ephesians 5:9–10:

The fruit produced by the Spirit is in all goodness (virtue, beneficence as its basic quality) and righteousness (justice in character and actions) and truth (examining, discerning, approving what is fully well pleasing to the Lord).

God speaks to my heart:

There are no bad apples in My barrel! My Spirit produces good fruit. Ask Him to stir up within you the ingredients.

"Being filled with the fruits of
righteousness. . . ."
Philippians 1:11 (KJV)

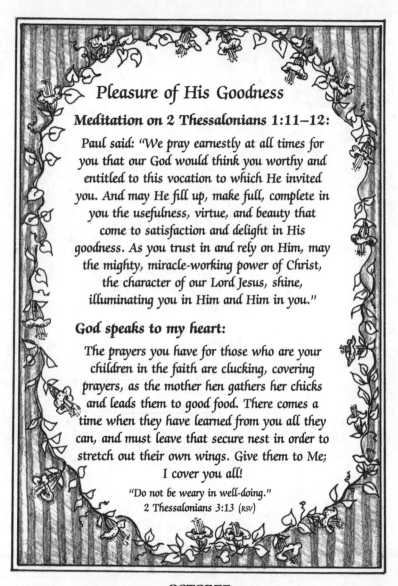

Pleasure of His Goodness

Meditation on 2 Thessalonians 1:11–12:

Paul said: "We pray earnestly at all times for you that our God would think you worthy and entitled to this vocation to which He invited you. And may He fill up, make full, complete in you the usefulness, virtue, and beauty that come to satisfaction and delight in His goodness. As you trust in and rely on Him, may the mighty, miracle-working power of Christ, the character of our Lord Jesus, shine, illuminating you in Him and Him in you."

God speaks to my heart:

The prayers you have for those who are your children in the faith are clucking, covering prayers, as the mother hen gathers her chicks and leads them to good food. There comes a time when they have learned from you all they can, and must leave that secure nest in order to stretch out their own wings. Give them to Me; I cover you all!

"Do not be weary in well-doing."
2 Thessalonians 3:13 (RSV)

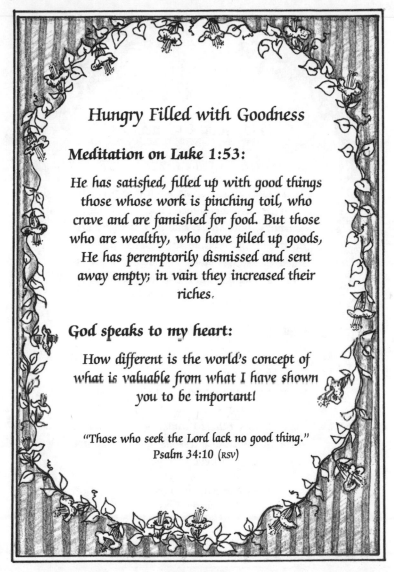

Hungry Filled with Goodness

Meditation on Luke 1:53:

He has satisfied, filled up with good things
those whose work is pinching toil, who
crave and are famished for food. But those
who are wealthy, who have piled up goods,
He has peremptorily dismissed and sent
away empty; in vain they increased their
riches.

God speaks to my heart:

How different is the world's concept of
what is valuable from what I have shown
you to be important!

"Those who seek the Lord lack no good thing."
Psalm 34:10 (RSV)

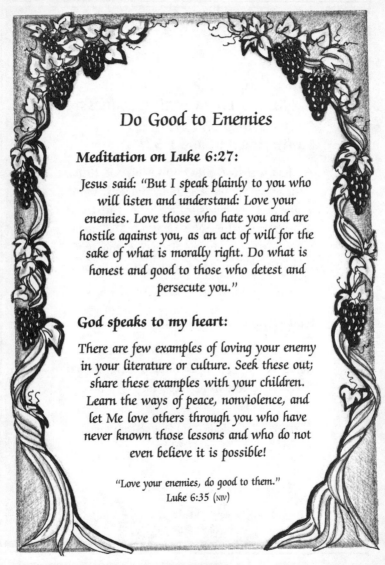

Do Good to Enemies

Meditation on Luke 6:27:

Jesus said: "But I speak plainly to you who will listen and understand: Love your enemies. Love those who hate you and are hostile against you, as an act of will for the sake of what is morally right. Do what is honest and good to those who detest and persecute you."

God speaks to my heart:

There are few examples of loving your enemy in your literature or culture. Seek these out; share these examples with your children. Learn the ways of peace, nonviolence, and let Me love others through you who have never known those lessons and who do not even believe it is possible!

"Love your enemies, do good to them."
Luke 6:35 (NIV)

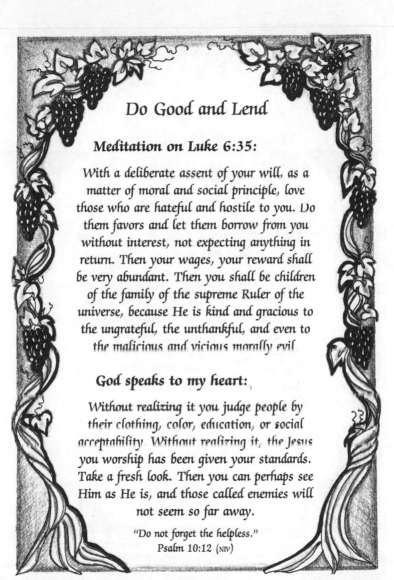

Do Good and Lend

Meditation on Luke 6:35:

With a deliberate assent of your will, as a matter of moral and social principle, love those who are hateful and hostile to you. Do them favors and let them borrow from you without interest, not expecting anything in return. Then your wages, your reward shall be very abundant. Then you shall be children of the family of the supreme Ruler of the universe, because He is kind and gracious to the ungrateful, the unthankful, and even to the malicious and vicious morally evil

God speaks to my heart:

Without realizing it you judge people by their clothing, color, education, or social acceptability. Without realizing it, the Jesus you worship has been given your standards. Take a fresh look. Then you can perhaps see Him as He is, and those called enemies will not seem so far away.

"Do not forget the helpless."
Psalm 10:12 (NIV)

OCTOBER
28

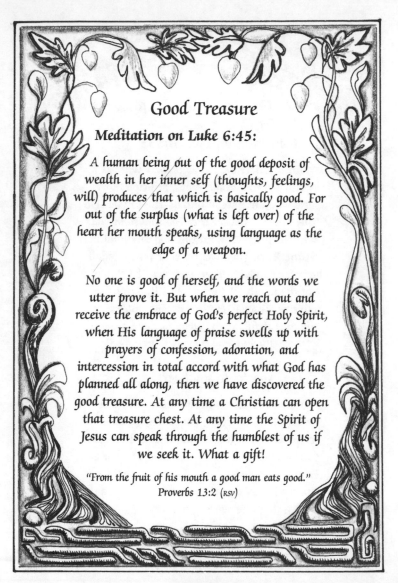

Good Treasure

Meditation on Luke 6:45:

A human being out of the good deposit of
wealth in her inner self (thoughts, feelings,
will) produces that which is basically good. For
out of the surplus (what is left over) of the
heart her mouth speaks, using language as the
edge of a weapon.

No one is good of herself, and the words we
utter prove it. But when we reach out and
receive the embrace of God's perfect Holy Spirit,
when His language of praise swells up with
prayers of confession, adoration, and
intercession in total accord with what God has
planned all along, then we have discovered the
good treasure. At any time a Christian can open
that treasure chest. At any time the Spirit of
Jesus can speak through the humblest of us if
we seek it. What a gift!

"From the fruit of his mouth a good man eats good."
Proverbs 13:2 (RSV)

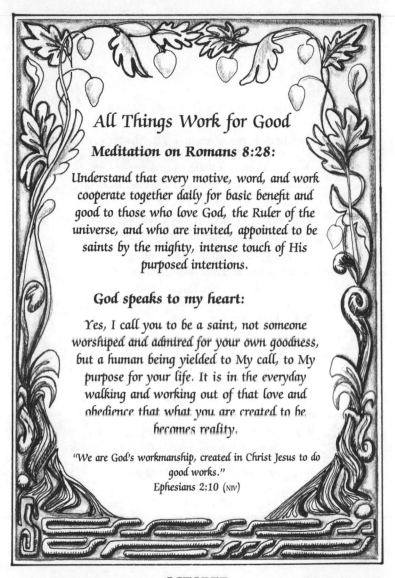

All Things Work for Good

Meditation on Romans 8:28:

Understand that every motive, word, and work
cooperate together daily for basic benefit and
good to those who love God, the Ruler of the
universe, and who are invited, appointed to be
saints by the mighty, intense touch of His
purposed intentions.

God speaks to my heart:

Yes, I call you to be a saint, not someone
worshiped and admired for your own goodness,
but a human being yielded to My call, to My
purpose for your life. It is in the everyday
walking and working out of that love and
obedience that what you are created to be
becomes reality.

"We are God's workmanship, created in Christ Jesus to do
good works."
Ephesians 2:10 (NIV)

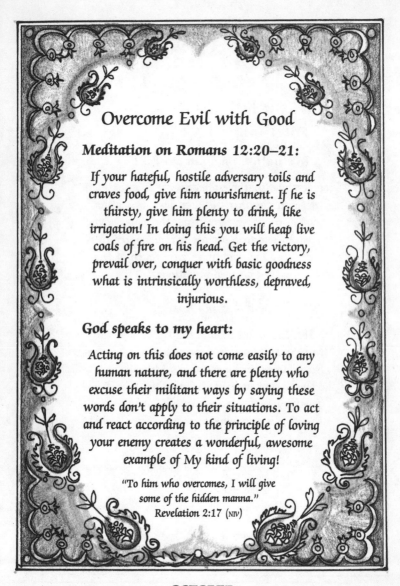

Overcome Evil with Good

Meditation on Romans 12:20–21:

If your hateful, hostile adversary toils and craves food, give him nourishment. If he is thirsty, give him plenty to drink, like irrigation! In doing this you will heap live coals of fire on his head. Get the victory, prevail over, conquer with basic goodness what is intrinsically worthless, depraved, injurious.

God speaks to my heart:

Acting on this does not come easily to any human nature, and there are plenty who excuse their militant ways by saying these words don't apply to their situations. To act and react according to the principle of loving your enemy creates a wonderful, awesome example of My kind of living!

"To him who overcomes, I will give some of the hidden manna."
Revelation 2:17 (NIV)

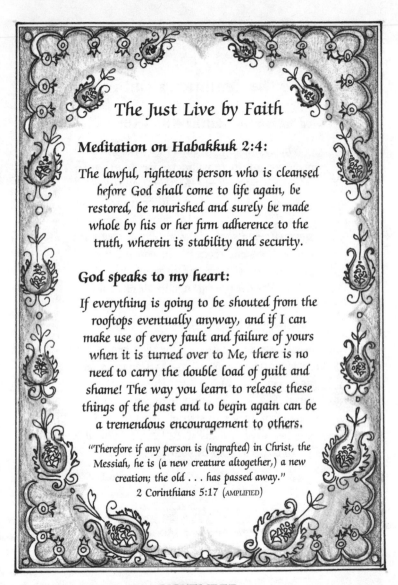

The Just Live by Faith

Meditation on Habakkuk 2:4:

The lawful, righteous person who is cleansed
before God shall come to life again, be
restored, be nourished and surely be made
whole by his or her firm adherence to the
truth, wherein is stability and security.

God speaks to my heart:

If everything is going to be shouted from the
rooftops eventually anyway, and if I can
make use of every fault and failure of yours
when it is turned over to Me, there is no
need to carry the double load of guilt and
shame! The way you learn to release these
things of the past and to begin again can be
a tremendous encouragement to others.

"Therefore if any person is (ingrafted) in Christ, the
Messiah, he is (a new creature altogether,) a new
creation; the old . . . has passed away."
2 Corinthians 5:17 (AMPLIFIED)

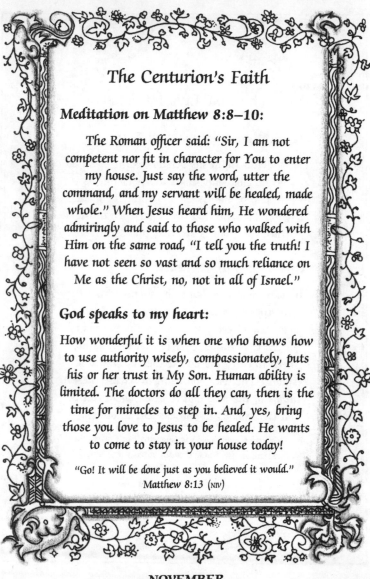

The Centurion's Faith

Meditation on Matthew 8:8–10:

The Roman officer said: "Sir, I am not competent nor fit in character for You to enter my house. Just say the word, utter the command, and my servant will be healed, made whole." When Jesus heard him, He wondered admiringly and said to those who walked with Him on the same road, "I tell you the truth! I have not seen so vast and so much reliance on Me as the Christ, no, not in all of Israel."

God speaks to my heart:

How wonderful it is when one who knows how to use authority wisely, compassionately, puts his or her trust in My Son. Human ability is limited. The doctors do all they can, then is the time for miracles to step in. And, yes, bring those you love to Jesus to be healed. He wants to come to stay in your house today!

"Go! It will be done just as you believed it would."
Matthew 8:13 (NIV)

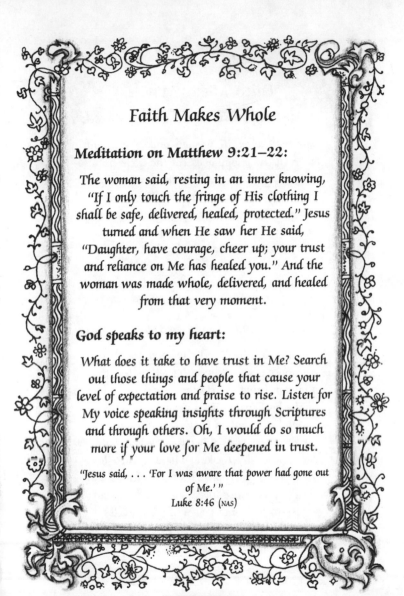

Faith Makes Whole

Meditation on Matthew 9:21–22:

The woman said, resting in an inner knowing, "If I only touch the fringe of His clothing I shall be safe, delivered, healed, protected." Jesus turned and when He saw her He said, "Daughter, have courage, cheer up; your trust and reliance on Me has healed you." And the woman was made whole, delivered, and healed from that very moment.

God speaks to my heart:

What does it take to have trust in Me? Search out those things and people that cause your level of expectation and praise to rise. Listen for My voice speaking insights through Scriptures and through others. Oh, I would do so much more if your love for Me deepened in trust.

"Jesus said, . . . 'For I was aware that power had gone out of Me.' "
Luke 8:46 (NAS)

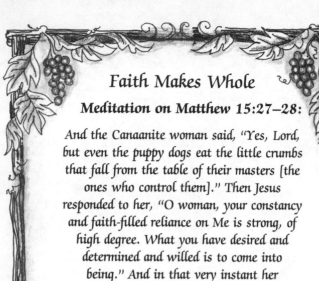

Faith Makes Whole

Meditation on Matthew 15:27–28:

And the Canaanite woman said, "Yes, Lord, but even the puppy dogs eat the little crumbs that fall from the table of their masters [the ones who control them]." Then Jesus responded to her, "O woman, your constancy and faith-filled reliance on Me is strong, of high degree. What you have desired and determined and willed is to come into being." And in that very instant her daughter was made whole.

God speaks to my heart:

Even though the Gentile woman accepted the cultural classification of herself as less than a human being in relation to Jesus, the love she had for her daughter and her utter confidence that in Jesus was healing and wholeness caused her to seek Him out face-to-face. Keep asking Me for greater love, for more compassion. Desire wholeness and healing for those loved ones. Seek Me out face-to-face, and you will see miracles!

"Don't be afraid; just believe."
Luke 8:50 (NIV)

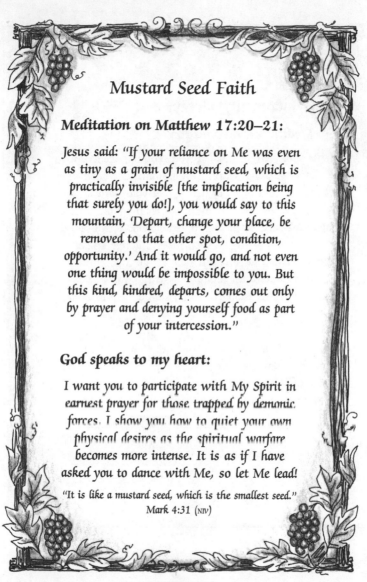

Mustard Seed Faith

Meditation on Matthew 17:20–21:

Jesus said: "If your reliance on Me was even as tiny as a grain of mustard seed, which is practically invisible [the implication being that surely you do!], you would say to this mountain, 'Depart, change your place, be removed to that other spot, condition, opportunity.' And it would go, and not even one thing would be impossible to you. But this kind, kindred, departs, comes out only by prayer and denying yourself food as part of your intercession."

God speaks to my heart:

I want you to participate with My Spirit in earnest prayer for those trapped by demonic forces. I show you how to quiet your own physical desires as the spiritual warfare becomes more intense. It is as if I have asked you to dance with Me, so let Me lead!

"It is like a mustard seed, which is the smallest seed."
Mark 4:31 (NIV)

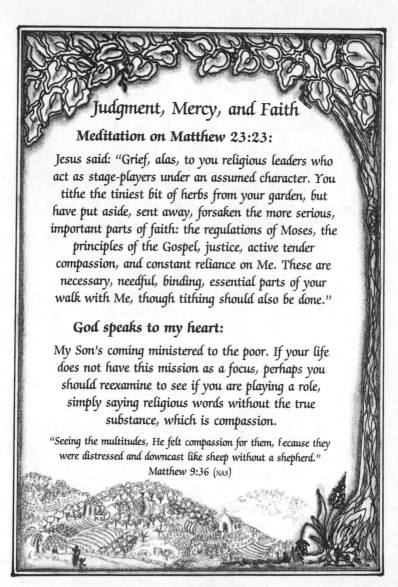

Judgment, Mercy, and Faith

Meditation on Matthew 23:23:

Jesus said: "Grief, alas, to you religious leaders who act as stage-players under an assumed character. You tithe the tiniest bit of herbs from your garden, but have put aside, sent away, forsaken the more serious, important parts of faith: the regulations of Moses, the principles of the Gospel, justice, active tender compassion, and constant reliance on Me. These are necessary, needful, binding, essential parts of your walk with Me, though tithing should also be done."

God speaks to my heart:

My Son's coming ministered to the poor. If your life does not have this mission as a focus, perhaps you should reexamine to see if you are playing a role, simply saying religious words without the true substance, which is compassion.

"Seeing the multitudes, He felt compassion for them, because they were distressed and downcast like sheep without a shepherd."
Matthew 9:36 (NAS)

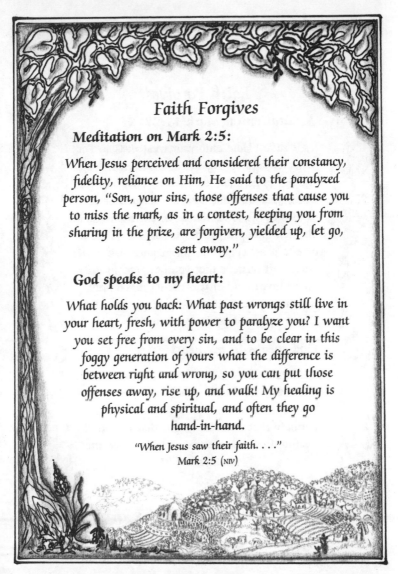

Faith Forgives

Meditation on Mark 2:5:

When Jesus perceived and considered their constancy, fidelity, reliance on Him, He said to the paralyzed person, "Son, your sins, those offenses that cause you to miss the mark, as in a contest, keeping you from sharing in the prize, are forgiven, yielded up, let go, sent away."

God speaks to my heart:

What holds you back: What past wrongs still live in your heart, fresh, with power to paralyze you? I want you set free from every sin, and to be clear in this foggy generation of yours what the difference is between right and wrong, so you can put those offenses away, rise up, and walk! My healing is physical and spiritual, and often they go hand-in-hand.

"When Jesus saw their faith. . . ."
Mark 2:5 (NIV)

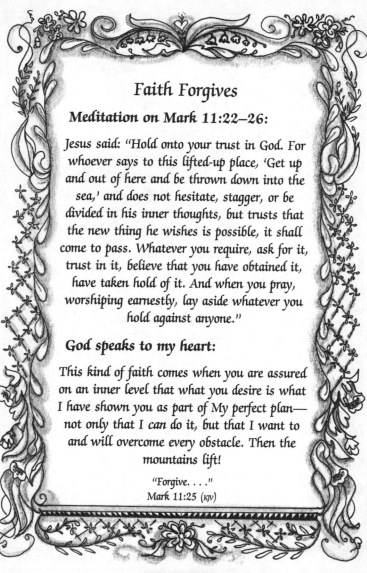

Faith Forgives

Meditation on Mark 11:22–26:

Jesus said: "Hold onto your trust in God. For whoever says to this lifted-up place, 'Get up and out of here and be thrown down into the sea,' and does not hesitate, stagger, or be divided in his inner thoughts, but trusts that the new thing he wishes is possible, it shall come to pass. Whatever you require, ask for it, trust in it, believe that you have obtained it, have taken hold of it. And when you pray, worshiping earnestly, lay aside whatever you hold against anyone."

God speaks to my heart:

This kind of faith comes when you are assured on an inner level that what you desire is what I have shown you as part of My perfect plan— not only that I *can* do it, but that I want to and will overcome every obstacle. Then the mountains lift!

"Forgive. . . ."
Mark 11:25 (kjv)

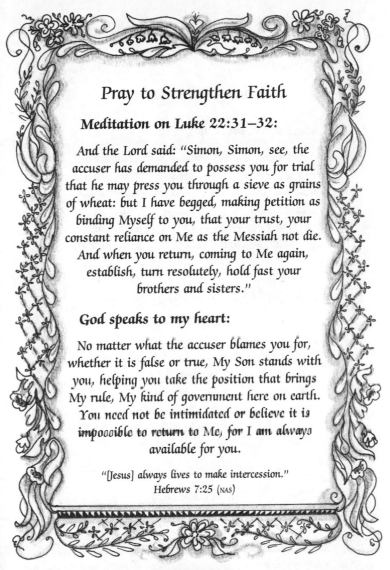

Pray to Strengthen Faith

Meditation on Luke 22:31–32:

And the Lord said: "Simon, Simon, see, the accuser has demanded to possess you for trial that he may press you through a sieve as grains of wheat: but I have begged, making petition as binding Myself to you, that your trust, your constant reliance on Me as the Messiah not die. And when you return, coming to Me again, establish, turn resolutely, hold fast your brothers and sisters."

God speaks to my heart:

No matter what the accuser blames you for, whether it is false or true, My Son stands with you, helping you take the position that brings My rule, My kind of government here on earth. You need not be intimidated or believe it is impossible to return to Me, for I am always available for you.

"[Jesus] always lives to make intercession."
Hebrews 7:25 (NAS)

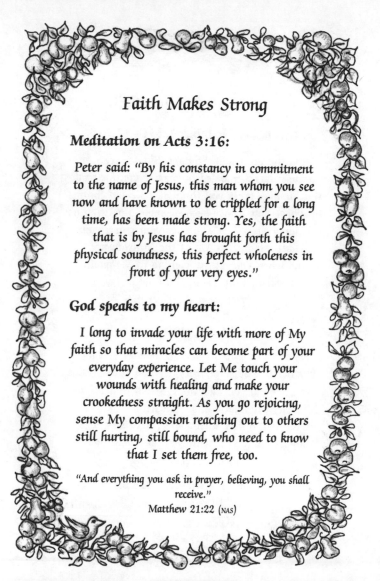

Faith Makes Strong

Meditation on Acts 3:16:

Peter said: "By his constancy in commitment to the name of Jesus, this man whom you see now and have known to be crippled for a long time, has been made strong. Yes, the faith that is by Jesus has brought forth this physical soundness, this perfect wholeness in front of your very eyes."

God speaks to my heart:

I long to invade your life with more of My faith so that miracles can become part of your everyday experience. Let Me touch your wounds with healing and make your crookedness straight. As you go rejoicing, sense My compassion reaching out to others still hurting, still bound, who need to know that I set them free, too.

"And everything you ask in prayer, believing, you shall receive."
Matthew 21:22 (NAS)

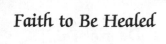

Faith to Be Healed

Meditation on Acts 14:8–10:

And there lived a certain man at Lystra, weak, crippled, unable to use his feet, being lame since birth, who had never walked at any time. That man heard Paul speak, gazing intently at him. Perceiving that the man had conviction of religious truth, a steady, constant reliance on Christ for his healing (salvation and deliverance in order to make him whole), Paul said with a mighty voice, "Stand up! Get up on your feet!" And the man jumped up and walked all around.

God speaks to my heart:

I love you. Of course My will is for your healing, health, wholeness. Keep on seeking to know Me. Keep on thanking Me, praising Me, looking to Me as the source, spring, and answer to your necessity. I am here for you and those you bring to Me.

"And he sprang up and walked."
Acts 14:10 (RSV)

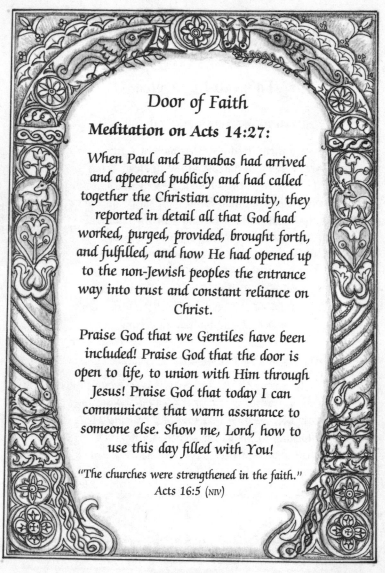

Door of Faith

Meditation on Acts 14:27:

When Paul and Barnabas had arrived and appeared publicly and had called together the Christian community, they reported in detail all that God had worked, purged, provided, brought forth, and fulfilled, and how He had opened up to the non-Jewish peoples the entrance way into trust and constant reliance on Christ.

Praise God that we Gentiles have been included! Praise God that the door is open to life, to union with Him through Jesus! Praise God that today I can communicate that warm assurance to someone else. Show me, Lord, how to use this day filled with You!

"The churches were strengthened in the faith."
Acts 16:5 (NIV)

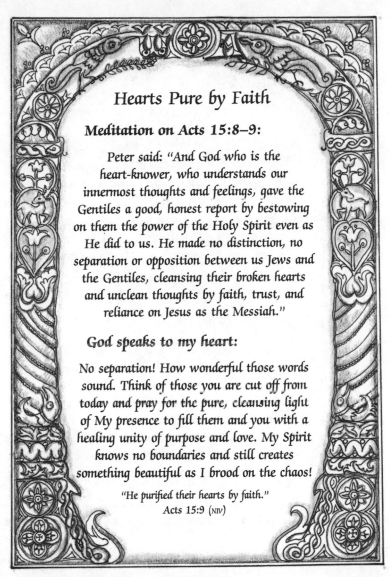

Hearts Pure by Faith

Meditation on Acts 15:8–9:

Peter said: "And God who is the heart-knower, who understands our innermost thoughts and feelings, gave the Gentiles a good, honest report by bestowing on them the power of the Holy Spirit even as He did to us. He made no distinction, no separation or opposition between us Jews and the Gentiles, cleansing their broken hearts and unclean thoughts by faith, trust, and reliance on Jesus as the Messiah."

God speaks to my heart:

No separation! How wonderful those words sound. Think of those you are cut off from today and pray for the pure, cleansing light of My presence to fill them and you with a healing unity of purpose and love. My Spirit knows no boundaries and still creates something beautiful as I brood on the chaos!

"He purified their hearts by faith."
Acts 15:9 (NIV)

Justified by Faith

Meditation on Romans 3:28:

Paul said: "Therefore we take an inventory and come to the conclusion that a human being is rendered free and innocent, is made righteous solely by trust and reliance on Jesus as the Messiah. This is separate and apart from any toil or effort regarding the regulations of Moses' law and the principles of the Gospel."

God speaks to my heart:

Laws and rituals do not cause one to enter into relationship with Me, but are guides pointing to a relationship. You can never on your own fulfill all the expectations or be "good enough" to stand proud in My presence. Choose My way, the humble way, that grabs hold of My hand and asks only to walk beside Me always. In this position, the servant's towel and basin become your indispensable tools, and your works have meaning beyond yourself.

"Therefore, having been justified by faith, we have peace."
Romans 5:1 (NKJ)

Faith by Hearing

Meditation on Romans 10:17:

Rely on Jesus as the Christ sent by God as Savior, Redeemer, Messiah. This trust grows and is accompanied by the act of hearing, and hearing by the command, the word of God (*rhema*) pouring forth.

God speaks to my heart:

Faith is not static or at a standstill. Faith is a moving, growing adventure that increases in your spirit so that you follow through with appropriate actions as you listen and soak in My Word. The Spirit of God speaks specific truth to your inner self in such clear tones that you know that you know. Isn't this the rock that I build on?

"See that you do not refuse him who is speaking."
Hebrews 12:25 (RSV)

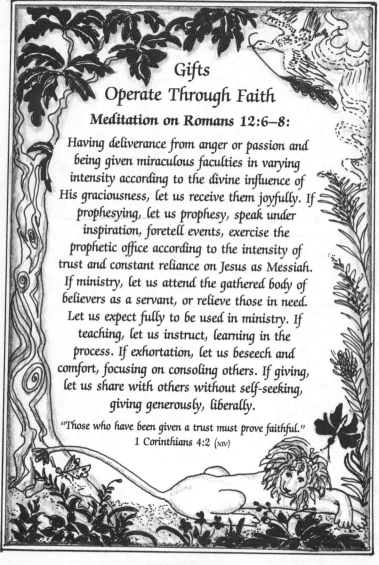

Gifts
Operate Through Faith

Meditation on Romans 12:6–8:

Having deliverance from anger or passion and being given miraculous faculties in varying intensity according to the divine influence of His graciousness, let us receive them joyfully. If prophesying, let us prophesy, speak under inspiration, foretell events, exercise the prophetic office according to the intensity of trust and constant reliance on Jesus as Messiah. If ministry, let us attend the gathered body of believers as a servant, or relieve those in need. Let us expect fully to be used in ministry. If teaching, let us instruct, learning in the process. If exhortation, let us beseech and comfort, focusing on consoling others. If giving, let us share with others without self-seeking, giving generously, liberally.

"Those who have been given a trust must prove faithful."
1 Corinthians 4:2 (NIV)

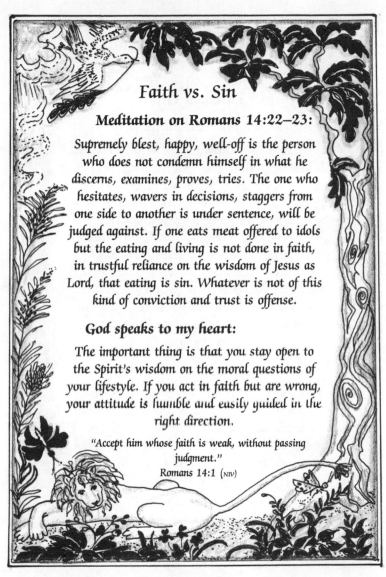

Faith vs. Sin

Meditation on Romans 14:22–23:

Supremely blest, happy, well-off is the person
who does not condemn himself in what he
discerns, examines, proves, tries. The one who
hesitates, wavers in decisions, staggers from
one side to another is under sentence, will be
judged against. If one eats meat offered to idols
but the eating and living is not done in faith,
in trustful reliance on the wisdom of Jesus as
Lord, that eating is sin. Whatever is not of this
kind of conviction and trust is offense.

God speaks to my heart:

The important thing is that you stay open to
the Spirit's wisdom on the moral questions of
your lifestyle. If you act in faith but are wrong,
your attitude is humble and easily guided in the
right direction.

"Accept him whose faith is weak, without passing
judgment."
Romans 14:1 (NIV)

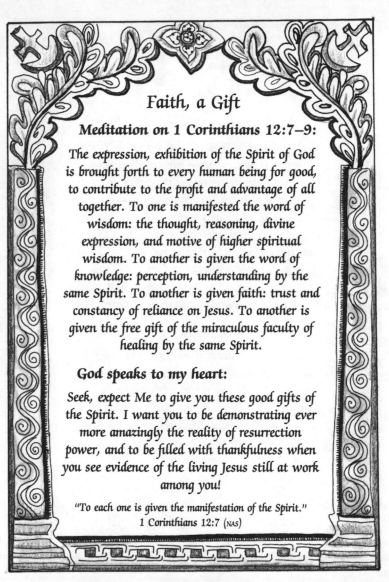

Faith, a Gift

Meditation on 1 Corinthians 12:7–9:

The expression, exhibition of the Spirit of God
is brought forth to every human being for good,
to contribute to the profit and advantage of all
together. To one is manifested the word of
wisdom: the thought, reasoning, divine
expression, and motive of higher spiritual
wisdom. To another is given the word of
knowledge: perception, understanding by the
same Spirit. To another is given faith: trust and
constancy of reliance on Jesus. To another is
given the free gift of the miraculous faculty of
healing by the same Spirit.

God speaks to my heart:

Seek, expect Me to give you these good gifts of
the Spirit. I want you to be demonstrating ever
more amazingly the reality of resurrection
power, and to be filled with thankfulness when
you see evidence of the living Jesus still at work
among you!

"To each one is given the manifestation of the Spirit."
1 Corinthians 12:7 (NAS)

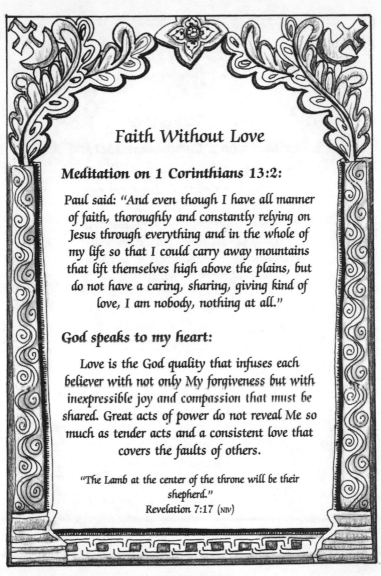

Faith Without Love

Meditation on 1 Corinthians 13:2:

Paul said: "And even though I have all manner of faith, thoroughly and constantly relying on Jesus through everything and in the whole of my life so that I could carry away mountains that lift themselves high above the plains, but do not have a caring, sharing, giving kind of love, I am nobody, nothing at all."

God speaks to my heart:

Love is the God quality that infuses each believer with not only My forgiveness but with inexpressible joy and compassion that must be shared. Great acts of power do not reveal Me so much as tender acts and a consistent love that covers the faults of others.

"The Lamb at the center of the throne will be their shepherd."
Revelation 7:17 (NIV)

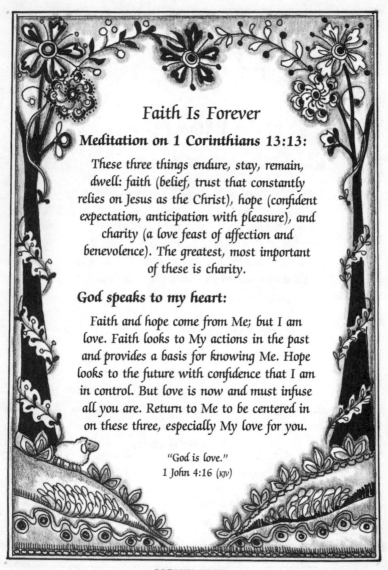

Faith Is Forever

Meditation on 1 Corinthians 13:13:

These three things endure, stay, remain, dwell: faith (belief, trust that constantly relies on Jesus as the Christ), hope (confident expectation, anticipation with pleasure), and charity (a love feast of affection and benevolence). The greatest, most important of these is charity.

God speaks to my heart:

Faith and hope come from Me; but I am love. Faith looks to My actions in the past and provides a basis for knowing Me. Hope looks to the future with confidence that I am in control. But love is now and must infuse all you are. Return to Me to be centered in on these three, especially My love for you.

"God is love."
1 John 4:16 (kjv)

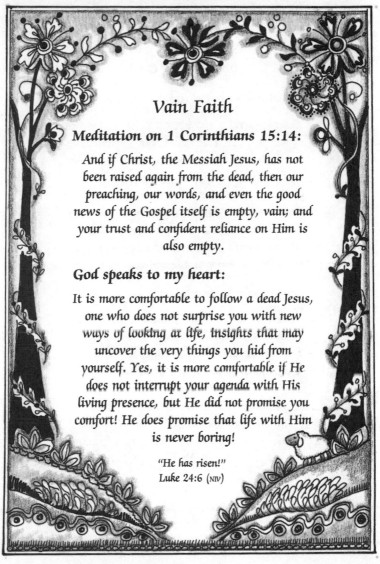

Vain Faith

Meditation on 1 Corinthians 15:14:

And if Christ, the Messiah Jesus, has not
been raised again from the dead, then our
preaching, our words, and even the good
news of the Gospel itself is empty, vain; and
your trust and confident reliance on Him is
also empty.

God speaks to my heart:

It is more comfortable to follow a dead Jesus,
one who does not surprise you with new
ways of looking at life, insights that may
uncover the very things you hid from
yourself. Yes, it is more comfortable if He
does not interrupt your agenda with His
living presence, but He did not promise you
comfort! He does promise that life with Him
is never boring!

"He has risen!"
Luke 24:6 (NIV)

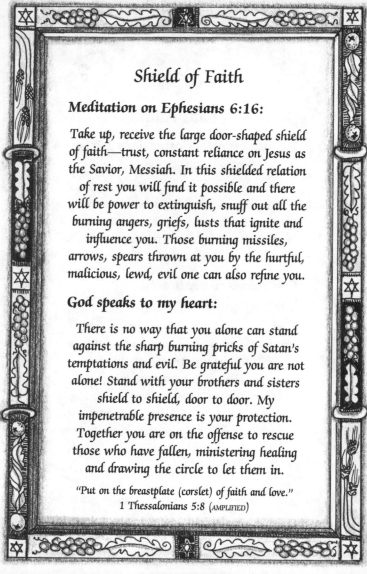

Shield of Faith

Meditation on Ephesians 6:16:

Take up, receive the large door-shaped shield
of faith—trust, constant reliance on Jesus as
the Savior, Messiah. In this shielded relation
of rest you will find it possible and there
will be power to extinguish, snuff out all the
burning angers, griefs, lusts that ignite and
influence you. Those burning missiles,
arrows, spears thrown at you by the hurtful,
malicious, lewd, evil one can also refine you.

God speaks to my heart:

There is no way that you alone can stand
against the sharp burning pricks of Satan's
temptations and evil. Be grateful you are not
alone! Stand with your brothers and sisters
shield to shield, door to door. My
impenetrable presence is your protection.
Together you are on the offense to rescue
those who have fallen, ministering healing
and drawing the circle to let them in.

"Put on the breastplate (corslet) of faith and love."
1 Thessalonians 5:8 (AMPLIFIED)

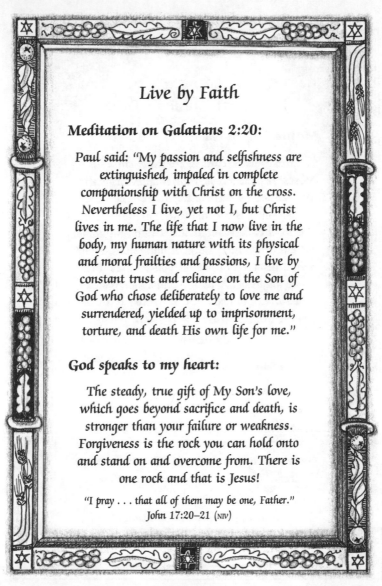

Live by Faith

Meditation on Galatians 2:20:

Paul said: "My passion and selfishness are extinguished, impaled in complete companionship with Christ on the cross. Nevertheless I live, yet not I, but Christ lives in me. The life that I now live in the body, my human nature with its physical and moral frailties and passions, I live by constant trust and reliance on the Son of God who chose deliberately to love me and surrendered, yielded up to imprisonment, torture, and death His own life for me."

God speaks to my heart:

The steady, true gift of My Son's love, which goes beyond sacrifice and death, is stronger than your failure or weakness. Forgiveness is the rock you can hold onto and stand on and overcome from. There is one rock and that is Jesus!

"I pray . . . that all of them may be one, Father."
John 17:20–21 (NIV)

The Spirit Through Faith

Meditation on Galatians 3:13–14:

Christ has rescued us from the curse of Moses' regulations and the rigid principles of the Gospel, by becoming Himself a curse for us. For it is written in the Scriptures, "Cursed is everyone that hangs on a tree." He did this that the benefit and consecration might be able to come on the Gentiles, that we might get hold of, obtain the divine assurance of good in the promise of the Spirit through trust and constant reliance upon Him.

God speaks to my heart:

Many today use Jesus' name as a curse. Let that remind you that He was cursed for you and for those others, also. Through the bitter, venomous words comes the pure sweetness of His response, "Father, forgive them. They don't know what they are doing."

"[We were redeemed] with the precious blood of Christ,
as of a lamb without blemish."
1 Peter 1:19 (kjv)

Children of God by Faith

Meditation on Galatians 3:26–27:

We are all sons and daughters produced by God because of our trust, our constant reliance on Jesus as the Messiah, the sent one of God. For as many as have been baptized, made fully wet, overwhelmed in Christ, we have put on Christ, have clothed ourselves as sinking into a garment, being arrayed with Him.

God speaks to my heart:

Confidence, faith in Me, is an inner decision based on a real relationship. This relationship is one in which you become part of God's family, exhibiting more and more qualities and characteristics that are God-like. As you change on the inside, you will desire the outside person, whom all can see, to represent Me also. You do not have to wear a beard and a bathrobe, but . . . think about it . . . put on love, joy, peace, humility, patience, gentleness, kindness to replace the rags of your own righteousness.

"And I will put a new spirit within you."
Ezekiel 11:19 (KJV)

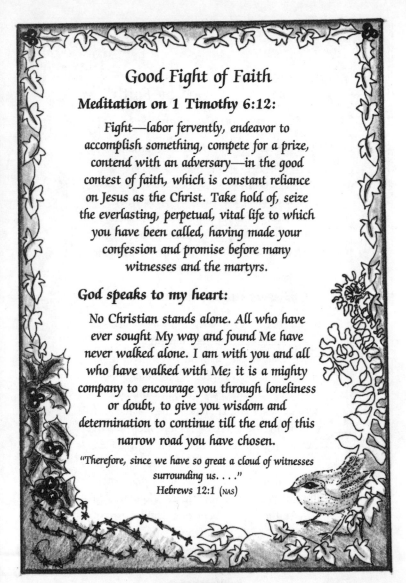

Good Fight of Faith

Meditation on 1 Timothy 6:12:

Fight—labor fervently, endeavor to accomplish something, compete for a prize, contend with an adversary—in the good contest of faith, which is constant reliance on Jesus as the Christ. Take hold of, seize the everlasting, perpetual, vital life to which you have been called, having made your confession and promise before many witnesses and the martyrs.

God speaks to my heart:

No Christian stands alone. All who have ever sought My way and found Me have never walked alone. I am with you and all who have walked with Me; it is a mighty company to encourage you through loneliness or doubt, to give you wisdom and determination to continue till the end of this narrow road you have chosen.

"Therefore, since we have so great a cloud of witnesses surrounding us. . . ."
Hebrews 12:1 (NAS)

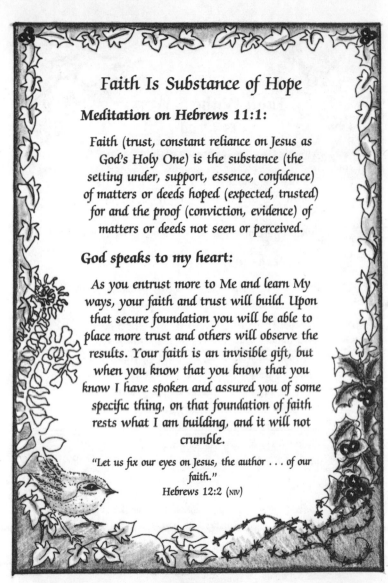

Faith Is Substance of Hope

Meditation on Hebrews 11:1:

Faith (trust, constant reliance on Jesus as
God's Holy One) is the substance (the
setting under, support, essence, confidence)
of matters or deeds hoped (expected, trusted)
for and the proof (conviction, evidence) of
matters or deeds not seen or perceived.

God speaks to my heart:

As you entrust more to Me and learn My
ways, your faith and trust will build. Upon
that secure foundation you will be able to
place more trust and others will observe the
results. Your faith is an invisible gift, but
when you know that you know that you
know I have spoken and assured you of some
specific thing, on that foundation of faith
rests what I am building, and it will not
crumble.

"Let us fix our eyes on Jesus, the author . . . of our
faith."
Hebrews 12:2 (NIV)

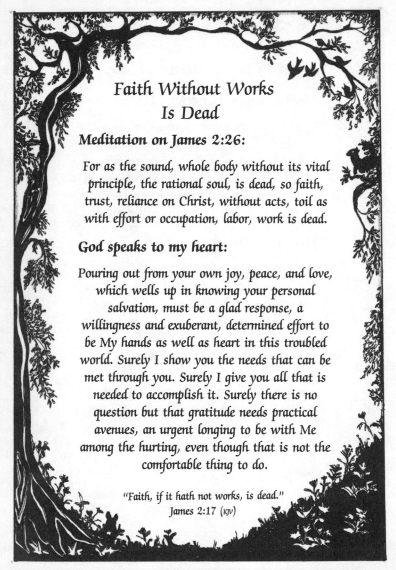

Faith Without Works Is Dead

Meditation on James 2:26:

For as the sound, whole body without its vital principle, the rational soul, is dead, so faith, trust, reliance on Christ, without acts, toil as with effort or occupation, labor, work is dead.

God speaks to my heart:

Pouring out from your own joy, peace, and love, which wells up in knowing your personal salvation, must be a glad response, a willingness and exuberant, determined effort to be My hands as well as heart in this troubled world. Surely I show you the needs that can be met through you. Surely I give you all that is needed to accomplish it. Surely there is no question but that gratitude needs practical avenues, an urgent longing to be with Me among the hurting, even though that is not the comfortable thing to do.

"Faith, if it hath not works, is dead."
James 2:17 (KJV)

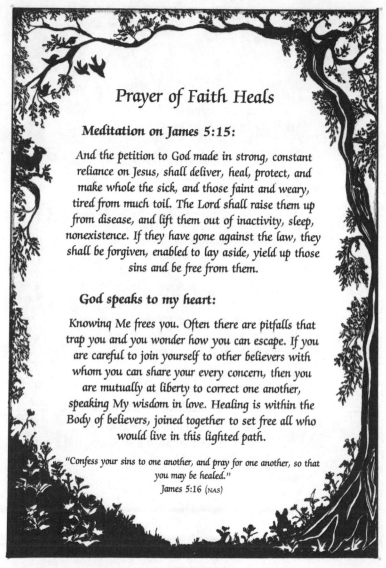

Prayer of Faith Heals

Meditation on James 5:15:

And the petition to God made in strong, constant reliance on Jesus, shall deliver, heal, protect, and make whole the sick, and those faint and weary, tired from much toil. The Lord shall raise them up from disease, and lift them out of inactivity, sleep, nonexistence. If they have gone against the law, they shall be forgiven, enabled to lay aside, yield up those sins and be free from them.

God speaks to my heart:

Knowing Me frees you. Often there are pitfalls that trap you and you wonder how you can escape. If you are careful to join yourself to other believers with whom you can share your every concern, then you are mutually at liberty to correct one another, speaking My wisdom in love. Healing is within the Body of believers, joined together to set free all who would live in this lighted path.

"Confess your sins to one another, and pray for one another, so that you may be healed."
James 5:16 (NAS)

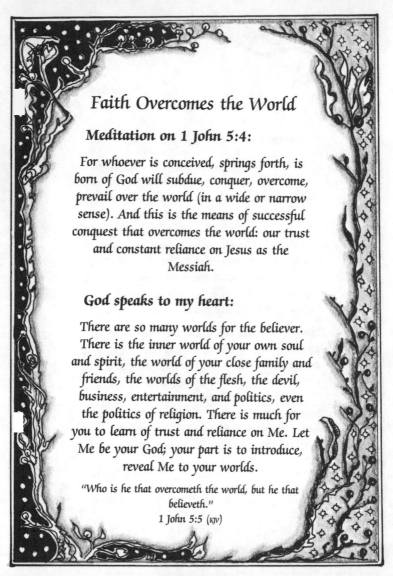

Faith Overcomes the World

Meditation on 1 John 5:4:

For whoever is conceived, springs forth, is born of God will subdue, conquer, overcome, prevail over the world (in a wide or narrow sense). And this is the means of successful conquest that overcomes the world: our trust and constant reliance on Jesus as the Messiah.

God speaks to my heart:

There are so many worlds for the believer. There is the inner world of your own soul and spirit, the world of your close family and friends, the worlds of the flesh, the devil, business, entertainment, and politics, even the politics of religion. There is much for you to learn of trust and reliance on Me. Let Me be your God; your part is to introduce, reveal Me to your worlds.

"Who is he that overcometh the world, but he that believeth."
1 John 5:5 (KJV)

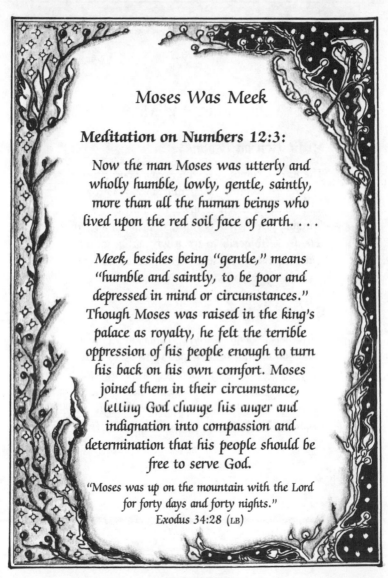

Moses Was Meek

Meditation on Numbers 12:3:

Now the man Moses was utterly and
wholly humble, lowly, gentle, saintly,
more than all the human beings who
lived upon the red soil face of earth. . . .

Meek, besides being "gentle," means
"humble and saintly, to be poor and
depressed in mind or circumstances."
Though Moses was raised in the king's
palace as royalty, he felt the terrible
oppression of his people enough to turn
his back on his own comfort. Moses
joined them in their circumstance,
letting God change his anger and
indignation into compassion and
determination that his people should be
free to serve God.

"Moses was up on the mountain with the Lord
for forty days and forty nights."
Exodus 34:28 (LB)

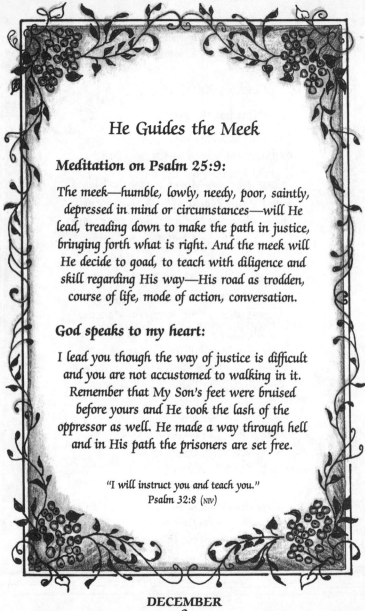

He Guides the Meek

Meditation on Psalm 25:9:

The meek—humble, lowly, needy, poor, saintly, depressed in mind or circumstances—will He lead, treading down to make the path in justice, bringing forth what is right. And the meek will He decide to goad, to teach with diligence and skill regarding His way—His road as trodden, course of life, mode of action, conversation.

God speaks to my heart:

I lead you though the way of justice is difficult and you are not accustomed to walking in it. Remember that My Son's feet were bruised before yours and He took the lash of the oppressor as well. He made a way through hell and in His path the prisoners are set free.

"I will instruct you and teach you."
Psalm 32:8 (NIV)

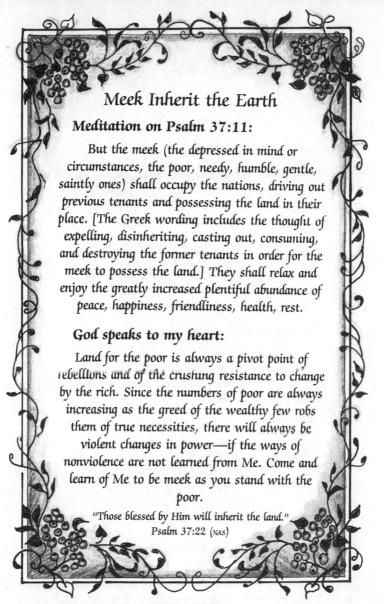

Meek Inherit the Earth

Meditation on Psalm 37:11:

But the meek (the depressed in mind or circumstances, the poor, needy, humble, gentle, saintly ones) shall occupy the nations, driving out previous tenants and possessing the land in their place. [The Greek wording includes the thought of expelling, disinheriting, casting out, consuming, and destroying the former tenants in order for the meek to possess the land.] They shall relax and enjoy the greatly increased plentiful abundance of peace, happiness, friendliness, health, rest.

God speaks to my heart:

Land for the poor is always a pivot point of rebellions and of the crushing resistance to change by the rich. Since the numbers of poor are always increasing as the greed of the wealthy few robs them of true necessities, there will always be violent changes in power—if the ways of nonviolence are not learned from Me. Come and learn of Me to be meek as you stand with the poor.

"Those blessed by Him will inherit the land."
Psalm 37:22 (NAS)

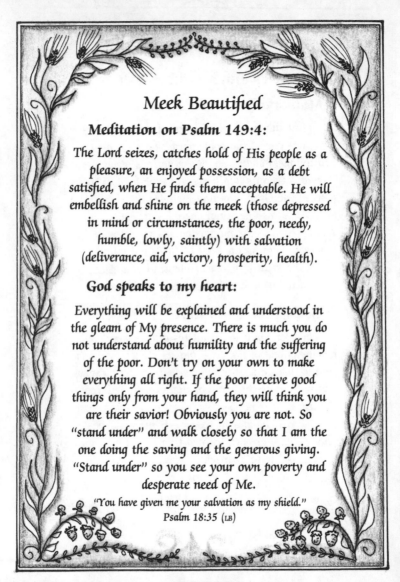

Meek Beautified

Meditation on Psalm 149:4:

The Lord seizes, catches hold of His people as a pleasure, an enjoyed possession, as a debt satisfied, when He finds them acceptable. He will embellish and shine on the meek (those depressed in mind or circumstances, the poor, needy, humble, lowly, saintly) with salvation (deliverance, aid, victory, prosperity, health).

God speaks to my heart:

Everything will be explained and understood in the gleam of My presence. There is much you do not understand about humility and the suffering of the poor. Don't try on your own to make everything all right. If the poor receive good things only from your hand, they will think you are their savior! Obviously you are not. So "stand under" and walk closely so that I am the one doing the saving and the generous giving. "Stand under" so you see your own poverty and desperate need of Me.

"You have given me your salvation as my shield."
Psalm 18:35 (LB)

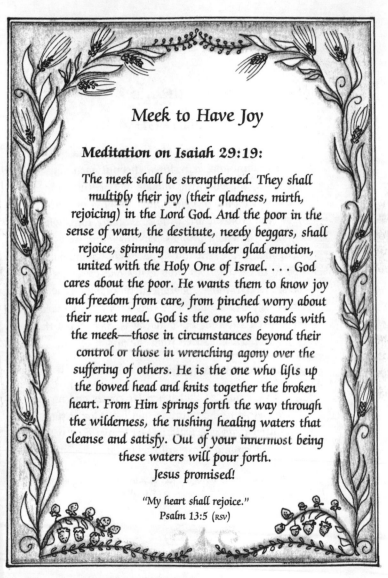

Meek to Have Joy

Meditation on Isaiah 29:19:

The meek shall be strengthened. They shall multiply their joy (their gladness, mirth, rejoicing) in the Lord God. And the poor in the sense of want, the destitute, needy beggars, shall rejoice, spinning around under glad emotion, united with the Holy One of Israel. . . . God cares about the poor. He wants them to know joy and freedom from care, from pinched worry about their next meal. God is the one who stands with the meek—those in circumstances beyond their control or those in wrenching agony over the suffering of others. He is the one who lifts up the bowed head and knits together the broken heart. From Him springs forth the way through the wilderness, the rushing healing waters that cleanse and satisfy. Out of your innermost being these waters will pour forth.
Jesus promised!

"My heart shall rejoice."
Psalm 13:5 (rsv)

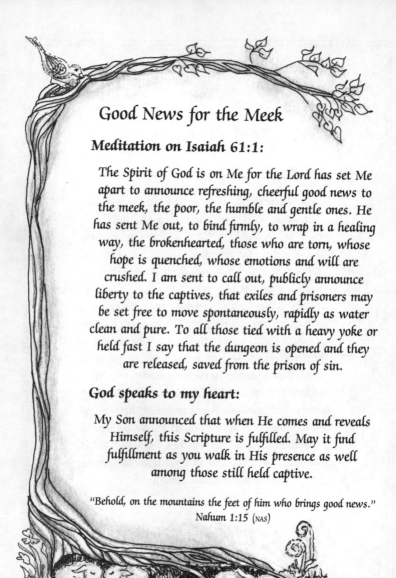

Good News for the Meek

Meditation on Isaiah 61:1:

The Spirit of God is on Me for the Lord has set Me apart to announce refreshing, cheerful good news to the meek, the poor, the humble and gentle ones. He has sent Me out, to bind firmly, to wrap in a healing way, the brokenhearted, those who are torn, whose hope is quenched, whose emotions and will are crushed. I am sent to call out, publicly announce liberty to the captives, that exiles and prisoners may be set free to move spontaneously, rapidly as water clean and pure. To all those tied with a heavy yoke or held fast I say that the dungeon is opened and they are released, saved from the prison of sin.

God speaks to my heart:

My Son announced that when He comes and reveals Himself, this Scripture is fulfilled. May it find fulfillment as you walk in His presence as well among those still held captive.

"Behold, on the mountains the feet of him who brings good news."
Nahum 1:15 (NAS)

Meek of the Earth

Meditation on Zephaniah 2:3:

Search out the Lord in worship and prayer, especially
you who are depressed in mind or circumstances from
whatever nation. Practice justice systematically and
habitually. Speak out what is right—national, moral,
and legal justice. Require gentleness, mercy, modesty,
humility. It may be you shall be kept close, hidden
under a covering in the age of the Lord's anger and
passion.

God speaks to my heart:

Be ready for My Son's coming. To make ready is to
prepare the way with justice at all levels of
government and to establish an environment where
the needs of the poor are taken seriously. Join with
those already involved in these tasks and let them see
that the God of the Old and New Covenants has
called you to demonstrate mercy.

"But seek ye first the kingdom of God."
Matthew 6:33 (KJV)

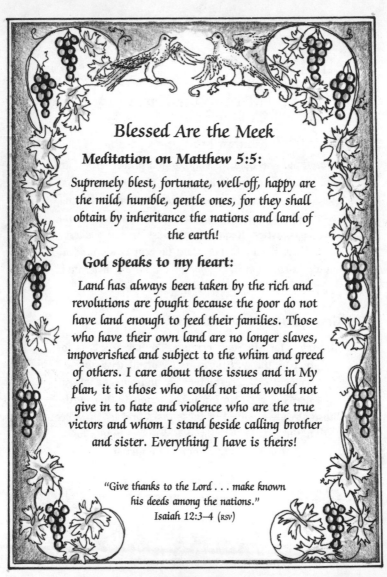

Blessed Are the Meek

Meditation on Matthew 5:5:

Supremely blest, fortunate, well-off, happy are
the mild, humble, gentle ones, for they shall
obtain by inheritance the nations and land of
the earth!

God speaks to my heart:

Land has always been taken by the rich and
revolutions are fought because the poor do not
have land enough to feed their families. Those
who have their own land are no longer slaves,
impoverished and subject to the whim and greed
of others. I care about those issues and in My
plan, it is those who could not and would not
give in to hate and violence who are the true
victors and whom I stand beside calling brother
and sister. Everything I have is theirs!

"Give thanks to the Lord . . . make known
his deeds among the nations."
Isaiah 12:3–4 (RSV)

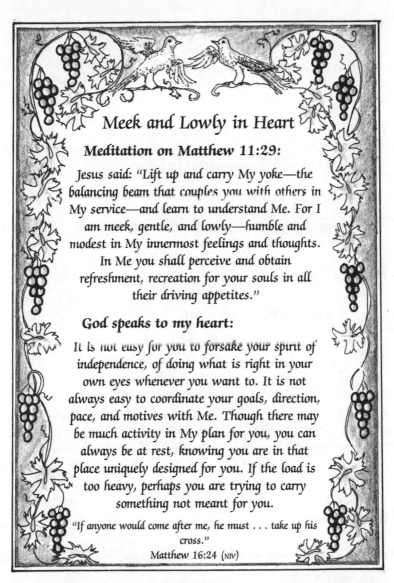

Meek and Lowly in Heart

Meditation on Matthew 11:29:

Jesus said: "Lift up and carry My yoke—the balancing beam that couples you with others in My service—and learn to understand Me. For I am meek, gentle, and lowly—humble and modest in My innermost feelings and thoughts. In Me you shall perceive and obtain refreshment, recreation for your souls in all their driving appetites."

God speaks to my heart:

It is not easy for you to forsake your spirit of independence, of doing what is right in your own eyes whenever you want to. It is not always easy to coordinate your goals, direction, pace, and motives with Me. Though there may be much activity in My plan for you, you can always be at rest, knowing you are in that place uniquely designed for you. If the load is too heavy, perhaps you are trying to carry something not meant for you.

"If anyone would come after me, he must . . . take up his cross."

Matthew 16:24 (NIV)

DECEMBER
9

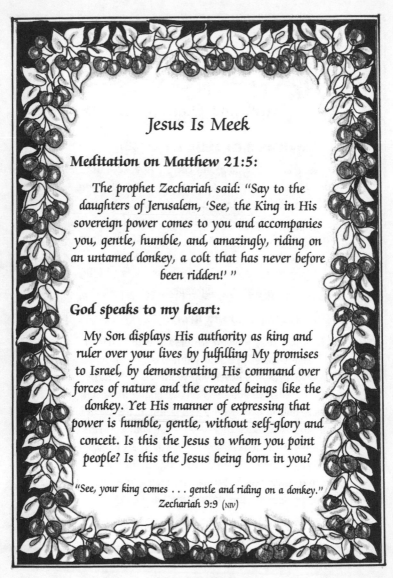

Jesus Is Meek

Meditation on Matthew 21:5:

The prophet Zechariah said: "Say to the daughters of Jerusalem, 'See, the King in His sovereign power comes to you and accompanies you, gentle, humble, and, amazingly, riding on an untamed donkey, a colt that has never before been ridden!' "

God speaks to my heart:

My Son displays His authority as king and ruler over your lives by fulfilling My promises to Israel, by demonstrating His command over forces of nature and the created beings like the donkey. Yet His manner of expressing that power is humble, gentle, without self-glory and conceit. Is this the Jesus to whom you point people? Is this the Jesus being born in you?

"See, your king comes . . . gentle and riding on a donkey."
Zechariah 9:9 (NIV)

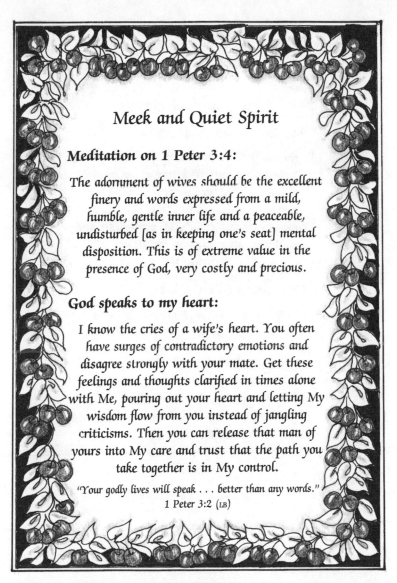

Meek and Quiet Spirit

Meditation on 1 Peter 3:4:

The adornment of wives should be the excellent
finery and words expressed from a mild,
humble, gentle inner life and a peaceable,
undisturbed [as in keeping one's seat] mental
disposition. This is of extreme value in the
presence of God, very costly and precious.

God speaks to my heart:

I know the cries of a wife's heart. You often
have surges of contradictory emotions and
disagree strongly with your mate. Get these
feelings and thoughts clarified in times alone
with Me, pouring out your heart and letting My
wisdom flow from you instead of jangling
criticisms. Then you can release that man of
yours into My care and trust that the path you
take together is in My control.

"Your godly lives will speak . . . better than any words."
1 Peter 3:2 (LB)

Truth and Meekness

Meditation on Psalm 45:4:

To the king: "And in your magnificent splendor and glorious beauty, ride forward in goodness and prosperity because you choose truth (stability, certainty, trustworthiness). You choose meekness (mildness, gentleness) and righteousness (national, moral, and legal justice)."

God speaks to my heart:

The people of every nation cry out for leadership that will remain true to promises held before taking office and ideals of righting wrongs. Inevitably leaders fail and greed overwhelms good intentions so that injustice reigns again.

Pray for your leaders to overcome those temptations and stand with those who would hold true to and flow with My living Word, shaping a reign of peace on earth as it is in heaven.

"Find a man, one who does justice
and seeks truth."
Jeremiah 5:1 (RSV)

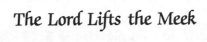

The Lord Lifts the Meek

Meditation on Psalm 147:6:

The Lord encompasses, relieves, restores the
depressed in mind or circumstances, the needy
and poor, the humble, gentle and saintly ones.
He puts down to the ground, humiliates, makes
low those who are morally wrong, actively bad,
guilty, ungodly.

God speaks to my heart:

You are a part of My arms stretched out to
comfort those in need. You are a part of My
voice making plain what is justice, what is
necessary to bring about a meaningful, decent
life for all My people. Yet never lose the
awareness of your own need for My correction
and My comfort. It is a two-way street.

"He will beautify the meek with salvation."
Psalm 149:4 (KJV)

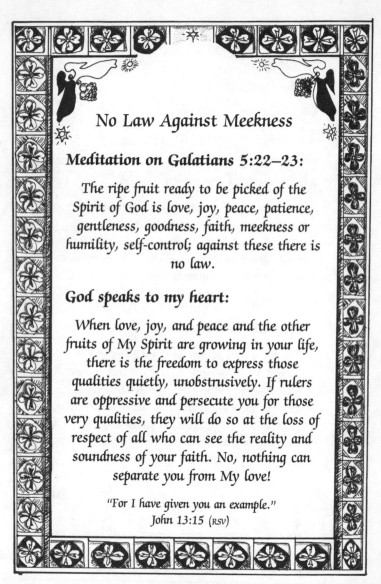

No Law Against Meekness

Meditation on Galatians 5:22–23:

The ripe fruit ready to be picked of the Spirit of God is love, joy, peace, patience, gentleness, goodness, faith, meekness or humility, self-control; against these there is no law.

God speaks to my heart:

When love, joy, and peace and the other fruits of My Spirit are growing in your life, there is the freedom to express those qualities quietly, unobstrusively. If rulers are oppressive and persecute you for those very qualities, they will do so at the loss of respect of all who can see the reality and soundness of your faith. No, nothing can separate you from My love!

"For I have given you an example."
John 13:15 (RSV)

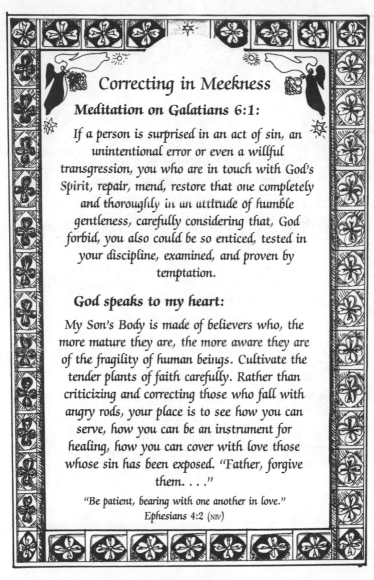

Correcting in Meekness

Meditation on Galatians 6:1:

If a person is surprised in an act of sin, an unintentional error or even a willful transgression, you who are in touch with God's Spirit, repair, mend, restore that one completely and thoroughly in an attitude of humble gentleness, carefully considering that, God forbid, you also could be so enticed, tested in your discipline, examined, and proven by temptation.

God speaks to my heart:

My Son's Body is made of believers who, the more mature they are, the more aware they are of the fragility of human beings. Cultivate the tender plants of faith carefully. Rather than criticizing and correcting those who fall with angry rods, your place is to see how you can serve, how you can be an instrument for healing, how you can cover with love those whose sin has been exposed. "Father, forgive them. . . ."

"Be patient, bearing with one another in love."
Ephesians 4:2 (NIV)

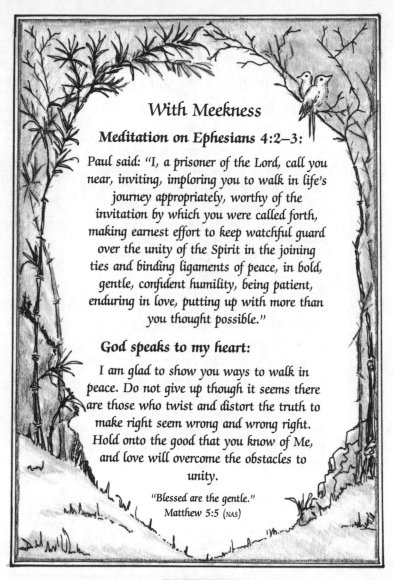

With Meekness

Meditation on Ephesians 4:2–3:

Paul said: "I, a prisoner of the Lord, call you near, inviting, imploring you to walk in life's journey appropriately, worthy of the invitation by which you were called forth, making earnest effort to keep watchful guard over the unity of the Spirit in the joining ties and binding ligaments of peace, in bold, gentle, confident humility, being patient, enduring in love, putting up with more than you thought possible."

God speaks to my heart:

I am glad to show you ways to walk in peace. Do not give up though it seems there are those who twist and distort the truth to make right seem wrong and wrong right. Hold onto the good that you know of Me, and love will overcome the obstacles to unity.

"Blessed are the gentle."
Matthew 5:5 (NAS)

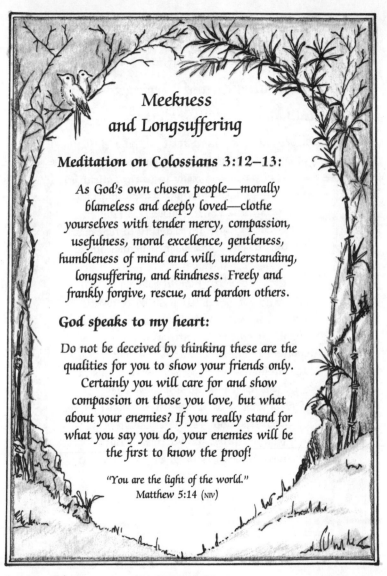

Meekness and Longsuffering

Meditation on Colossians 3:12–13:

As God's own chosen people—morally blameless and deeply loved—clothe yourselves with tender mercy, compassion, usefulness, moral excellence, gentleness, humbleness of mind and will, understanding, longsuffering, and kindness. Freely and frankly forgive, rescue, and pardon others.

God speaks to my heart:

Do not be deceived by thinking these are the qualities for you to show your friends only. Certainly you will care for and show compassion on those you love, but what about your enemies? If you really stand for what you say you do, your enemies will be the first to know the proof!

"You are the light of the world."
Matthew 5:14 (NIV)

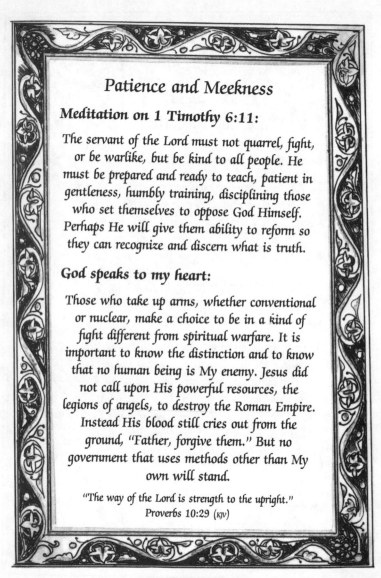

Patience and Meekness

Meditation on 1 Timothy 6:11:

The servant of the Lord must not quarrel, fight, or be warlike, but be kind to all people. He must be prepared and ready to teach, patient in gentleness, humbly training, disciplining those who set themselves to oppose God Himself. Perhaps He will give them ability to reform so they can recognize and discern what is truth.

God speaks to my heart:

Those who take up arms, whether conventional or nuclear, make a choice to be in a kind of fight different from spiritual warfare. It is important to know the distinction and to know that no human being is My enemy. Jesus did not call upon His powerful resources, the legions of angels, to destroy the Roman Empire. Instead His blood still cries out from the ground, "Father, forgive them." But no government that uses methods other than My own will stand.

"The way of the Lord is strength to the upright."
Proverbs 10:29 (KJV)

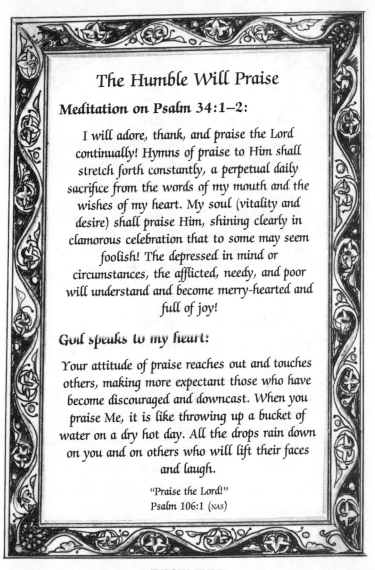

The Humble Will Praise

Meditation on Psalm 34:1–2:

I will adore, thank, and praise the Lord continually! Hymns of praise to Him shall stretch forth constantly, a perpetual daily sacrifice from the words of my mouth and the wishes of my heart. My soul (vitality and desire) shall praise Him, shining clearly in clamorous celebration that to some may seem foolish! The depressed in mind or circumstances, the afflicted, needy, and poor will understand and become merry-hearted and full of joy!

God speaks to my heart:

Your attitude of praise reaches out and touches others, making more expectant those who have become discouraged and downcast. When you praise Me, it is like throwing up a bucket of water on a dry hot day. All the drops rain down on you and on others who will lift their faces and laugh.

"Praise the Lord!"
Psalm 106:1 (NAS)

Meekness to All

Meditation on Titus 3:1–2:

Quietly remind the believer to be obedient to
those in power, those who have privilege and
force at their command, to submit to the
authority of their rulers, and to be prepared to
carry out every good deed, every just labor and
work. Be gentle and patient, acting in
moderation, showing meekness, gentleness, and
humility by word and actions to all human
beings.

God speaks to my heart:

People in power often do not see the suffering of
the poor, do not feel with compassion the results
of their acts of war. As you stand with the poor,
sharing in their lot, you will feel that tension of
injustice and want to lash out. Instead you can
determine that these injustices will not be done
through you or through your people. In secret
intercession and in public acts you will
respectfully say no to the evil ordered by
authority, yet encourage and praise the good.

"Whoever exalts himself shall be humbled."
Matthew 23:12 (NAS)

Receive with Meekness

Meditation on James 1:21:

Cast off and put away all dirtymindedness, all filthiness, and all overflowing abundance of depraved, malicious badness. Accept, take hold of the implanted, engrafted word, the Christlike reasoning and way of thinking that enables your very souls to be healed and delivered, made safe and whole.

God speaks to my heart:

Evil thoughts come, whether or not you open doors for them by what you watch on TV or read. Satan wants to ensnare your mind. But you can decide to shove out those thoughts and slam the door on them. Even if you still hear their mutterings, they have no power over you if you fill up the cracks and closets of your mind with the brilliant light of praise and the insights I share with you as we speak together intimately. My Word is an active lover of your soul, and jealous protector of your thoughts.

"[We] do not walk according to the flesh, but according to the Spirit."
Romans 8:4 (NAS)

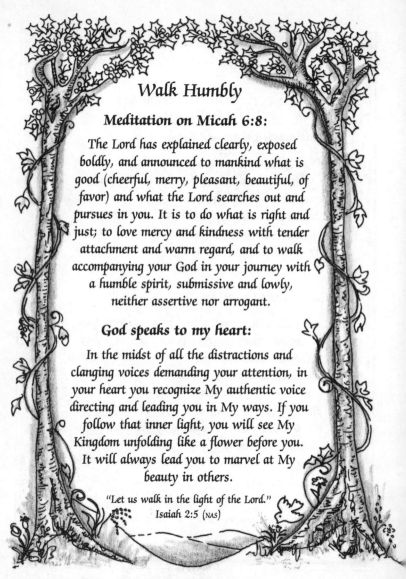

Walk Humbly

Meditation on Micah 6:8:

The Lord has explained clearly, exposed
boldly, and announced to mankind what is
good (cheerful, merry, pleasant, beautiful, of
favor) and what the Lord searches out and
pursues in you. It is to do what is right and
just; to love mercy and kindness with tender
attachment and warm regard, and to walk
accompanying your God in your journey with
a humble spirit, submissive and lowly,
neither assertive nor arrogant.

God speaks to my heart:

In the midst of all the distractions and
clanging voices demanding your attention, in
your heart you recognize My authentic voice
directing and leading you in My ways. If you
follow that inner light, you will see My
Kingdom unfolding like a flower before you.
It will always lead you to marvel at My
beauty in others.

"Let us walk in the light of the Lord."
Isaiah 2:5 (NAS)

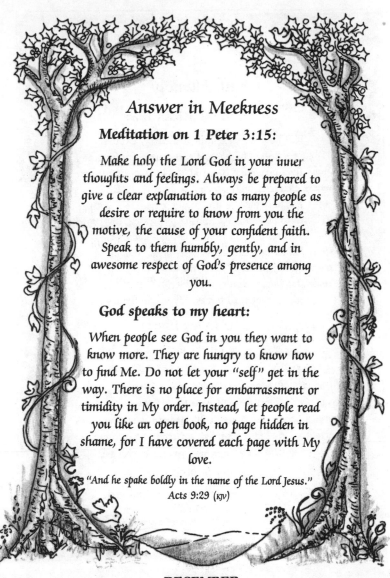

Answer in Meekness

Meditation on 1 Peter 3:15:

Make holy the Lord God in your inner
thoughts and feelings. Always be prepared to
give a clear explanation to as many people as
desire or require to know from you the
motive, the cause of your confident faith.
Speak to them humbly, gently, and in
awesome respect of God's presence among
you.

God speaks to my heart:

When people see God in you they want to
know more. They are hungry to know how
to find Me. Do not let your "self" get in the
way. There is no place for embarrassment or
timidity in My order. Instead, let people read
you like an open book, no page hidden in
shame, for I have covered each page with My
love.

"And he spake boldly in the name of the Lord Jesus."
Acts 9:29 (KJV)

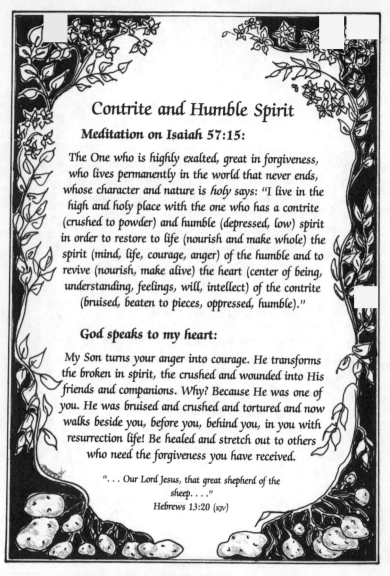

Contrite and Humble Spirit

Meditation on Isaiah 57:15:

The One who is highly exalted, great in forgiveness, who lives permanently in the world that never ends, whose character and nature is *holy* says: "I live in the high and holy place with the one who has a contrite (crushed to powder) and humble (depressed, low) spirit in order to restore to life (nourish and make whole) the spirit (mind, life, courage, anger) of the humble and to revive (nourish, make alive) the heart (center of being, understanding, feelings, will, intellect) of the contrite (bruised, beaten to pieces, oppressed, humble)."

God speaks to my heart:

My Son turns your anger into courage. He transforms the broken in spirit, the crushed and wounded into His friends and companions. Why? Because He was one of you. He was bruised and crushed and tortured and now walks beside you, before you, behind you, in you with resurrection life! Be healed and stretch out to others who need the forgiveness you have received.

"... Our Lord Jesus, that great shepherd of the
sheep...."
Hebrews 13:20 (kjv)

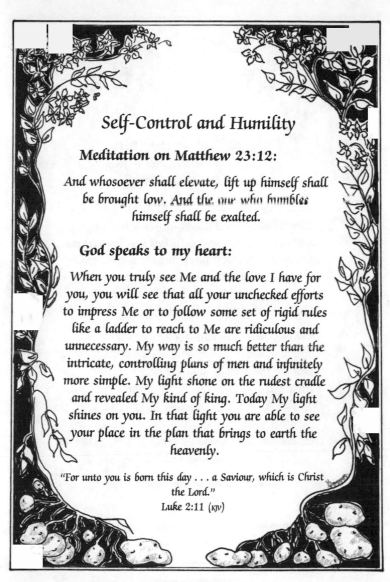

Self-Control and Humility

Meditation on Matthew 23:12:

And whosoever shall elevate, lift up himself shall
be brought low. And the one who humbles
himself shall be exalted.

God speaks to my heart:

When you truly see Me and the love I have for
you, you will see that all your unchecked efforts
to impress Me or to follow some set of rigid rules
like a ladder to reach to Me are ridiculous and
unnecessary. My way is so much better than the
intricate, controlling plans of men and infinitely
more simple. My light shone on the rudest cradle
and revealed My kind of king. Today My light
shines on you. In that light you are able to see
your place in the plan that brings to earth the
heavenly.

"For unto you is born this day . . . a Saviour, which is Christ
the Lord."
Luke 2:11 (kjv)

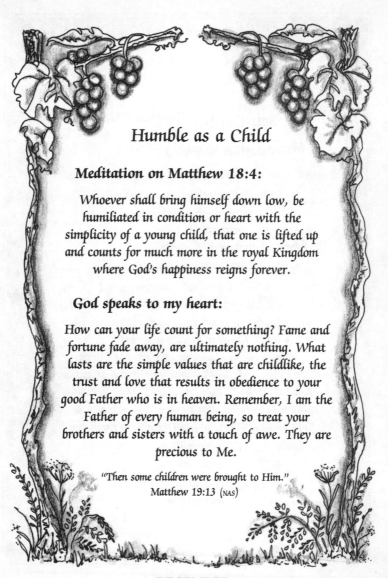

Humble as a Child

Meditation on Matthew 18:4:

Whoever shall bring himself down low, be humiliated in condition or heart with the simplicity of a young child, that one is lifted up and counts for much more in the royal Kingdom where God's happiness reigns forever.

God speaks to my heart:

How can your life count for something? Fame and fortune fade away, are ultimately nothing. What lasts are the simple values that are childlike, the trust and love that results in obedience to your good Father who is in heaven. Remember, I am the Father of every human being, so treat your brothers and sisters with a touch of awe. They are precious to Me.

"Then some children were brought to Him."
Matthew 19:13 (NAS)

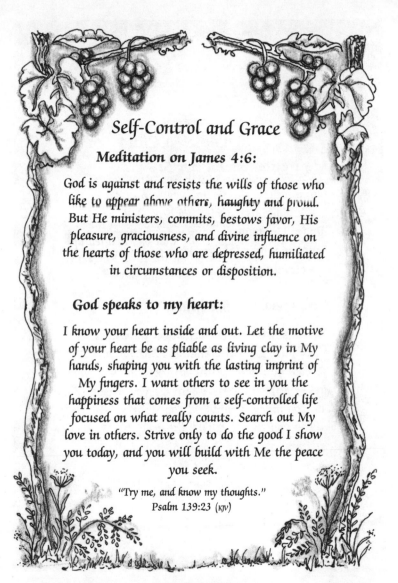

Self-Control and Grace

Meditation on James 4:6:

God is against and resists the wills of those who like to appear above others, haughty and proud. But He ministers, commits, bestows favor, His pleasure, graciousness, and divine influence on the hearts of those who are depressed, humiliated in circumstances or disposition.

God speaks to my heart:

I know your heart inside and out. Let the motive of your heart be as pliable as living clay in My hands, shaping you with the lasting imprint of My fingers. I want others to see in you the happiness that comes from a self-controlled life focused on what really counts. Search out My love in others. Strive only to do the good I show you today, and you will build with Me the peace you seek.

"Try me, and know my thoughts."
Psalm 139:23 (KJV)

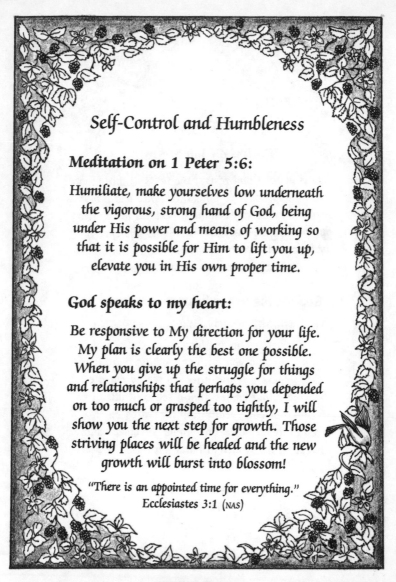

Self-Control and Humbleness

Meditation on 1 Peter 5:6:

Humiliate, make yourselves low underneath
the vigorous, strong hand of God, being
under His power and means of working so
that it is possible for Him to lift you up,
elevate you in His own proper time.

God speaks to my heart:

Be responsive to My direction for your life.
My plan is clearly the best one possible.
When you give up the struggle for things
and relationships that perhaps you depended
on too much or grasped too tightly, I will
show you the next step for growth. Those
striving places will be healed and the new
growth will burst into blossom!

"There is an appointed time for everything."
Ecclesiastes 3:1 (NAS)

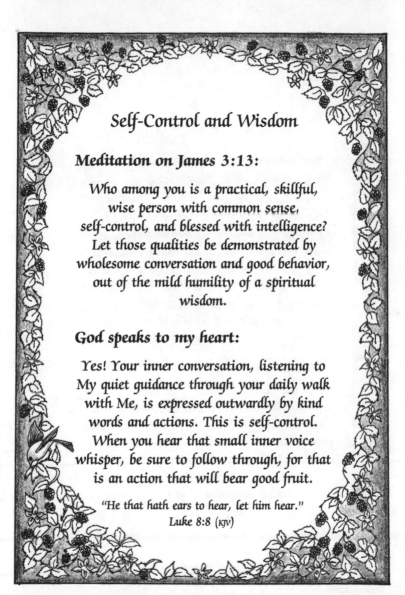

Self-Control and Wisdom

Meditation on James 3:13:

*Who among you is a practical, skillful,
wise person with common sense,
self-control, and blessed with intelligence?
Let those qualities be demonstrated by
wholesome conversation and good behavior,
out of the mild humility of a spiritual
wisdom.*

God speaks to my heart:

*Yes! Your inner conversation, listening to
My quiet guidance through your daily walk
with Me, is expressed outwardly by kind
words and actions. This is self-control.
When you hear that small inner voice
whisper, be sure to follow through, for that
is an action that will bear good fruit.*

"He that hath ears to hear, let him hear."
Luke 8:8 (KJV)

Instructing with Meekness

Meditation on 2 Timothy 2:25:

In meekness, gentleness, humility, the servant of
the Lord must train up with discipline and
correction those who are argumentative so that
perhaps God will enable them to repent, reverse
their decision, to regain self-control, and reform to
the full discernment and recognition of what is
true. Pray they may become sane again, recovered
from the tricks, traps, temptations of the devil,
who has ensnared, taken them alive as prisoners of
war for his purposes.

God speaks to my heart:

Those tricked and deluded by Satan need to see the
standard in you of one who does not have all the
answers, but who, choosing to remain steadfast,
without wavering, holds on to all you know of My
Son and His ways. This is self-control! Satan
would have you use his violent methods to
accomplish the purposes of Jesus, which is a
contradiction in terms.

"As they were coming down the mountain, Jesus instructed
them. . . ."
Matthew 17:9 (NIV)

Clothed with Humility

Meditation on 1 Peter 5:5:

Obey, subordinate yourselves to one another and be
clothed for labor (the apron being a badge of servitude to
wear as a token of mutual deference) with modesty and
humbleness of mind. For God puts Himself in opposition
to those who appear conspicuously above others in a
haughty manner. He is gracious and gives benefits,
pleasure, and divine influence on the heart to the
humble—those cast down or of low estate.

God speaks to my heart:

After a year of learning about the fruits of My Spirit,
after a year of listening to My voice tell you quietly
about the kind of life that results from My breath
pulsing through you, we close these pages with a perfect
description from Peter of the harmonious Christian life.
Filled with Me, you put on the apron and serve, not
from a sense of inferiority, but from genuine love,
respect, and desire to benefit others.

"He poured water into the basin, and began to wash the disciples' feet."
John 13:5 (NAS)